# Tyndale New Testament Commentaries

Volume 12

# Colossians and Philemon

To David and Lloyd,
faithful friends

# Tyndale New Testament Commentaries

## Volume 12

Series Editor: Eckhard J. Schnabel
Consulting Editor: Nicholas Perrin

# Colossians and Philemon

An Introduction and Commentary

Alan J. Thompson

An imprint of InterVarsity Press
Downers Grove, Illinois

**InterVarsity Press**
P.O. Box 1400 | Downers Grove, IL 60515-1426
ivpress.com | email@ivpress.com

**Inter-Varsity Press, England**
36 Causton Street | London SW1P 4ST, England
ivpbooks.com | ivp@ivpbooks.com

©2022 by Alan J. Thompson

All rights reserved. No part of this book may be reproduced in any form without written permission from InterVarsity Press.

InterVarsity Press® is the publishing division of InterVarsity Christian Fellowship/USA®. For more information, visit intervarsity.org.

Inter-Varsity Press, England, originated within the Inter-Varsity Fellowship, now the Universities and Colleges Christian Fellowship, a student movement connecting Christian Unions in universities and colleges throughout Great Britain, and a member movement of the International Fellowship of Evangelical Students. That historic association is maintained, and all senior IVP staff and committee members subscribe to the UCCF Basis of Faith. Website: www.uccf.org.uk.

Unless otherwise indicated, Scripture quotations are taken from The Holy Bible, New International Version (Anglicized edition). Copyright © 1979, 1984, 2011 by Biblica. Used by permission of Hodder & Stoughton Ltd, an Hachette UK company. All rights reserved. 'NIV' is a registered trademark of Biblica. UK trademark number 1448790.

Quotations marked ESV are taken from the ESV Bible (The Holy Bible, English Standard Version), copyright © 2001 by Crossway, a publishing ministry of Good News Publishers. Used by permission. All rights reserved.

First published 2022

USA ISBN 978-1-5140-0560-6 (print) | USA ISBN 978-1-5140-0561-3 (digital)

UK ISBN 978-1-78974-304-3 (print) | UK ISBN 978-1-78974-403-3 (digital)

Typeset in Great Britain by CRB Associates, Potterhanworth, Lincolnshire

Printed in the United States of America ∞

---

**Library of Congress Cataloging-in-Publication Data**
A catalog record for this book is available from the Library of Congress.

**British Library Cataloguing-in-Publication Data**
A catalogue record for this book is available from the British Library.

---

30  29  28  27  26  25  24  23  22   |   12  11  10  9  8  7  6  5  4  3  2  1

# CONTENTS

| | |
|---|---|
| General preface | vii |
| Author's preface | ix |
| Abbreviations | xi |
| Select bibliography | xiv |

## COLOSSIANS

**Introduction**     1

1. Who wrote this letter?     2
2. Where is Colossae and who is Paul writing to?     8
3. Where is Paul when he writes to the Colossians (and Philemon)?     11
4. Why did Paul write to the Colossians?     15
5. How does Paul's argument develop?     23

**Analysis**     25

**Commentary**     27

## PHILEMON

**Introduction**     205

1. Why was this letter written to Philemon?     207

**Analysis**     211

**Commentary**     213

# GENERAL PREFACE

The Tyndale Commentaries have been a flagship series for evangelical readers of the Bible for over sixty years. Both the original New Testament volumes (1956–74) as well as the new commentaries (1983–2003) rightly established themselves as a point of first reference for those who wanted more than is usually offered in a one-volume Bible commentary, without requiring the technical skills in Greek and in Jewish and Greco-Roman studies of the more detailed series, with the advantage of being shorter than the volumes of intermediate commentary series. The appearance of new popular commentary series demonstrates that there is a continuing demand for commentaries that appeal to Bible study leaders in churches and at universities. The publisher, editors and authors of the Tyndale Commentaries believe that the series continues to meet an important need in the Christian community, not the least in what we call today the Global South with its immense growth of churches and the corresponding need for a thorough understanding of the Bible by Christian believers.

In the light of new knowledge, new critical questions, new revisions of Bible translations, and the need to provide specific guidance on the literary context and the genre of the individual passages as well as on theological emphases, it was time to publish new commentaries in the series. Three authors have revised their commentaries that appeared in the second series. The original aim remains. The new commentaries are neither too short nor unduly long. They are exegetical and thus root the interpretation of the text in its historical context. They do not aim to solve all critical questions, but they are written with an awareness of major scholarly debates which may be treated in the Introduction, in Additional Notes or in the commentary itself. While not specifically homiletic in aim, they want to help readers to understand the passage under consideration in such a way that they begin to see points of relevance and application, even though the commentary does not explicitly offer these. The authors base their exegesis on the Greek text, but they write for readers who do not know Greek; Hebrew and Greek terms that are discussed are transliterated. The English translation used for the first series was the Authorized (King James) Version, the volumes of the second series mostly used the Revised Standard Version; the volumes of the third series use either the New International Version (2011) or the New Revised Standard Version as primary versions, unless otherwise indicated by the author.

An immense debt of gratitude for the first and second series of the Tyndale Commentaries was owed to R. V. G. Tasker and L. Morris, who each wrote four of the commentaries themselves. The recruitment of new authors for the third series proved to be effortless, as colleagues responded enthusiastically to be involved in this project, a testimony to the larger number of New Testament scholars capable and willing to write commentaries, to the wider ethnic identity of contributors, and to the role that the Tyndale Commentaries have played in the church worldwide. It continues to be the hope of all those concerned with this series that God will graciously use the new commentaries to help readers understand as fully and clearly as possible the meaning of the New Testament.

Eckhard J. Schnabel, Series Editor
Nicholas Perrin, Consulting Editor

# AUTHOR'S PREFACE

I am very grateful to Eckhard Schnabel for the invitation to contribute to this series, and for his invaluable editorial suggestions. The opportunity to spend time focused on the text of Colossians and Philemon is a great blessing, especially since these letters point us to the sufficiency of Christ (and they are a little shorter than Luke and Acts!). I am also thankful for Philip Duce, Rima Devereaux and Jenny Roberts at Inter-Varsity Press for their gracious and helpful guidance through the editorial process. IVP authors who have interacted with Philip over his twenty-two years at IVP are enormously grateful for his many years of faithful service. My own interest in studying the details of these letters goes back to my first Greek exegesis class in seminary with Doug Moo as my teacher and Murray Harris's EGGNT volume as my guide. Not surprisingly then, I have been greatly helped by their two commentaries. My procedure for writing this commentary was to begin with the (Greek) text, lexicons and tools, before reading as much as I could to check or correct my initial conclusions. I have focused on studies that have been published since Tom Wright's 1986 volume in this series, although in this short commentary there is no space to interact with all of the interpretive options. I have sought to explain the text and flow of thought of the text, based on the NIV.

Throughout this process many have supported or encouraged me. I am grateful to the board of Sydney Missionary and Bible College for a sabbatical that helped me complete this project. I particularly wish to thank my wife Alayne Thompson and our girls,

Deborah and Rebekah, as well as Sigurd Grindheim, Jeff Aernie, Alex Prentice, Meagan Prabhakar, Em Wynne and Kassie Thomson, who read earlier portions of this work. They have 'refreshed my heart' (Philemon 7) along the way. While reflecting on the fellow workers Paul mentions at the end of Colossians, I was reminded of how especially grateful I am for two long-term, dear and faithful friends, David Frost and Lloyd Vivian. It is to them that I dedicate this commentary.

Alan J. Thompson

# ABBREVIATIONS

## General

| | |
|---|---|
| AB | Anchor Bible |
| *ABD* | *Anchor Bible Dictionary*, ed. D. N. Freedman (New York: Doubleday, 1992) |
| BDAG | *A Greek-English Lexicon of the New Testament and Other Early Christian Literature*, ed. W. Bauer, F. W. Danker, W. F. Arndt and F. W. Gingrich, 3rd edn. (Chicago: University of Chicago Press, 2000) |
| BECNT | Baker Exegetical Commentary on the New Testament |
| BHGNT | Baylor Handbook on the Greek New Testament |
| BNTC | Black's New Testament Commentaries |
| ECC | Eerdmans Critical Commentary |
| *EDNT* | *Exegetical Dictionary of the New Testament*, ed. H. Balz and G. Schneider (Grand Rapids: Eerdmans, 1990–1993) |
| EFN | Estuios de filología neotestamentaria |
| EGGNT | Exegetical Guide to the Greek New Testament |
| EVV | English Versions |
| ICC | International Critical Commentary |
| *JETS* | *Journal of the Evangelical Theological Society* |
| *JSNT* | *Journal for the Study of the New Testament* |
| JSNTSup | Journal for the Study of the New Testament Supplement series |

| | |
|---|---|
| *JSOT* | *Journal for the Study of the Old Testament* |
| L&N | *A Greek-English Lexicon of the New Testament Based on Semantic Domains*, ed. Johannes P. Louw and Eugene A. Nida, 2nd edn. (New York: United Bible Societies, 1989) |
| LNTS | Library of New Testament Studies |
| LSJ | *A Greek-English Lexicon*, ed. H. G. Liddell, R. Scott and H. S. Jones, 9th edn., with rev. supplement by Peter G. W. Glare (Oxford: Oxford University Press, 1996) |
| LXX | Septuagint (Greek translation of the Hebrew Scriptures) |
| MM | *The Vocabulary of the Greek Testament* by J. H. Moulton and G. Milligan (London: Hodder & Stoughton, 1930. Repr. Peabody, MA: Hendrickson, 1997) |
| MT | Masoretic (Hebrew) Text |
| NA$^{28}$ | E. Nestle and K. Aland (eds.), *Novum Testamentum Graece* (28th ed.) |
| NICNT | New International Commentary on the New Testament |
| *NIDNTTE* | *New International Dictionary of New Testament Theology and Exegesis,* ed. Moisés Silva, 2nd edn., 5 vols (Grand Rapids: Zondervan, 2014) |
| NIGTC | New International Greek Testament Commentary |
| NT | New Testament |
| NTC | New Testament Commentary |
| *NTS* | *New Testament Studies* |
| OT | Old Testament |
| PNTC | Pillar New Testament Commentary |
| SNTSMS | Society for New Testament Studies Monograph Series |
| *TDNT* | *Theological Dictionary of the New Testament*, 10 vols., ed. G. Kittel and G. Friedrich (Grand Rapids: Eerdmans, 1964–1976) |
| THNTC | The Two Horizons New Testament Commentary |
| TNTC | Tyndale New Testament Commentary |
| UBS$^{5}$ | United Bible Societies Greek New Testament (5th ed.) |

| | |
|---|---|
| *VE* | *Vox evangelica* |
| WUNT | Wissenschaftliche Untersuchungen zum Neuen Testament |
| ZECNT | Zondervan Exegetical Commentary on the New Testament |
| ZNW | *Zeitschrift für die neutestamentliche Wissenschaft und die Kunde der älteren Kirche* |

## Bible versions

| | |
|---|---|
| ASV | American Standard Version (1901) |
| Cassirer | *God's New Covenant: A New Testament Translation*, translated by H. W. Cassirer (1989) |
| CSB | Christian Standard Bible (2017) |
| ESV | English Standard Version (2007) |
| KJV | King James Version (1901) |
| LSB | Legacy Standard Bible (2021) |
| MLB:BV | The Modern Language Bible: Berkeley Version (1969) |
| NASB | New American Standard Bible (2020) |
| NET | New English Translation (2005) |
| NIV | New International Version (2011) |
| NIV84 | New International Version (1984) |
| NJB | New Jerusalem Bible (1985) |
| NKJV | New King James Version (1982) |
| NLT | New Living Translation (1996) |
| NRSV | New Revised Standard Version (1989) |
| RSV | The Revised Standard Version of the Bible (1971) |

# SELECT BIBLIOGRAPHY

## Commentaries on Colossians and Philemon

Barth, Markus and Helmut Blanke (1994), *Colossians*, AB 34B (New York: Doubleday).
—— (2000), *The Letter to Philemon*, ECC (Grand Rapids: Eerdmans).
Beale, G. K. (2019), *Colossians and Philemon*, BECNT (Grand Rapids: Baker Academic).
Bird, Michael F. (2009), *Colossians and Philemon: A New Covenant Commentary* (Eugene: Cascade).
Bruce, F. F. (1984), *The Epistles to the Colossians, to Philemon, and to the Ephesians*, 2nd edn., NICNT (Grand Rapids: Eerdmans).
Campbell, Constantine R. (2013), *Colossians and Philemon: A Handbook on the Greek Text*, BHGNT (Waco: Baylor University Press).
Dunn, James D. G. (1996), *The Epistles to the Colossians and to Philemon: A Commentary on the Greek Text*, NIGTC (Grand Rapids: Eerdmans).
Felder, Cain Hope (2000), *Philemon*, The New Interpreter's Bible, vol. 11 (Nashville: Abingdon), pp. 881–905.
Foster, Paul (2016), *Colossians*, BNTC (London: T&T Clark).
Harris, Murray J. (2010), *Colossians and Philemon*, EGGNT (Nashville: B&H Academic).
Hendriksen, W. (1964), *Colossians and Philemon*, NTC (Grand Rapids: Baker).

Lightfoot, J. B. (1879), *Saint Paul's Epistles to the Colossians and to Philemon* (London: Macmillan).
Lohse, Eduard (1971), *Colossians and Philemon* (Philadelphia: Fortress).
McKnight, Scot (2017), *The Letter to Philemon*, NICNT (Grand Rapids: Eerdmans).
—— (2018), *The Letter to the Colossians*, NICNT (Grand Rapids: Eerdmans).
Moo, Douglas J. (2008), *The Letters to the Colossians and to Philemon*, PNTC (Grand Rapids: Eerdmans).
Nordling, John G. (2004), *Philemon*, Concordia Commentary (Saint Louis: Concordia).
Pao, David W. (2012), *Colossians & Philemon*, ZECNT (Grand Rapids: Zondervan).
Talbert, C. H. (2007), *Ephesians and Colossians*, Paideia Commentaries (Grand Rapids: Baker).
Thompson, Marianne Meye (2005), *Colossians and Philemon*, THNTC (Grand Rapids: Eerdmans).
Wilson, R. McL. (2005), *Colossians and Philemon: A Critical and Exegetical Commentary*, ICC (London: T&T Clark).
Witherington, Ben (2007), *The Letters to Philemon, the Colossians, and the Ephesians: A Socio-Rhetorical Commentary on the Captivity Epistles* (Grand Rapids: Eerdmans).
Wright, N. T. (1986), *The Epistles of Paul to the Colossians and to Philemon*, TNTC (Leicester: Inter-Varsity Press).

## Other books, monographs and articles

Arnold, Clinton E. (1996), *The Colossian Syncretism: The Interface Between Christianity and Folk Belief at Colossae* (Grand Rapids: Baker).
Balchin, John F. (1985), 'Colossians 1:15–20: An Early Christian Hymn? The Arguments from Style', *VE* 15, pp. 65–94.
Bartchy, S. Scott (1973), *Mallon Chrēsai: First-Century Slavery and the Interpretation of 1 Corinthians 7:21* (Missoula, MT: Scholars' Press).
—— (1992), 'Slavery: New Testament', *ABD*, vol. 6, pp. 65–73.

Bauckham, Richard (2008), *Jesus and the God of Israel:* God Crucified *and Other Studies on the New Testament's Christology of Divine Identity* (Grand Rapids: Eerdmans).
—— (2020), 'Confessing the Cosmic Christ (1 Corinthians 8:6 and Colossians 1:15–20', in Matthew V. Novenson (ed.), *Monotheism and Christology in Greco-Roman Antiquity*, Novum Testamentum Supplements 180 (Leiden: Brill), pp. 139–171.
Beale, G. K. and B. L. Gladd (2014), *Hidden but Now Revealed: A Biblical Theology of Mystery* (Downers Grove: InterVarsity Press; Nottingham: Apollos).
Beavis, Mary Ann (2021), *The First Christian Slave: Onesimus in Context* (Eugene: Cascade).
Beetham, C. A. (2008), *Echoes of Scripture in the Letter of Paul to the Colossians*, Biblical Interpretation Series 96 (Leiden: Brill).
Brauns, Chris (2008), *Unpacking Forgiveness: Biblical Answers for Complex Questions and Deep Wounds* (Wheaton: Crossway).
Brogdon, Lewis (2018), *A Companion to Philemon* (Eugene: Cascade).
Cadwallader, Alan H. (2011), 'Refuting an Axiom of Scholarship on Colossae: Fresh Insights from New and Old Inscriptions', in Alan H. Cadwallader and Michael Trainor (eds.), *Colossae in Space and Time: Linking to an Ancient City* (Göttingen: Vandenhoeck & Ruprecht), pp. 151–179.
—— (2015), *Fragments of Colossae* (Hindmarsh: ATF Press).
Carson, D. A. (2004), 'Mystery and Fulfillment: Toward a More Comprehensive Paradigm of Paul's Understanding of the Old and the New', in D. A. Carson, Peter T. O'Brien and Mark A. Seifrid (eds.), *Justification and Variegated Nomism,* vol 2: *The Paradoxes of Paul* (Grand Rapids: Baker), pp. 390–436.
Clark, B. T. (2015), *Completing Christ's Afflictions*, WUNT 2/383 (Tübingen: Mohr Siebeck).
Edsall, Benjamin and Jennifer R. Strawbridge (2015), 'The Songs we Used to Sing? Hymn "Traditions" and Reception in Pauline Letters', *JSNT* 37, pp. 290–311.
Fee, Gordon (2007), *Pauline Christology: An Exegetical-Theological Study* (Peabody, MA: Hendrickson).
Gibson, David (2012), 'Sacramental Supersessionism Revisited: A Response to Martin Salter on the Relationship between Circumcision and Baptism', *Themelios* 37, pp. 191–208.

Gordley, Matthew E. (2007), *The Colossian Hymn in Context: An Exegesis in Light of Jewish and Greco-Roman Hymnic and Epistolary Conventions*, WUNT 2/228 (Tübingen: Mohr Siebeck).

Grindheim, Sigurd (2001), 'The Law Kills but the Gospel Gives Life: The Letter-Spirit Dualism in 2 Corinthians 3.5–18', *JSNT* 84, pp. 97–115.

—— (2013), 'A Deutero-Pauline Mystery? Ecclesiology in Colossians and Ephesians', in Stanley E. Porter and Gregory P. Fewster (eds.), *Paul and Pseudepigraphy* (Leiden: Brill), pp. 173–195.

Harris, Murray J. (1999), *Slave of Christ: A New Testament Metaphor for Total Devotion to Christ* (Leicester: Apollos; Downers Grove: InterVarsity Press).

Hurtado, Larry W. (2003), *Lord Jesus Christ: Devotion to Jesus in Earliest Christianity* (Grand Rapids: Eerdmans).

Knox, J. (1960), *Philemon Among the Letters of Paul* (London: Collins).

Kümmel, Werner Georg (1975), *Introduction to the New Testament*, rev. edn. (London: SCM Press).

McDonough, Sean M. (2009), *Christ as Creator: Origins of a New Testament Doctrine* (Oxford: Oxford University Press).

McFadden, Kevin W. (2021), *Faith in the Son of God: The Place of Christ-Oriented Faith Within Pauline Theology* (Wheaton: Crossway).

Nes, J. van (2018), '*Hapax Legomena* in Disputed Pauline Letters: A Reassessment', *ZNW* 109, pp. 118–137.

Porter, Stanley (1994), *Καταλλάσσω in Ancient Greek Literature, with Reference to the Pauline Writings*, EFN 5 (Córdoba: Ediciones el Almendro).

Ridderbos, Herman (1975), *Paul: An Outline of His Theology*, translated by John Richard De Witt (Grand Rapids: Eerdmans).

Rosner, Brian (2007), *Greed as Idolatry: The Origin and Meaning of a Pauline Metaphor* (Grand Rapids: Eerdmans).

Routley, J. J. (2021), 'On the Brink of Discovery: New Testament Colossae', *Bible and Spade* 34, pp. 4–9.

Salter, Martin (2010), 'Does Baptism Replace Circumcision? An Examination of the Relationship between Circumcision and Baptism in Colossians 2:11–12', *Themelios* 35, pp. 15–29.

—— (2012), 'Response to David Gibson', *Themelios* 37, pp. 209–210.

Schnabel, E. J. (2012), 'Paul, Timothy, and Titus: The Assumption of a Pseudonymous Author and of Pseudonymous Recipients in the Light of Literary, Theological, and Historical Evidence', in J. K. Hoffmeier and D. R. Magary (eds.), *Do Historical Matters Matter to Faith? A Critical Appraisal of Modern and Postmodern Approaches to Scripture* (Wheaton: Crossway), pp. 383–403.

Smith, Ian K. (2006), *Heavenly Perspective: A Study of the Apostle Paul's Response to a Jewish Mystical Movement at Colossae*, LNTS 326 (London: T&T Clark).

Thompson, Alan J. (2008), 'Unity in Acts: Idealization or Reality?', *JETS* 51, pp. 523–542.

—— (2017), '"Consolation for the Despairing": C. H. Spurgeon's Endorsement of Lament Psalms in Public Worship', in G. Geoffrey Harper and Kit Barker (eds.), *Finding Lost Words: The Church's Right to Lament* (Eugene: Wipf & Stock), pp. 37–51.

Weima, Jeffrey A. D. (2016), *Paul the Ancient Letter Writer: An Introduction to Epistolary Analysis* (Grand Rapids: Baker).

White, Joel (2016), 'Paul Completes the Servant's Sufferings (Colossians 1:24)', *Journal for the Study of Paul and His Letters* 6, pp. 181–198.

—— (2018), 'The Imprisonment that Could Have Happened (And the Letters Paul Could Have Written There): A Response to Ben Witherington', *JETS* 61, pp. 549–558.

Wilson, Mark (2020), *Biblical Turkey: A Guide to the Jewish and Christian Sites of Asia Minor* (Istanbul: Ege Yayinlari).

Wink, W. (1984), *Naming the Powers: The Language of Power in the New Testament* (Philadelphia: Fortress).

Witherington, Ben (2017), 'The Case of the Imprisonment that Did Not Happen: Paul at Ephesus', *JETS* 60, pp. 525–532.

—— (2018), 'Was Paul a Jailbird? A Response to the Response', *JETS* 61, pp. 559–561.

Young, Stephen E. (2021), *Our Brother Beloved: Purpose and Community in Paul's Letter to Philemon* (Waco: Baylor University Press).

# COLOSSIANS

## INTRODUCTION

Paul's letter to the Colossians has long been one of the most loved letters in the New Testament for Christians. It has the wonderful combination of teaching about the greatness of the Lord Jesus as well as application for Christian living, and all within four succinct chapters. The perennial temptation to minimize the person of Christ and find strength for Christian living in sources other than the gospel means that this letter continues to teach and challenge us today. The letter to the Colossians contains one of the two passages in all of Paul's letters that focus on the person of Christ in detail (1:15–20; see also Philippians 2:6–11) and it unfolds a grand vision of the universal significance of Christ and the good news about him. Universal claims pervade this short letter so that the claims of Christ and the relevance of the gospel explained in Colossians have held appeal to Christians down through the ages. The claims of the gospel are challenging, the vision of the church is vast, the description of the Christian life is encouraging and the concerns of the apostle Paul are inspiring. All of this is intertwined with the main theme of this letter: Christ, in particular his sovereignty and sufficiency, and his supremacy in everything. Before we get into the riches of this letter, however, we need to orient ourselves to the questions surrounding who wrote the letter, who the author is writing to, where the author is as he writes and why he is writing this letter?

## 1. Who wrote this letter?

Unlike some of the following matters, this first question is one that was not in any doubt throughout most of church history. Paul, after all, identifies himself as the author in the very first verse (1:1), not to mention another two times later on in the letter (1:23; 4:18), one of which, the 'signature' at the end of the letter in 4:18, is a distinguishing mark of Paul's letters (1 Cor. 16:21; Gal. 6:11; 2 Thess. 3:17; cf. Phlm. 19). On this count Paul identifies himself more times in this letter than he does in most of his other letters, including Romans. Of the thirteen letters with Paul's name, only Philemon and 1 Corinthians have more references to the name 'Paul' (with Philemon having three very similar references, cf. vv. 1, 9, 19). But we have more than just Paul's name scattered throughout this letter. Many of the first person references in this letter give detailed personal information about Paul.[1] Paul refers, for example, to his view of his suffering (1:24), his own personal commission (1:25), the content, means, and goal of his preaching (1:28), his personal struggle and effort in this proclamation (1:29), his personal concern and struggle for those at Colossae and Laodicea (2:1), his ultimate purposes in this struggle (2:2–3), his own reasons for why he tells them his personal purposes and goals (2:4) and his own delight in them (2:5). Later he asks for prayer (4:3–4), and reveals personal details and his estimation of fellow believers and co-workers (4:7–17), ending with a final personal ('I, Paul') appeal about his own circumstances (4:18). Would the original audience, after reading the warnings in the letter against deception (2:4, 8; 3:9) in contrast to truth (1:5, 6), agree that a pseudonymous letter would be acceptable, that all of these references

---

1. Moo, p. 28.

and claims for Paul could be made by someone other than Paul?[2] The view that Paul wrote Colossians was held from the early church (e.g. Irenaeus, *Against Heresies*, 3.14.1; Origen, *Against Celsus*, 5.8) through to the mid-nineteenth century when claims that this letter was written in the second century and contained ideas that were deemed 'un-Pauline' developed.[3] Arguments against the Pauline authorship of Colossians since then have largely revolved around the same recurring issues which we will briefly summarize here: language and style of writing and the theology of the letter.

Those who think the letter could not have been written by Paul typically point to what they claim is evidence of irregular vocabulary. There are thirty-four words in Colossians that only occur once in the New Testament (called 'hapax legomena'; e.g. *philosophia*, 2:8; *ethelothrēskia*, 2:23) and another twenty-eight words that are not found in any of Paul's other letters.[4] Conversely, words common to Paul's letters such as righteousness, justification, promise, law and believe are not found here. There are a number of problems with this kind of analysis on the basis of word statistics, however. The most obvious problem is that we are dealing with such a small range for analysis and the same conclusion for an assumption of pseudonymity could be drawn from any New Testament letter. Galatians, recognized by all to be Pauline, has a similar number of unique words (30), as does Philippians (36) which has an additional forty-six words that appear elsewhere in the New Testament but

---

2. For the problems of attributing pseudonymity to NT letters, see Beale, pp. 5–8; Moo, pp. 37–40; Schnabel, 'Paul', pp. 383–403.
3. For a succinct summary of the developments arising from E. T. Mayerhoff's claims in 1838, see Kümmel, *Introduction*, p. 340. The following discussion in favour of Pauline authorship draws at times from Kümmel's succinct summary on pp. 340–346 and can be seen more recently in expanded form in Moo, pp. 28–41; Pao, pp. 20–23; Beale, pp. 1–8. Foster (who thinks the letter was written by a follower of Paul, after Paul's death), pp. 73–78, provides a table of those for and against Pauline authorship.
4. Cf. Kümmel, *Introduction*, p. 341.

not in Paul's letters.[5] These kinds of statistics are what one would expect from (mostly) short letters written to different locations with different audiences and different pastoral concerns since these believers are facing different challenges. In Colossians much of the unique vocabulary is found in the section where Paul warns more pointedly of false teaching (2:16–23). Since the same kinds of issues are not being faced by the believers in Rome, Galatia or Philippi, it is not surprising to find a selection of other words here. On the other hand, there are eleven words in Colossians that are only found in Paul's writings in the New Testament (e.g. *hikanoō*, 1:12 [2 Cor. 3:6]; *hedraioi*, 1:23 [1 Cor. 7:37; 15:58]; *synthaptomai*, 2:12 [Rom. 4:4]; *thriambeuō*, 2:15 [2 Cor. 2:14]). In addition to the differing destinations, it must also be remembered that Paul's letters were written over a span of approximately fifteen years (depending on the dating of some letters), during which time Paul lived through a wide range of experiences and traversed an enormous amount of the Roman empire by land and sea, visiting numerous cities and towns along the way. It is reasonable to expect that he might have acquired new vocabulary and expressions during this time.

Some have argued that the style of Colossians points to an author other than Paul. Features of Colossians such as long sentences (e.g. 218 words in 1:9–20) that unfold with connecting participles, relative clauses ('who is . . .'), many genitives (e.g. 'the riches of full assurance of understanding', 2:2), and synonymous repetition ('wisdom and understanding', 'holy and blameless') are said to be un-Pauline. In addition to what we noted above regarding the size of the sample we are dealing with, it is also possible that some of this is overblown. Long sentences are not unknown in Paul's other letters (e.g. Rom. 1:1–7). Furthermore, in light of Paul's signature in the final greeting of Colossians 4:18, it is likely that apart from the final greeting, this, like other letters of Paul, was written by a secretary or amanuensis (cf. 1 Cor. 16:21; Gal. 6:11) and it is difficult to recreate the setting in which these letters were written with the presence and perhaps occasional input from others, including Timothy (e.g. the plural 'we' in Colossians,

---

5. Pao, p. 20 n. 6; cf. Beale, p. 5; Nes, '*Hapax*', pp. 118–137.

e.g. 1:3–4, 9–10). For example, the letter to the believers in Rome, although from Paul (Rom. 1:1), was 'written' by Tertius (Rom. 16:22). More positively, Kümmel lists a range of stylistic features of Colossians that are only found in Paul's writings, indicating that the differences between Colossians and Paul's other letters are exaggerated by some.[6]

In terms of language and style, the similarities between Colossians and Philemon form another strong argument in favour of the Pauline authorship of Colossians. Philemon is one of the so-called seven 'undisputed' letters of Paul (Romans, 1–2 Corinthians, Galatians, Philippians, 1 Thessalonians and Philemon). Given the specific and personal nature of Philemon no one doubts that it was written by Paul, who is the author named in that letter.[7] As the table in the Introduction to Philemon shows, there are a number of names and greetings common to both letters that strongly suggest common authorship and a common destination. These greetings are not found in the same order or in the same formulations and do not give an indication of literary dependence or mere copying. Furthermore, apart from Romans 16:7, the rare term 'fellow prisoner' is used only in Colossians 4:10 (for Aristarchus) and Philemon 23 (for Epaphras) in the New Testament. Both letters refer to Paul being in chains (Col. 4:3, 10, 18; Phlm. 9–10, 13), and with Timothy (Col. 1:1; Phlm. 1). The comparatively longer instructions to slaves in Colossians 3:22–25 also makes sense if the letter is written by Paul at the time of Philemon and going to the same destination in Colossae. It is more likely that a person who knows those named in 4:7–17 is actually sending greetings from them to people who also know them than that either a forger is deceptively copying and creatively adjusting random greetings and instructions to names of people he didn't know, or that a later Pauline school is seeking authorization of Paul's co-workers with a literary technique that no one else in the early church recognized.[8]

---

6. Kümmel, *Introduction*, pp. 341–342.
7. Dunn notes that it is difficult to come up with a rationale for why a later author would seek to use Paul's name for the letter to Philemon (p. 300).
8. Beale, p. 7; Moo, pp. 37–40.

The other main objection to Pauline authorship focuses on apparent differences in theology in Colossians with that of Paul's other letters. The Christology of 1:19 and 2:9 is high and Christ's supremacy is cosmic (1:16, 20), the resurrection eschatology of 2:12 and 3:1 is more realized than future, the ecclesiology of the church as the body in 1:18, 24 is universal rather than local, and the letter lacks the great Pauline doctrines of justification, the imminent return of Christ and the future resurrection of the dead and final judgment. In response to this, we note, first, as with the matter of vocabulary, it is strange to insist on the same topics being treated the same way in several short letters to differing audiences in differing locations facing differing concerns. Paul surely does not need to include everything in every letter. Conversely, why would someone seeking to imitate Paul omit referring to apparently classic Pauline doctrines? One only needs to compare the widely held authentic letters of Romans, 1 Corinthians, Philippians and Philemon to see that different occasions require differing approaches to differing topics.

Second, it is likely that these claims are also a little overblown. True, the Christology of Colossians is exalted and cosmic, the ecclesiology is broad, and the eschatology emphasizes some of the blessings 'already' received in Christ. Yet Paul's Christology is similarly cosmic in passages such as 1 Corinthians 8:6 ('one Lord Jesus Christ, through whom all things came and through whom we live') and Philippians 2:10 ('at the name of Jesus every knee should bow, in heaven and on earth and under the earth').[9] Paul's resurrection eschatology is not too dissimilar in passages such as Romans 6:4 (believers have new life) and there are many references to future eschatology in Colossians (e.g. 1:5, 12, 22–23, 27, 28; 3:4, 6, 24, 25). It is common to use metaphors differently in different settings for different rhetorical purposes (Paul describes Christ as 'head' in different contexts even in Colossians, see 1:18; 2:10, 19). Yet even Paul's more universal description of the church as a body is not too dissimilar to what he says about the body in 1 Corinthians (e.g. 12:12–13, 27–28), Christ as head (11:3; though not specifically

---

9. Cf. also Rom. 9:5; 10:6–13; 2 Cor. 4:4; Gal. 4:4; Phil. 2:6.

'of the body'), and the church as part of a wider people of God (e.g. 1:2; 3:21–22; 6:15; 10:32; 15:9, 22). The references to 'church' in a more local sense in Colossians 4:15–16 show continuity with Paul's other uses of the word. Although the doctrine of justification is not expressed in the same way as in Romans or Galatians, this letter contrasts a reliance on Christ with a teaching that focuses on a reliance on rules that are the basis of other's judgment (2:16, 20–21). The gospel in this letter still concerns redemption by grace (1:6, 14) through faith (1:4), on the basis of Christ's death on the cross (1:22; 2:14), in which he takes our punishment of death (2:13–14), and through which we receive reconciliation and forgiveness of sins (1:14; 2:13) and a secure hope for the future judgment, knowing that we no longer face God's wrath (3:6), but will appear before him as holy, blameless and without accusation (1:22). Thus, although different issues are addressed and correspondingly different emphases are present, I do not see the theology of Colossians as fundamentally different from that of 1 Corinthians. In response to the claims of the false teachers, Paul emphasizes the supremacy of Christ, and the sufficiency of Christ's provision already received by all who belong to him.[10]

Finally, it is evident that Colossians has some kind of direct relationship with Ephesians so the issue of authorship is tied in some ways to the authorship of Ephesians. This is not the place to outline all of the similarities, but a comparison of the two letters reveals a similar sequence of topics and often with similar or even identical wording (see e.g. regarding Tychicus in Ephesians 6:21–22 and Colossians 4:7–8). However, beyond recognizing similarities it is impossible at this vantage point to determine if there is literary dependence in which Ephesians was based on Colossians, or if Colossians was based on Ephesians, or if it is just that the same author wrote both letters at about the same time, which seems likely, both being sent with Tychicus to Asia Minor and the Lycus

---

10. See White, who argues for an (earlier) Ephesian imprisonment along these lines ('Imprisonment', pp. 556–558). Grindheim, 'Ecclesiology', sees a 'complex reapplication of familiar Pauline terms and themes in a way that is consistent with the apostle's earlier letters' (p. 173).

Valley (where Colossae is located). The order in which Paul wrote them, however, is impossible to tell. When the household instructions of Ephesians 5:22 – 6:9 are compared with Colossians 3:18 – 4:1 it is evident that the instructions for each group in Colossians is very brief except for the instructions to slaves. It seems possible that the longer material (Ephesians) was written first and then abbreviated (Colossians), but there is no way of knowing. Accordingly, throughout this commentary I will primarily (though not exclusively) focus on interpreting Colossians and each passage in the flow of argument in its literary context in Colossians rather than write a combined Colossians/Ephesians commentary.

## 2. Where is Colossae and who is Paul writing to?

Before we get to the question of where Paul was when he wrote the letters to the Colossians and Philemon, it will help if we first get our bearings on Colossae and where it was in relation to the possible locations for where Paul was. Colossae was in the Lycus Valley at the foot of Mount Cadmus (modern day snow-capped Mount Honaz, in southwestern Turkey) in the region of Phrygia in the Roman province of Asia.[11] It was located on the road running east to Ephesus, which was approximately 120 miles away (193 km). Paul mentions two nearby cities in this letter, Laodicea (2:1; 4:13, 15–16), famous for its wealth, was about 11 miles (18 km) northwest, and Hierapolis (4:13), famous for its hot springs, was about 15 miles (24 km) north-northwest. Today one can still look across the valley from Laodicea and see in the distance the white limestone formed from the mineral springs at Hierapolis. Herodotus calls Colossae, 'a great city of Phrygia' (*Histories* 7.30) when Xerxes visited in 480 BC. Likewise Xenophon describes Colossae as 'an inhabited city, prosperous and large' (*Anabasis* 1.2.6) when Cyrus came to the city in 400 BC. Josephus describes an occasion in the third century BC when Antiochus III ordered 2,000 Jewish families to be sent from Babylon to Phrygia (*Antiquities* 12.3.4; cf. also Acts 2:9–10). Thus a significant Jewish population in the region, together with

---

11. See Cadwallader, *Fragments*.

Greeks, Romans and Phrygian locals, made for a bustling cosmopolitan town. Unfortunately Colossae remains unexcavated, but the evidence from coins and inscriptions found nearby points to the worship of gods common to cities of the area such as Zeus, Artemis, Mēn, Tyche, Dionysos and possibly a god of the Lycus river.[12]

Many commentators contrast the previously 'great' city of Colossae with its first-century decline to a small and insignificant town with little influence compared to its great past.[13] Much of the reason for this is due to a passing comment made by the first-century historian Strabo as he names Colossae in his description of the region of Phrygia. Having described Apameia and Laodicea as the two 'largest of the Phrygian cities [*poleis*]', Strabo adds that in the neighbourhood of these two cities there are situated 'towns [*polismata*] and . . . , Aphrodisias, Colossae, Thermisonium,' (*Geography*, 12.8.13). However, this need not mean that Colossae was an insignificant town.[14] This comment may just mean that Colossae was not as large as nearby Laodicea. Since there is a gap in the text that we have after the words 'towns and . . .', it is possible that 'cities' or 'places' was in the original text here. More importantly, before adding Colossae to his list, Strabo includes Aphrodisias. This nearby city was not exactly insignificant, with its three-storied porticoes lining a street in honour of Caesar Augustus that had a twenty-four-column gate at the end, a large stadium (able to hold approximately 30,000 people), bouleuterion (for city council meetings, with an inscription referring to a place for the Hebrew elders) and temples, and its reputation as a centre for sculptures (evidenced in the many sculptures seen in the museum there today). Strabo later also states that Colossae earned substantial revenue from the well-known wool produced in the area of Laodicea, the

---

12. Ibid., pp. 45–73. For surveying and excavation plans see Routley, 'Discovery', pp. 4–9.
13. E.g. Lightfoot, pp. 15–16.
14. Those questioning the consensus that Colossae was small and insignificant include Bruce, p. 5; Dunn, p. 20–21; and more extensively Cadwallader, 'Refuting', pp. 151–179, cf. Cadwallader's chronology on pp. 302–303.

red-purple colour of which was called *colossinus* (*Geography*, 12.8.16). Thus, although not as large as its famous neighbour Laodicea, Colossae may still have been a prosperous town at least until an earthquake in approximately AD 60/61 or 63/64 and perhaps for some time beyond.[15] Today, while there is much tourist interest in and archaeological excavation of neighbouring sites Laodicea and Hierapolis, the site of the town of Colossae is an unexcavated mound before the scenic mountain range behind it just waiting to provide archaeologists, historians, and Bible readers a wealth of information to fill in some of these unanswered questions about the city. The preceding historical discussion does not affect the exegesis of any passage in the letter to the Colossians, but it may at least help to temper homiletic comments about the insignificance or obscurity of the city in which the Colossian believers lived.

Turning to what we know of the church, from the letter itself we discover that the church was founded by Epaphras, who brought the gospel to them and who continued to have a deep concern for the church (1:7; 4:12–13). Paul does not seem to have met them (2:1). Given that Epaphras was originally from Colossae (4:12), and that he came as a representative of Paul's (1:7), it is probable that he came to Colossae during Paul's two-to-three years of gospel ministry in Ephesus (AD 53–55), during which time 'all the Jews and Greeks who lived in the province of Asia heard the word of the Lord' (Acts 19:10). The church met in Philemon's house (see comments on Philemon 1–2), had close connections with the church in Laodicea (Col. 4:15–16) and was probably largely made up of believers from a Gentile background (1:21, 27; 2:13). The references to the Jewish elements of the false teaching may indicate that some Jews, proselytes and Godfearers were in the congregation too

---

15. Bruce, p. 5. Tacitus, *Annals* 14.27.1 mentions an earthquake affecting Laodicea only (AD 60/61), and Eusebius, *Chronicon* (Olympiad) 210 (preserved in Jerome) mentions Laodicea, Hierapolis and Colossae as three cities that were ruined in an earthquake (AD 63/64). On the possible continuing significance of Colossae after the earthquake see Foster, pp. 4–8 (drawing on recent inscriptions published by Cadwallader).

(2:16). Since Paul calls Epaphras a 'fellow prisoner' in Philemon 23 (cf. also Col. 4:10), it is likely that he has since come to visit Paul and has told him about the Colossian believers, particularly about their faith in Christ and their love for fellow believers (1:4, 8; Phlm. 5), but also probably about the dangers facing them from the false teaching.

## 3. Where is Paul when he writes to the Colossians (and Philemon)?

On the assumption that Paul is the author of both Colossians and Philemon, another debated question concerns where Paul was when he wrote these letters. Unlike the question of authorship, there is no place name mentioned in the letters that could guide us in knowing the answer to this question (and none was needed for the original readers; cf. 4:8–9). As we will see below, the matter is complicated further when the letter to Philemon is factored into the discussion as Onesimus has travelled to Paul from Colossae and is due to return to Philemon in Colossae (Phlm. 10–11, 12, 15–16). If we start with what Paul says about his circumstances in the letter we learn that he is 'in chains', perhaps under house arrest (Col. 4:3, 18; Phlm. 10, 13), as a 'prisoner' (Philemon 1, 9), and he refers to 'fellow prisoners' (Col. 4:10; Phlm. 23). The question is, where is Paul 'in chains' (and therefore, when were these letters written)? The similarities with Ephesians and Philemon place all three letters together, and the similar references to imprisonment in Philippians (Phil. 1:13–14; 4:22) mean that all four letters are traditionally called 'Prison Epistles'. Three options have generally been proposed for this imprisonment: Caesarea, Ephesus and Rome.

Caesarea has been proposed because the book of Acts states that Paul spent some time imprisoned there (Acts 23:33–27:1). This proposal has not won many adherents as a setting for this letter, since there is no evidence that Paul wrote any letters from Caesarea and the situation in Acts seems more restrictive than the way he speaks about his ministry in Colossians (4:3–4) and his travel plans in Philemon (vv. 10, 22).

Ephesus has been suggested largely on the basis of its closer proximity to Colossae and because of the travels mentioned in

Philemon.[16] In Philemon Paul says that Onesimus had come to him and Paul was sending him back to Philemon in Colossae (vv. 10–16). On the assumption that Onesimus fled from Philemon it is thought to be more likely that he would not travel so far and risk getting caught on the way to Rome. Furthermore, Paul requests that a guest room be prepared for him (v. 22). This too is thought to make more sense if Paul is coming from relatively nearby Ephesus, rather than distant Rome, over 1,200 miles (1,930 km) away. Some also suggest that since Paul wanted to continue west to Spain (Rom. 15:24), it would be unlikely that he would now say (in Rome) that he would turn east to visit Colossae.

Rome, however, has been the traditional location for Paul's references to his 'chains' in these letters, and I think this is the most compelling option.[17] This view goes back to the subscriptions of some early manuscripts and was the view of early church fathers such as Jerome, John Chrysostom and Theodoret.[18] Although some object that the Marcionite prologue places Paul in Ephesus for Colossians (White, 'Imprisonment', p. 550), this same prologue places Paul in Rome for Philemon (and Ephesians), and Philemon is one of the main reasons for objecting to Paul writing from Rome. No such imprisonment in Ephesus is mentioned in Acts, nor (apart from the debatable reference in the Marcionite prologue) do we have any record anywhere else of an imprisonment in Ephesus.[19] If Rome is the location then this would place this letter during Paul's (first) Roman imprisonment described at the end of Acts where

---

16. For recent defences for Ephesus see: Beale, p. 8; McKnight, pp. 34–39.
17. See the recent defence by Witherington, 'Imprisonment', pp. 525–532; the response by White, 'Imprisonment', pp. 549–558; and again Witherington, 'Response', pp. 559–561. See also Moo, pp. 41–46; Pao, pp. 23–24.
18. Pao, p. 24, cites, for example (following Metzger), mss. Bc (4th century), K (9th century) and P (6th century), and church fathers (following Barth and Blanke, p. 127). Metzger also adds mss. A (5th century). Manuscripts K and P refer to Rome in the subscription for Philemon.
19. Though 2 Cor. 11:23 suggests other imprisonments.

Paul was under house arrest for two years (Acts 28:16, 30). The greater freedom entailed in a house arrest in which Paul stayed in his own rented accommodation in Rome (Acts 28:16, 30) accords with the sense of gospel opportunities together with a potential visit we noted above. The evidence for a Roman imprisonment can be deduced from the names stated in these letters when corroborated with the book of Acts. In Colossians Aristarchus is with Paul as a 'fellow prisoner' (4:10) and this is likely to be the same Aristarchus, the Macedonian from Thessalonica, who joins Paul on his journey from Caesarea to Rome (Acts 27:2).[20] Luke is also mentioned in Colossians 4:14 (and Philemon 24 with Aristarchus) as sending greetings, which means that he is with Paul. Assuming this is the Luke who authored Acts, and that the (first person plural) 'we' passages in Acts indicate his presence in the accounts described (Acts 16:10–17; 20:5–21:18; 27:1–28:16), then it is likely that he too is with Paul in Rome as this journey in Acts 27–28 is one of those 'we' passages (cf. Acts 27:1, 2, 3; 28:16, etc). Furthermore, on the basis of Acts 16:10, 16, 40 and 20:6 it appears that Luke remained in Philippi during Paul's visit to Ephesus, which means that he was not present in Ephesus for the alleged imprisonment of Paul there. Mark may also be added to this list since (according to Acts 15:39) he was not in Ephesus and (apparently, according to 1 Pet. 5:13) may have been in Rome (Col. 4:10; Phlm. 24).[21] That Paul expressed a plan to travel to Spain when he wrote to the Romans from Corinth a few years earlier does not preclude a later plan to travel east to Colossae from Rome (Phlm. 22). This would not be the first time that Paul's desire to travel somewhere had been changed in God's providence (Acts 16:6–10). Paul readily included his understanding of providence in articulating his plans (e.g. Acts 18:21), and he incorporated this understanding into his letter to Philemon (cf. vv. 15, 22). Furthermore the letter to Titus indicates that Paul

---

20. Aristarchus is seized in Ephesus (Acts 19:29) but this is not an arrest or imprisonment. He also joins Paul on his travel to Jerusalem (Acts 20:4).
21. References in 2 Timothy to Mark (4:11) and Tychicus (4:12) in Ephesus are from Paul's last letter, a later Roman imprisonment, and therefore not referring to Paul's time in Ephesus in Acts 19.

did travel east again, most likely between this first and his second Roman imprisonment (Titus 1:5; 3:12), and early church references indicate that he did eventually get to Spain (e.g. 1 Clement 5:7).

The question of travel between Colossae and Rome is not as much of an objection when the frequency of ancient travel is kept in mind. There is an inscription on the tomb of a certain Flavius Zeuxis and his sons in nearby Hierapolis, dating from the first century, stating that the merchant Zeuxis 'had rounded Cape Malea [on the Peloponnese peninsula, south of Corinth] 72 times on voyages to Italy'. This is often calculated at about two trips a year for 36 years (or 36 round trips), and adds up to more travel than Paul.[22] If we assume that Onesimus was running from his master (or seeking out a mediator, see the notes on Philemon 10–16), it is possible that he would have wanted to get further away to Rome than to somewhere closer where his master could potentially find him. Rome, with its large population of slaves, might have been the best place to disappear without a trace. Some argue that it would be unlikely for Paul to ask Philemon to send Onesimus back to him in Rome if Onesimus had only just arrived back in Colossae from Rome. In the commentary I will argue that Paul is not actually asking Philemon to send Onesimus to him in Rome (see Philemon 15–16). Paul's central request is that Philemon welcome Onesimus (v. 17). The reference to Paul's visit in Philemon 22 should be interpreted as a general request and should be understood also in light of its purpose in the context of Paul's central request of the letter in verse 17 (see comments on Philemon 22). Thus the distance between Rome and Colossae is not a convincing objection against a Roman imprisonment.

The similarities between Colossians and Ephesians only raise more questions against the Ephesian hypothesis given that Tychicus would deliver the letters and tell the recipients news about Paul and how he is doing (Eph. 6:21–22; Col. 4:7–9). Even if Ephesians is a

---

22. See for example, the tomb and translation in Wilson, *Biblical Turkey*, p. 236. Wilson also notes the many goods listed in Rev. 18:11–13 that merchants brought to Rome, highlighting the profits and travels of merchants from the province of Asia.

circular letter, this seems a strange comment to have in a letter if it is written from Ephesus to recipients that would include those also in Ephesus. In summary, in the absence of any evidence for an imprisonment in Ephesus, and given the number of correspondences to Rome along with supporting external evidence, I think it is most likely that Paul is in Rome. This accordingly, dates the letter to some time in AD 60–62.

## 4. Why did Paul write to the Colossians?

This question takes us into the twin topics of the nature of the false teaching Paul is combating and the theological themes that are raised in Colossians, or to put it another way, the problem that Paul seeks to address and the solution that he points them to. There has been much discussion about the nature of the false teaching Paul warns against in Colossians, largely because, as is often the case in these matters, we only have access to Paul's response and not the false teachings themselves. Furthermore, although some specific teachings are mentioned (e.g. 2:16, 20–23), Paul does not specify the origin or background of these teachings. So, methodologically, we must start with the known rather than speculate from the unknown. In the letter itself the warnings against the false teaching in their most specific sense all come in chapter 2. It will help to see the relevant references laid out here first before we make some observations.

> I tell you this so that no one may deceive you by fine-sounding arguments.
> (2:4)

> See to it that no one takes you captive through hollow and deceptive philosophy, which depends on human tradition and the elemental spiritual forces [elementary principles, NASB] of this world rather than on Christ.
> (2:8)

> Do not let anyone judge you by what you eat or drink, or with regard to a religious festival, a New Moon celebration or a Sabbath day.
> (2:16)

> Do not let anyone who delights in false humility and the worship of angels disqualify you. Such a person goes into great detail about what they have seen; they are puffed up with idle notions by their unspiritual mind.
> (2:18)

> Since you died with Christ to the elemental spiritual forces [elementary principles, NASB] of this world ... why ... do you still submit to its rules: 'Do not handle! Do not taste! Do not touch!' These rules, which have to do with things that are all destined to perish with use, are based on merely human commands and teachings.
> (2:20–22)

> Such regulations indeed have an appearance of wisdom, with their self-imposed worship, their false humility and their harsh treatment of the body, but they lack any value in restraining sensual indulgence.
> (2:23)

Based on these statements by Paul we can conclude the following (all of which will be developed further in the commentary): first, the references to 'no one' or 'anyone' in 2:4, 8, 16, and 18 indicate that Paul has particular people in view who are spreading the teaching he is warning against. Second, in the context of the letter as a whole, the first hint that there is another teaching that Paul is concerned about arises in 2:4. Then specific instructions become the focus of the letter from 2:6, with the first imperative of the letter appearing there (the positive exhortation to 'continue to live' in Christ) and the second imperative, a prohibition, occurring in 2:8. There are three prohibitions in this section: 2:8, 16, and 18, with the most sustained focus on the false teaching found in 2:16–23. Third, whereas the first prohibition in 2:8 is a general warning to be sure that no one takes them captive by this teaching, the second and third prohibitions in 2:16 and 18 are more specific warnings not to let anyone 'judge you'. These bring us close to the nature of this false teaching. At the heart of this false teaching there appears to be, at least in part, a claim that the Colossians were inadequate or lacked something that the false teachers were requiring and the false teachers are positioned as superior spiritually. Fourth, at the heart of the teaching is adherence to a set of practices or rules (2:16, 20–23). The implication is that these rules were necessary to avoid the 'judgment' or 'condemnation' of the false teachers, and were therefore spiritually necessary. Fifth, the nature of the rules in 2:16 indicates that the teaching is derived from some Old Testament laws. Sixth, the nature of the rules in 2:21 and 2:23 appear to go beyond just Old Testament laws with an added emphasis on ascetic practices and restrictions for the body, and perhaps outward appearances only with no genuine wisdom, worship, humility and godliness. Seventh, this is confirmed by the sustained critique of this teaching as essentially 'this-worldly' and of human origin in 2:8, 20, and 22. Leaving aside the debated phrase *ta stoicheia tou kosmou* in 2:8 and 20 for now (see the comments on 2:8), the focus of Paul's critique is that this teaching is merely human. Eighth, therefore, since Paul would not say this about God's law, he must be opposing a novel (human-invented) blend of Old Testament and additional ascetic rules designed to appease the judgments of the false teachers. Thus the Old Testament alone does not explain their teaching. Ninth, although the teaching appears to be a blend of Old Testament and additional ascetic rules, Paul's salvation-historical appeal to the shadow–body/reality contrast undercuts the teaching at its source. If the laws the teachers were basing their regulations on were from the shadows that anticipate Christ, then their instructions lose their force. Tenth, strictly speaking, the description in 2:18–19a (which is probably the most debated verse of this section) is not primarily about what the teachers were requiring of the Colossian believers. This verse describes the false teachers themselves and mainly draws attention to the pride and separation from Christ that is characteristic of the false teachers. Finally, Paul's fundamental critique of the false teaching with its rules and regulations is that it is not 'according to Christ' (2:8 [NRSV], 17, 19). Thus in these warnings Paul also looks back to all that he has said in chapters 1 and 2 about the supremacy and sufficiency of Christ. Paul's concluding comment on the inability of the regulations to restrain the flesh also looks forward to what Paul says next about the change that comes when one has died and risen with Christ through faith (2:12, applied in 3:1ff.).

In addition to the specific references, many point to more implicit references throughout Colossians as further hints about the false teachings. Adding to the explicit references to Old Testament laws in 2:16 some see a reference to circumcision in 2:11, 13 and the law in 2:14 as another possible indicator that the main issue is Jewish. To this may be added references to 'inheritance' (1:12), 'holy' (1:2, 12; 3:12), and the 'chosen' (3:12) as evidence of Old Testament language reserved for Israel that is being applied to this largely Gentile congregation. However, it is difficult to tell if any of these, including the reference to circumcision, are being used in a specifically polemical way in Colossians. The reference to the worship of angels in 2:18 has led many to focus on a mystical element in the teaching, perhaps supported by references to invisible powers in 1:16 and 2:10, the defeat of powers in 2:15, and the possible interpretation of 'spiritual forces' in 2:8 and 20. It is likely that there was fear of evil spirits in ancient Phrygia. However, this does not appear to be Paul's explicit concern in his summary of their requirements in 2:16, 20–21, and it is unclear how the angels who are worshipped (or who are worshipping) in 2:18 relate to the powers that are disarmed through the cross in 2:15. The many references to wisdom, knowledge and understanding throughout Colossians (1:9–10, 26–28; 2:2–3; 3:10, 16) as well as the description of the teaching as a 'philosophy' in 2:8 may also point to an emphasis of the false teachers. Some also see significance in the use of terms such as 'fullness' (2:9–10) and 'mystery' (1:27; 2:2; 4:3). However, the use of this language elsewhere in Scripture, and elsewhere by Paul (e.g. 1 Cor. 1–4; Rom. 11; 15:29), makes it difficult to be sure that these terms are employed specifically to respond to uses of them by the false teachers (see the commentary on those verses).

In light of the above, we will now briefly evaluate some of the proposals that have been put forward for what the false teaching might be.[23] First, the specific Old Testament references in 2:16

---

23. For the vast amount of secondary literature on this see the overview in Smith, *Heavenly*, pp. 1–6, 19–38, 143–145. Accessible summaries can be found in Pao, pp. 25–31 and Moo, pp. 46–60, esp. 53–59.

(explained more in the commentary), together with the allusions noted above, rule out a purely Gentile pagan philosophical background, whether Hellenistic mystery cults or Platonic or Cynic philosophy.

Second, a growing consensus sees the influence as from some kind of Judaism. But there is still debate about the kind of mix involved here. The description of the teaching as 'human tradition' or 'human commands and teachings' (2:8, 22) makes it unlikely that the issue is merely a Judaism that was proud of its identity markers of sabbath, food laws and circumcision. Thus the rules that are emphasized specifically in the verses listed above, together with the Old Testament allusions throughout the letter and the descriptions Paul gives to this teaching as of human origin, point to a predominant emphasis on adherence to laws and regulations that the false teachers have developed from and taken further than the Old Testament. But what has influenced the particular adaptation of these rules and regulations in Colossae?

Third, this has led to a variety of overlapping suggestions about the kind of influences that may have characterized Judaism in Phrygia. The same language in 2:8 ('human tradition') as Jesus' use of Isaiah 29:13 in Mark 7:6–9 indicates a similar blend of human-originated rules with God's commands. Still, the asceticism of 2:23 suggests that the blend here, although similar in principle, differs in its particular emphases. Some suggest the focus of Paul's concern is Jewish mysticism. However, this appears to depend in large part on a particular interpretation of 2:18 (entering into heavenly visions of angelic worship, or an initiation rite) that is debatable. This verse does not specifically identify the teaching or regulations that the Colossians are being pressured with (these are found in Paul's explicit identification of behaviours in 2:16, 20–21). Rather, it describes what is characteristic of the false teachers themselves and what they 'delight in' ('idle notions' their own minds have made up). In other words, a focus on a possible interpretation of the description of the false teachers in 2:18 (and the reference to what they think they see) may overshadow Paul's more explicit statements about what the false teachers were actually requiring. Arnold has argued that there is likely to be a mix of various influences, probably from 'Phrygian folk belief, local folk

Judaism, and Christianity' in which angels were venerated or called upon for protection.[24] As Moo correctly observes, however, the focus of Paul's polemic is more on their 'preoccupation with rules' than veneration of angels (or, we might add, mystic visions centred around angels).[25] Also, as many have pointed out, apart from the debated reference to angels in 2:18, Colossians does not refer to magic, or spells or other features such as amulets. Thus, although the influence of local beliefs is likely, the Old Testament language of 2:16 indicates that the dominant framework does not appear to be derived from the pagan elements of Phrygian folk religions.[26] In summary, we are left with a rather general conclusion that their teaching focused on regulations and practices, some of which were ascetic and some of which revolved around calendar observances, developed and adapted from the Old Testament under the influence of more localized priorities that were said to help or elevate the Colossian believers spiritually, perhaps also to protect them, but primarily to appease the demands and judgment of the false teachers concerning their spiritual life and status. I tentatively conclude, therefore, that the teaching was a localized form of 'legalism' (in the sense of a reliance upon certain 'rules' as the means to be spiritually advanced) that included elements of asceticism from teachers who boasted of their superior (mystical?) spiritual status.[27]

Paul does not respond in the same way that he does in Galatians because, unlike with the Galatians, he does not think the Colossian believers are 'so quickly deserting the one who called them' (Gal. 1:6). In contrast to Galatians 1:6–7; 3:1, Paul is overflowing with thankfulness for the Colossians' faith and love (Col. 1:3–5). He expresses gratitude for the fruit and growth of the gospel among them (1:6). Indeed, the reason why he continually prays for them is not because of the false teachers, but because he has heard of their

---

24. Arnold, *Syncretism*, p. 243.
25. Moo, p. 59.
26. Pao, p. 30.
27. Paul's imperatives, for example in 3:1–4:6, flow out of the 'indicative' of what Christ has accomplished for the believer already.

embrace of the gospel (1:9). The content of his prayer in 1:9–12 is shaped by what he has said that God has been doing already in 1:3–7. In 2:5, just before the central command of the letter, Paul even says that he 'rejoices' or 'delights' that their faith is neither misplaced nor unsure; their faith is in Christ and it is firm. What Paul wants them to do is to 'continue to live' in Christ (2:6). Thus Paul's concern here is more preventative than it is corrective. 'The epistle is a vaccination against heresy, not an antibiotic for those already afflicted.'[28]

We may now summarize the main themes of Colossians, with implied contrasts to the false teachers following each summary. With the danger of the false teaching lurking in the background the solution Paul provides throughout this letter centres on the supremacy of Christ. Any teaching that suggests that believers need 'Christ plus . . .' effectively diminishes the supremacy of Christ since it either implies or asserts that he is not enough for forgiveness, reconciliation with God and the Christian life. Christ is the sovereign Lord, there is nothing that is greater than him. He is the head over every ruler and authority, he is the fullness of God and in him are all the treasures of wisdom and knowledge. The false teachers, by contrast, seek to take the Colossian believers captive, and want to judge and condemn them.

What Christ has accomplished in his death and resurrection is also fully sufficient. Therefore, those who belong to him by faith, that is, those who rely upon him alone, receive redemption and forgiveness of sins because he took the penalty for their sin upon himself in his death on the cross. They are reconciled to God because his death on the cross has made peace. As Creator he is the ultimate Lord of all powers, and his death and resurrection show that he has triumphed over all hostile powers. By his resurrection he is the Lord not only of creation, but also of his people, those who belong to the new creation. Consequently, it is because of him and the blessings received through him that believers have a secure hope, they can look forward to their presentation before the

---

28. Moo, p. 175 provides this quote (which many have cited) from Wink, *Powers*, p. 73.

judgment as holy, without blemish and free from accusation. They have no need to fear the wrath to come. Therefore, the additional rules do not help, and the 'judgment' from the false teachers is of no consequence.

The Colossians heard about all of this in the gospel that Epaphras proclaimed to them. Because of this, to hear and understand this gospel is to hear and understand God's grace. It is this gospel that is the message of truth because it is God's message. His saving plan is revealed in this message of good news about the Messiah who is the hope of glory. Only this gospel enables hope and assurance. It is because of the hope announced in this gospel that Paul labours to proclaim only this gospel to everyone everywhere. It is Christ that Paul proclaims and it is Christ that the Colossians have received. Epaphras was a reliable and faithful servant of the gospel in contrast to the false teachers, even though they claim to have something new and extra. The teaching focused on rules is false and deceptive rather than true, and it is an instrument of judgment, not grace or good news; it leads to uncertainty rather than the hope and assurance of the gospel, and is merely human rather than from God.

It follows then that all who belong to Christ enjoy these blessings because they have all heard and responded by faith to the Christ proclaimed in this gospel. Because of Christ they are all 'holy and faithful', they are all one family, he is everything and they all alike have one master. The gospel of grace enables love for all of God's people since they are not divided according to the rules and judgment of the false teachers.

As those who belong to Christ they too share in his death and resurrection. They have, therefore, died to who they once were outside of Christ and they have new life in him. The way to live the Christian life, therefore, is to look to Christ, to seek him and to set one's mind and priorities on him, doing all to the honour of him. Christ is the one who enables believers to know God and live lives pleasing to him. To live the Christian life is essentially to continue as they began, relying on him alone for every spiritual need. These human-originated rules don't help, they only end up hurting the Colossian believers themselves and others. Christ is, therefore, in a word, sufficient.

## 5. How does Paul's argument develop?

A variety of outlines proposed by commentators can be conveniently seen in Beale (pp. 18–21) and McKnight (*Colossians*, pp. 66–72). My outline seeks to highlight the overall emphasis in the letter on the supremacy of Christ and is closest to Moo's outline (p. vi). Further explanation for the main divisions is provided in the introduction to each section below. The centre and turning point of the letter is found in 2:6–7 where Paul introduces a series of imperatives and states that his main concern is for the Colossian believers to continue to centre their lives on Christ, just as they began. The whole letter, therefore, can be read in light of that central concern. The preceding chapters emphasize the supremacy of Christ in the gospel message that they heard and believed, and that Paul proclaims. Because of Christ's supremacy it is only this God-given gospel that provides hope (1:3–2:5). Following the exhortation of 2:6–7, Paul shows that, in contrast to the gospel of Christ, the regulations of the false teachers are of merely human origin, and provide no spiritual help (2:8–23). It is Christ, therefore, who enables spiritual change evidenced in love for fellow believers and seen in the everyday realities and relationships of life and work (3:1–4:6).

# ANALYSIS

**1. OPENING GREETING (1:1–2)**

**2. THE SUPREMACY OF CHRIST IN THE GOSPEL (1:3 – 2:5)**
    A. The gospel bears fruit (1:3–14)
        i. Thanksgiving for the Colossians' response to the gospel (1:3–8)
        ii. Prayer for the Colossians' continued growth in the gospel (1:9–14)
    B. The gospel centres on the Son's supremacy (1:15–20)
        i. The Son's supremacy over creation (1:15–17)
        ii. The Son's supremacy over the new creation (1:18–20)
    C. The gospel provides hope in the Son for the final judgment (1:21–23)
    D. The gospel of Christ is the centre of Paul's ministry (1:24 – 2:5)
        i. Paul labours to proclaim Christ with the final judgment in view (1:24–29)
        ii. Paul labours to see the Colossians remain firm in Christ (2:1–5)

## 3. THE SUPREMACY OF CHRIST IN THE CHRISTIAN LIFE (2:6 – 4:6)

   A. The heart of the matter: continue to be centred on Christ (2:6–7)
   B. Threats to Christ-centred living from the false teachers (2:8–23)
      i. Fullness is found in Christ (2:8–15)
      ii. The regulations of the false teaching offer no spiritual good (2:16–23)
   C. Living a Christ-centred life (3:1 – 4:6)
      i. Heavenly thinking (3:1–4)
      ii. Putting off the practices of the 'old self' (3:5–11)
      iii. Putting on the practices of the 'new self' (3:12–17)
      iv. The supremacy of Christ in earthly relationships (3:18 – 4:1)
      v. Prayerful presentation of Christ to those outside the community (4:2–6)

## 4. CONCLUDING GREETINGS AND INSTRUCTIONS (4:7–18)

# COMMENTARY

## 1. OPENING GREETING (1:1–2)

*Context*

In keeping with his usual letter openings, Paul identifies himself as an apostle, says who is with him as he writes and who he is writing to, and he greets the recipients of the letter. Although these letter openings contain common elements, they still need to be understood in the particular context in which they are found. In this particular letter Paul will highlight the supremacy and sufficiency of the Lord Jesus and so even these common elements of this letter opening are enriched in light of what follows. Thus Paul describes everyone in these opening greetings in light of the difference the Lord Jesus has made. This is of course unsurprising in the light of Pauline theology that centres on Jesus. Still, in this context these descriptions should be read in the context of what Paul will go on to say to the Colossians.

*Comment*

**1.** Paul begins this letter by identifying himself as *an apostle of Christ Jesus*. In other contexts this term 'apostle' can simply refer to a messenger (cf. e.g. 2 Cor. 8:23; Phil. 2:25) or to those 'commissioned' (cf. e.g. Barnabas, Acts 14:4, 14; 1 Cor. 9:6) without any reference to this unique authority that the apostles chosen by Jesus had.[1] In this context, however, the designation *apostle* means that Paul is an authorized and personally chosen representative of the promised Messiah, the risen Jesus, to proclaim the good news, along with the twelve (Acts 1:21–22; 1 Cor. 9:1–2; 15:5, 7, 9), and whose foundational role in the new covenant people of God enables him to speak with the authority of Christ (1 Cor. 14:37; Eph. 2:20). The Greek word, *Christos*, translates the Hebrew word *mashiach*, which in this context identifies Jesus as the Messiah. Paul's primary task is to make Christ known, with the authority of Christ, as Christ himself had commanded him (cf. Acts 26:15–23). Thus Paul did not see himself as operating independently of Christ or setting himself up as a founder of something other than what Christ came to earth to do (cf. Gal. 1:10). Although Paul usually opens his letters with reference to his apostleship (see comments on Philemon 1), this laser focus on Christ is especially prominent in this letter as Paul will unpack with great detail the significance of the supremacy of Christ for the world in general, and for the Colossians in particular. When he adds that this apostleship is *by the will of God*, Paul recognizes, as he often does, God's sovereign purposes (Rom. 1:10; 15:32; 1 Cor. 4:19; 2 Cor. 2:14), particularly in his own conversion by Christ and commission to proclaim Christ (Acts 22:14; Gal. 1:15–16).

Timothy is mentioned in the opening greetings of 1 and 2 Thessalonians, 2 Corinthians, Philippians and Philemon. Timothy was also with Paul and sent greetings when Paul wrote to the Romans (16:21); he was sent by Paul to the believers in Thessalonica (1 Thess. 3:2), Corinth (1 Cor. 4:17; 16:10) and Philippi (Phil. 2:19), and he was known to the recipients of the letter to the Hebrews (Heb. 13:23). Paul variously calls Timothy his 'co-worker' (Rom. 16:21; 1 Thess. 3:2; cf. 1 Cor. 16:10), a 'servant of Christ' along with Paul (Phil. 1:1), Paul's 'son' (1 Tim. 1:18), 'dear son' (2 Tim. 1:2), 'true son in the faith' (1 Tim. 1:2) and his 'son' whom he loves and who is 'faithful

---

1. Cf. Harris, p. 7.

in the Lord' (1 Cor. 4:17). The 'son' language implies that Timothy came to faith through Paul (see on Philemon 10) and the 'co-worker/ servant' language points to a long and precious partnership in gospel ministry.[2] Paul calls Timothy *our brother* here, in Philemon 1 and in 1 Thessalonians 3:2 (cf. Heb. 13:23).[3] Timothy was a close labourer in gospel ministry who reflected Paul's passion for Christlike sacrificial service. His inclusion here may indicate that he helped Paul as a scribe or amanuensis and since he was with Paul during his two to three years of ministry in nearby Ephesus (Acts 19:10, 22; see below on 1:7) it is likely that Timothy met some people from Colossae during that time. Since Timothy's name does not reappear in the letter, and since Paul's name reoccurs without further reference to Timothy in Colossians 1:23 and again in the final greeting in 4:18, the first person singular pronouns and verbs in crucial texts such as 1:24, 2:4, 4:4 and 4:7–15 all point to Paul as the ultimate author of the letter.[4] The simple designation of Timothy as *our brother* focuses on Timothy's spiritual family identity as a member of the family of God, and the equal status that he and all believers have because Christ has brought them together and they now know God as their Father (cf. 1:2). In the following verse all the believers at Colossae are called *brothers and sisters in Christ* (1:2). Later, Tychicus is called a *dear brother* (4:7), as is Onesimus (4:9) and all the believers across the valley at Laodicea (4:15). The significance of what it means to be a 'brother' in the family of God is especially significant in Philemon (see comments on Philemon 7, 16, 20).

**2.** Having described himself and Timothy in light of the impact of Christ in their lives, Paul proceeds to describe the believers at Colossae in a similar way. They are *God's holy people and faithful brothers and sisters in Christ*. The designation *God's holy people* ('saints', e.g. ESV, NRSV) is a description of the status that all believers have

---

2. See Acts 16:1 (and Paul's work in Lystra in 14:6–18, 21).
3. The article functions as a pronoun here and in Philemon, whereas the pronoun 'our' is used in 1 Thess. 3:2 and Heb. 13:23.
4. Beale, pp. 24–25. For an emphasis on co-authorship see McKnight, p. 81.

before God as people who belong to God rather than a description of their performance or level of holy living (i.e. the word 'saints' and the expression 'holy people' should not be misunderstood to refer to a special level of Christian who is above all others). Position in Christ and subsequent conformity to Christ are of course inseparable. Yet this description of believers as holy, occurring another four times in this letter (cf. 1:4, 12, 26; 3:12), refers to who believers are because of Christ. As Paul will state later in this letter, Christ died on the cross in order to present us 'holy . . . without blemish and free from accusation' (1:22). Paul's use of the word 'holy' draws on the use of the word in the Old Testament to refer to that which is set apart to be dedicated to or to belong to God. The word was used at times to describe the people of God in the Old Testament (e.g. Pss 16:3; 34:9; Dan. 7:18, 22, 27), and is often used by Paul for God's new covenant people (e.g. outside his opening greetings, Rom. 15:25; 1 Cor. 6:2; 16:15; 2 Cor. 13:12; Eph. 3:18; Phil. 4:22).

The description of the Colossians as *faithful* is also a description of who they are as believers in Christ rather than a reference to their level of faithfulness. Although faithfulness is expected for believers and can be a description of some (cf. 1:7; 4:7, 9), since in this context this term refers to all of those who are holy rather than a select number of them, it is more likely that this description also refers to who they are.[5] Because they have trusted in Christ (see the ref. to 'faith' in 1:4), they are 'believers', the *faithful* ones, they belong to God by faith.[6] Like *our brother* Timothy (1:1), because of the Lord Jesus, they enjoy the family identity and equal status that all believers, not just a select few, have as brothers and sisters because of Christ. In applying the terms 'holy', 'believers/faithful' and 'brothers and sisters' to all of the people of God in Colossae, Paul draws attention to the unity of the one people of God. It is not

---

5. Taking the word 'and' between 'saints' and 'faithful' as epexegetical (and taking the word 'holy ones' as a noun); cf. Harris, p. 9; Pao, p. 48; Beale, p. 28. For 'holy' as an adjective see Campbell, p. 2 (the explanation above is not affected by this).

6. Cf. the use of *pistos* (believing) in 1 Tim. 4:3.

some who are holy, some who believe, some who have more privileged access, because they follow extra special rules or practices. Rather, this is true for all of them because they are *in Christ*. This phrase is significant for understanding Paul's theology in general as well as the emphases of this letter. It is such a common phrase, along with variations such as 'in him', 'in the Lord', that it is impossible to boil it down to just one definition that covers all uses. In this context the phrase 'in Christ' means that all this is true of the people of God because they belong to Christ. What is true of him is true of them and of all who trust in Christ. In the broader salvation-historical framework of Paul's gospel all humanity can be broadly defined by who they belong to – Adam or Christ (Rom. 5:12–21). The actions of each one affects all who belong to them. Those who belong to Christ by grace through faith are essentially transferred from the realm in which Adam's sinful trespass holds sway (sin, death, condemnation) to the realm in which Christ's obedience holds sway (righteousness, life, justification). Thus there is often a 'new realm' in view when this phrase is used (cf. Col. 1:13).

At the same time that they are spiritually *in Christ* they are also geographically *in Colossae*. The former has eternal significance regardless of the earthly significance of the latter. Colossae was not as large as other destinations of Paul's letters such as Rome, Corinth and nearby Ephesus, and it was becoming overshadowed by its near neighbour Laodicea (cf. Col. 2:1; 4:13, 15, 16; see the Introduction above for more on Colossae). Still, regardless of the geographical location of believers, Christ is sufficient for them. What matters is that they are 'in Christ', the Creator and Sustainer of all creation, the Saviour of all who trust in him and the hope of glory (1:16–17, 22–23, 27; 3:4).

Paul concludes his letter opening with his greeting to the believers in which he, as usual, transforms a standard letter opening in light of Christ. Rather than open with the standard word 'greetings' (*chairein*, cf. Acts 15:23), Paul wishes the believers *grace* (*charis*). In Colossians, 'God's grace' is something one only comes to know through the gospel (1:6). In this context, Paul wants the Colossians to know by experience that their continuing Christian life is also only lived out by God's undeserved favour. Since he begins and ends the letter with 'grace' (4:18), it is the gospel of grace that frames the letter and drives Paul's hopes for the Colossians that they will live by this in contrast to the demands of the false teachers. Similarly, Paul's wish for the believers to know *peace* arises out of the framework expressed elsewhere in Colossians that believers have been reconciled to God through Christ (1:20–22). It is because of Christ's death that believers are no longer at enmity with God and thus live out their lives now in harmony with God.

This *grace and peace* comes to the believers from God *our Father*. Unlike his other opening greetings, Paul does not add something like 'and our Lord Jesus Christ'.[7] The focus, therefore, in this greeting is on the reality that since all believers know God as their grace-and-peace-giving *Father* they are now *brothers and sisters*.[8] The privilege of knowing that the Creator of the universe is our Father, and that as believers we are his children living under his grace and peace, is something that Paul returns to throughout this letter, particularly as he expresses thanksgiving in the following verses (1:3, 12; 3:17).

*Theology*
These opening verses are filled with references to God's gracious purposes in the lives of his people. Paul is an apostle 'by the will of God', believers are the recipients of grace and peace 'from God', and this God is 'our Father'. It follows then that God's people are understood in relation to him. God's people are a family – Timothy is 'our brother' – and all believers are 'brothers and sisters'. The defining characteristics of believers are in relation to God: they belong to him ('holy') and they are his by believing in him ('faithful/believers'). All of this is possible through Jesus who is the Messiah. Thus by God's will Paul is an authorized representative of, and missionary for, Jesus the Messiah, and God's people are those who belong to Christ ('in Christ'). The reference to Jesus

---

7. Although there is good external manuscript support for the inclusion of this phrase (cf. NKJV), there is also good manuscript support for its omission. Conformity to the standard Pauline greeting explains the scribal addition rather than accidental omission here.
8. Beale, p. 29.

as the Messiah also alludes to the continuity and discontinuity of the Testaments. On the one hand, reference to one God and the description of his people as holy uses standard Old Testament language. Yet a development has taken place. The promised Messiah has come and he is Jesus. God's people are those who have faith and submit to teaching from him and about him from his authorized representatives, the apostles.

## 2. THE SUPREMACY OF CHRIST IN THE GOSPEL (1:3 – 2:5)

Paul's primary concern in this letter is for the Colossian believers to continue trusting in Christ and living their lives focused on Christ. This is evident in the central appeal of 2:6–7 where he urges them to 'continue' in Christ just as they received him. The reason for this appeal is because there are some who are seeking to distract the believers from the sufficiency of Christ with new teaching centred on rules and regulations. Before combatting this teaching directly, Paul begins by pointing the Colossians to their original reception of the gospel. In summary, Paul outlines in this section that this gospel is that which they received by God's grace, which Epaphras brought to them, and which bears fruit in their lives, centres on the supremacy of Christ, provides hope for the future and defines Paul's ministry. This Christ-centred gospel is what they have received and is what they must 'continue' to depend upon.

### A. The gospel bears fruit (1:3–14)

Paul focuses here on God's work of grace in the Colossian's lives. They have come to know God's grace in the gospel proclaimed to them by Epaphras. It is this work of God that is the basis for Paul's prayer that they continue to grow in their knowledge of him. Therefore, thankfulness permeates Paul's prayers for them, and Paul prays that thankfulness will permeate their lives too. Such thankfulness is based on what the Father has done for believers through his Son. The majesty of the Son then becomes Paul's focus, especially in 1:15–20.

### i. Thanksgiving for the Colossians' response to the gospel (1:3–8)
*Context*
Before Paul turns to address the specific needs of the Colossians he begins, as he often does, with prayer and thanksgiving. Paul's characteristic triad of faith, hope and love also feature in this opening thanksgiving. Yet these are not mere formulaic opening formalities for Paul. They have their own purpose and arrangement. Prayer and thanksgiving appear again in 1:9 and 12, and are connected more directly at the end of the letter in 4:2–4. Since prayer and thanksgiving occur together here and in 4:2–4 with reference to the spread of the gospel message and God's initiative in enabling that gospel spread, it is likely that these two sections frame the body of the letter. The following layout, explained below, may help to see the flow of thought here.

>faith and love from hope
>>heard in the gospel that came to you
>>>the gospel that bears fruit in the whole world
>>the day you heard the gospel
>Epaphras is the one you learned the gospel from and
>the one who tells us of your love

Thus there is a broad movement in which Paul begins by expressing his thanks to God for their love and faith (1:3–4) that springs from the hope that they heard about in the gospel (1:5). Then from 1:5b the main focus is on the gospel which came to them and bears fruit among them and everywhere (1:6). Then Paul moves to the human messenger of the gospel (1:7). They came to faith through Epaphras, and Epaphras, who is himself faithful and beloved, has reported of their love (1:7–8). Thus Paul highlights the impact the gospel has and in particular looks back to the way in which this gospel came to, and gave rise to, the church in Colossae.

*Comment*
**3.** Paul begins by saying that *we always thank God . . . when we pray for you*.[1] The occasion for Paul's constant thankfulness is whenever he prays for the wellbeing of the Colossians.[2] Because Paul views all of life in light of God's good and sovereign purposes, before he transitions to the heart of his concerns for the Colossians he expresses his thankfulness for God's work in their lives. Even here, however, his thankfulness for the effects of the gospel of Christ in their lives may anticipate his warning later in the letter not to be deceived by teachings that detract from the supremacy and sufficiency of Christ. Thankfulness permeates the letter as a constant reminder to look to Christ.[3] The implication is that Paul thanks God for their faith in Christ and their love for the believers (1:4) because God is the one who is the source of their faith and their love in their lives.

The God to whom Paul prays is specifically *the Father of our Lord Jesus Christ*. Having described all believers in the previous verse as 'brothers and sisters' who receive grace and peace from 'God our Father', Paul continues to focus on the Father. However, the juxtaposition of 1:2 and 3 serves to distinguish Jesus in his relationship to the Father. Jesus is the unique Son of the Father (1:13), and as Son he is the one who reveals the invisible God (1:15). Although the title 'Son' only occurs once in this letter (1:13), it is followed by sixteen pronouns that look back to the word 'Son' in 1:13. The full title *Lord Jesus Christ* may serve to emphasize the authority of the Son and the uniqueness of his relationship with the Father. This is the only occasion in Colossians where the full name 'Lord Jesus Christ' is used, indicating that the man Jesus was and is the Messiah (Greek *Christos*), and also the risen and reigning sovereign Lord.

---

1. The plural 'we' may include Timothy, or it could be an 'epistolary plural' that just refers to Paul himself (see 1:1).
2. Harris, p. 14.
3. See comments on 1:4, 12; 2:6; 3:15, 17; 4:2.

Elsewhere in Colossians the name Jesus never occurs by itself but does appear five times in combination with the other terms 'Christ' and 'Lord'.[4] The term Christ occurs twenty-five times, though more could be added if the pronoun 'him' that often follows a reference to Christ is added.[5] As noted above on 1:1, 'Christ' has in view the Old Testament hopes for the promised Messiah, and functions here as a title rather than merely a name. The term 'Lord' occurs fourteen times, though seven occur in 3:18 – 4:1.[6] In view of the use of this word in the context of the high Christology of this letter in which Jesus is the Creator and Sustainer of all things (1:16–17), having all the fullness of God (1:19; 2:9), the title Lord is to be understood in light of its regular usage in the Greek translation of the Old Testament (LXX) to refer to the sovereign Lord, Yahweh.[7]

**4–5.** Paul specifies two reasons for his thanksgiving to God (1:4) and indicates the basis for both (1:5a).[8] In these verses Paul returns to his familiar triad of faith, hope and love, but again anticipates themes that will arise later in the letter. In this context the two reasons for Paul's thankfulness are specifically their *faith in Christ Jesus* and their *love . . . for all God's [holy] people* ('saints', ESV; see on 1:2). Although it is their faith and love that they exercise, God must be the source and initiator of these since Paul gives thanks to God for their presence in the Colossians' lives.

---

4. See 1:1, 3, 4; 2:6; 3:17 (var. in 4:12).
5. See 1:2, 7, 24, 27, 28; 2:2, 5, 8, 11, 17, 20; 3:1 (x2), 3, 4, 11, 15, 16; 4:3, 12; 'Christ Jesus' (1:1, 4; 2:6); 'Lord Christ' (3:24); 'Lord Jesus Christ' (1:3); 'Christ' is followed by eight pronouns in 2:8–15.
6. See 'the Lord' (1:10; 3:13, 18, 20, 22 [and earthly 'lords'], 23, 24; 4:1 [and earthly 'lords'], 7, 17); 'Lord Jesus' (3:17); 'Christ Jesus the Lord' (2:6); 'the Lord Christ' (3:24); 'Lord Jesus Christ' (1:3).
7. Cf. e.g. Rom. 10:13 (Joel 2:32); 1 Cor. 8:6 (Deut. 6:4); Phil. 2:11 (Isa. 43:23).
8. The participle translated 'having heard' (1:4) is probably causal, hence the translation 'because we have heard' (NIV). See below on the connection between 'hope' in 1:5a and faith and love in 1:4.

First, *faith in Christ Jesus* identifies when they became God's people (cf. 1:2a; 2:12; Eph. 2:8) and is also the continuing characteristic of God's people since genuine faith is persevering faith (1:23; 2:5, 7).[9] Faith, whether initial or continuing, is the act of trusting in or relying upon what has been accomplished by God in Christ (cf. 2:12). Thus, for example, in 1:22 Paul speaks of God's reconciling work in Christ's death and in 1:23 he speaks of the need to rely upon that. The prepositional phrase *in Christ Jesus* shows that the sphere in which true faith operates is Christ Jesus.[10] Paul's concern for the Colossians is that some might be deceived and tragically turn away from relying upon the sufficiency of Christ, hence his emphasis throughout this letter on the superiority of Christ and the need for continuing faith in him.

Second, their *love for all God's people* is outward 'horizontal' evidence of their internal transformation and 'vertical' relationship with God through Christ (see comments on Philemon 5). Love is described further in the rest of this letter (see especially 3:14). Love for other believers holds all other virtues together since each of them displays love (3:12–14). This both reflects God's love in Christ (1:21–22; 3:12) and characterizes the new humanity in Christ (3:10–11) in contrast to the disregard for others that was characteristic of who they were in their 'earthly nature' (3:5–9). By contrast, those peddling the false teaching are characterized by a condemning attitude to others if certain rules are not kept (2:16, 18), and false humility (2:23). For the false teachers, since faith in Christ is not enough, and since they insist that their own rules ought to be

---

9. See McFadden, *Faith*, pp. 121–122.
10. The preposition *en* in the phrase 'in Christ Jesus' may not primarily describe the 'object' of their faith, but rather the one who determines the operation and meaning of genuine faith. This of course does not then exclude the notion that Christ is the object of genuine faith, it is just that Paul uses other constructions to focus on that aspect whereas this construction includes this broader reality (e.g. 2:5 *eis Christon pisteōs*; cf. Phlm. 5; however, see Eph. 1:15; 1 Tim. 3:13; 2 Tim. 3:15; and McFadden, *Faith*, p. 122). See Harris, pp. 14–15; Moo, p. 84; Pao, p. 51. Cf. 'love in (*en*) the Spirit' (1:8).

followed, it is a corollary that instead of love for *all* of God's people, there is a disdain for those not in line with their particular rules. Love for God's people, of course, doesn't mean overlooking the harmful effects of deceit and false teaching. Paul exhibits love for the Colossians by urging them to continue in faith in Christ and warning them not to depart from Christ for the lies of the false teachers whose teachings are merely of human origin.

Paul concludes this triad with reference to *hope* (1:5a). Although the triad of faith, hope and love is common in the New Testament, not every combination of the three terms functions in the same way. The opening words of 1:5, 'because of the hope' in most versions, is clarified in the NIV to show that in this context hope gives rise to both faith and love (*the faith and love that spring from the hope*; cf. also NET). Just as the pair 'faith' and 'love' are both the basis of Paul's thanksgiving, so too are they viewed together here.[11] Although the word 'faith' is not mentioned later in 1:6–7, the idea is referred to in the description of the Colossians' coming to 'understand' God's grace, having 'learned' of this from Epaphras (who is both 'beloved' and 'faithful'). In this context, therefore, hope is the reason for and basis for the Colossians' faith in Christ and love for Christ's people.

Hope is further described as that which is *stored up for you in heaven*. Hope in this sense then is not so much their subjective sense of confidence in God's promises, but the object of what they hope for, the reality of God's presence for eternity (cf. 4:1). Although some commentators react against popular emphases on the hope of going to heaven when you die,[12] this verse provides some justification for just such a hope for believers (cf. Phil. 1:23). Even Revelation 21–22, which begins with reference to a 'new heaven and a new earth' goes on to describe in symbolic language the transformed people of God in God's holy presence (cf. Rev. 21:3–4, 9; the cube of 21:16 alludes to the holy of holies). There is a sense in which this future heavenly hope is already a reality for those who belong to Christ (3:1–3). Since this is *stored up* ('reserved for

---

11. Harris, p. 15.
12. E.g. McKnight, *Colossians*, pp. 95–96.

you', CSB), the focus here is on the security of that future that those who belong to Christ can confidently look forward to. This again anticipates Paul's concerns in this letter that the Colossians do not turn from Christ and therefore this hope (1:23, 27; 3:4). It is the security of this promise that has led the Colossians to rely upon Christ (i.e. their faith). It seems likely then that this same secure hope has led them away from self-focused lives in selfish gain for themselves and disdain for others and instead freed them to serve one another (i.e. their love).

Hope is then further defined as that which the Colossians heard about in *the true message of the gospel* (1:5b). Knowledge of what is beyond the grave in eternity is only gained by revelation from God, it is not able to be discovered by human ingenuity or speculation. Thus the Colossians found out about this heavenly hope when they heard the good news. The gospel is an announcement of the good news about God's saving purposes to provide forgiveness of sins in the Lord Jesus, the crucified and resurrected Messiah, one who had come from heaven, defeated death and returned to heaven (cf. Isa. 52:7; Acts 13:26; 1 Cor. 15:1–5). This message, because it is centred on who Christ is as the Son of the Father and what he has done, is a firm basis for this hope. Indeed, it is *the true message* ('the word of the truth', ESV), elsewhere in Colossians described as 'the word of God' (1:25) and 'the word of Christ' (3:16).[13] That is, the message is objectively true despite its detractors. This again contrasts with the 'hollow and deceptive' and merely human speculations of the false teachers (2:8, 18, 22). It is only in God's gospel message about Christ that hope can be found, a true and certain hope that is therefore trustworthy and the basis of faith and love.

**6.** Although Paul has been talking about the gospel earlier in 1:3–5 with reference to their faith in Christ and their heavenly hope, in 1:6–7 Paul turns to focus more specifically on the fruit-bearing effect of the gospel (1:6, 8) and the messenger who brought

---

13. The phrase is more woodenly translated as 'the word of the truth of the gospel'. I have taken 'the gospel' here to be in apposition to 'the word of the truth' and 'truth' as a description of the message.

the gospel to them and has reported of this fruit to Paul (1:7). The gospel is not a message that is either ineffective or only informational. Nor is it only effective for limited locations or groups of people. The gospel Paul proclaims is God's 'word of truth' (NASB; cf. ESV, NRSV) and therefore comes with God's life-giving power. Where the gospel is present, so also is there fruit and growth, meaning people of every nation are 'rescued from the dominion of darkness' and brought 'into the kingdom of the Son' (1:13) when they hear the gospel and *truly understand God's grace*. In the parable of the soils Jesus likewise combines references to the growth and fruit-bearing effect of the word in explaining the mystery of the kingdom (Matt. 13:23, 32; Mark 4:8–20). Similarly the book of Acts plots the spread of 'the word' and its 'growth' (Acts 6:7; 12:24; 19:20). It is possible that in this letter which looks back to Genesis 1–2 with references to creation (1:16–17), and Christ as the 'image' of God (1:15; 3:10), these references to 'growth' and 'fruit' in 'the whole world' also look back to God's plans for humanity which are now fulfilled in the new humanity that belongs to Christ.[14]

In stating the effectiveness of the gospel in this way, Paul may again have the false teachers and their schismatic, works-based, deceitful and ultimately ineffective lies in view (particularly since this is his second reference to truth in two verses). It is the gospel that is powerful to save and transform, not the human-derived rules of the false teachers. Furthermore, rather than divide the Colossian believers into 'haves' and 'have nots', the gospel unites them with believers *throughout the whole world* in God's grace. Paul's reference to 'God's grace' is another complementary summary of the gospel message that he referred to in 1:5 as 'the word of truth'. To understand this message is to understand 'God's grace' because the message announces forgiveness of sins (1:14; 2:13) and peace

---

14. Cf. Moo, p. 88 with reference to the words 'grow' and 'multiply' (not 'bear fruit') in Gen. 1:28 (creation); 28:3; 35:11 (Abraham and seed); Exod. 1:7 (the exodus); Jer. 3:16; 23:3 (promises for beyond the exile). See Beale, pp. 47–50 for an expanded discussion of an allusion to Gen. 1:28.

with God (1:20–21) even though we were at enmity with God (1:21) and deserving of God's wrath (3:6).

**7–8.** As the previous verse implied, although the gospel effects fruit and growth, nevertheless it is brought and carried by human instruments and requires a response. The Colossians have 'heard' the word of truth (1:5), 'heard and truly understood' the gospel of God's grace (1:6), and they have 'learned' this message from Epaphras (1:7). All of this indicates that the gospel message, although 'effective' in the sense that it changes lives, nevertheless is mediated through human messengers who proclaim and articulate this message in a way that is coherent and understandable. Thus Paul turns to Epaphras, the human instrument responsible for the arrival of the gospel in Colossae. Before unpacking the flow of thought, let us pause to note all the ways Paul describes Epaphras, both here and again towards the conclusion of the letter in 4:12–13. Epaphras is: the one from whom they 'learned' the gospel; 'beloved'; a 'fellow slave'; a 'faithful servant of Christ's'; represents Paul (on 'our behalf'); from Colossae ('one of you'); a 'slave of Christ'; always wrestling in prayer for them; Paul 'testifies' about him; and he has deep concern and works hard for the Colossians. Why this emphasis on Epaphras in 1:7–8 (and again in 4:12–13)? Perhaps Paul simply emphasizes the reliability of the faithful servant who brought the gospel as a way of reminding the Colossians of the power of the gospel they first heard and that this gospel is the 'real deal' being delivered by a genuine apostolic associate and therefore one with Christ's approval. In a context in which Paul highlights the truth and power of the gospel message, probably with an eye on the false teachings, his emphasis on the messenger's reliability and commitment to Christ may also have an eye on the false teachers. Perhaps they were undermining the messenger that brought the gospel to the Colossians, or implying some inadequacy in the Colossian church's beginnings compared to the 'advances' these new teachings would bring to the Colossians. It is not uncommon for false teachers to claim that everything a person has understood about the gospel up to now is mistaken or misguided.

We learn (from vv. 7–8; as well as Col. 4:12; Phlm. 23) that Epaphras was originally from Colossae; the one who brought the gospel to Colossae; and Paul's 'fellow prisoner' (Phlm. 23). Since Paul describes him as *our dear fellow servant* and *a faithful minister of Christ on our behalf*, it seems likely that Epaphras was commissioned by Paul to bring the gospel to Colossae.[15] Epaphras could have been sent to Colossae during Paul's two to three years in Ephesus when 'all who lived in the province of Asia heard the word of the Lord' (Acts 19:10). Paul's description of Epaphras as a 'fellow slave' (*syndoulos*; NET) is only used elsewhere by Paul in 4:7 of Tychicus.[16] This rare description points to the lordship of Jesus and indicates that even if Epaphras returned to Colossae at the initiative of Paul, they both serve a common master (cf. 4:1). The 'servant-hearted' nature of Epaphras is reiterated with Paul's additional description of him as a 'faithful servant of Christ' (NASB).[17] The term 'servant' (*diakonos*) is used in this context in the sense of one who is an intermediary in bringing the gospel.[18] Paul speaks of his own commitments similarly in terms of service of the gospel, and service of the church, in 1:23–25. Furthermore, although all the Colossians who belonged to Christ can be called 'faithful' in view of their faith in Christ (1:2, 4), the term is used here to refer in particular to Epaphras' reliability in passing on the truth of the

---

15. For more on these terms see 4:7. There is a textual variant here reflected in the translation 'your behalf' (ESV). The manuscript evidence favours the first person pronoun 'our' (NIV).
16. The term appears only ten times in the NT, four of them in Matt. 18:28–33.
17. The translation 'minister' (e.g. NIV) could be misunderstood in some modern church settings to refer to an ordained position in a church.
18. BDAG, p. 230 (meaning #1). The term can refer to the government (Rom. 13:4, for God), false apostles (2 Cor. 11:15, for Satan), Christ (Gal. 2:17, for sin), Paul and others for the gospel (1 Cor. 3:5–6; Eph. 3:7; 6:21 and Col. 4:7 [Tychicus]; 1 Tim. 4:6); 'deacons' (Phil. 1:1; 1 Tim. 3:8, 12); and all who follow Jesus' example in 'becoming great' by 'becoming a servant' (Matt. 20:26; 23:11; Mark 9:35; 10:43). BDAG also defines the term as 'assistant' to a superior in some contexts (meaning #2).

gospel.[19] Epaphras was 'dearly loved' (CSB) by Paul, faithful to Christ and he clearly loved the Colossian believers as is evident in his prayerful concern for them (4:12).[20]

Now present with Paul again, Epaphras has told him about the Colossians' love: the love for all of God's people that Paul has just been describing in 1:4–5. In the only explicit reference to the Holy Spirit in Colossians (though cf. 1:9; 3:16), Paul describes their love for one another as a love *in the Spirit* (1:8). In this context this probably means the Holy Spirit is the one producing this fruit in their lives (Gal. 5:22).

*Theology*

Paul has a lot to say in these few verses about God and the gospel and the people of God that the gospel produces. Continuing from the opening verses there is much here again about the initiative of God in the lives of the Colossian believers. He is the one that Paul thanks for the presence of faith in their lives and the evidence of this faith in their love. God's goodness is also why understanding the gospel message can be summarized as understanding 'God's grace' (1:6). Yet a trinitarian framework is also evident here since even though the gospel message is summarized as 'God's grace', those who bring the gospel are described as servants of Christ, and even though God is the one being thanked for their love, it is the Spirit who enabled their love (1:8). The work of the triune God is oriented towards the creation of a people belonging to God ('saints' 1:4) and thus it is a corollary that there is one people of God. Love for his people is to extend to 'all' of his people, and the gospel that came to the Colossians is the same gospel that bears fruit throughout the world because it is 'the word of truth' (1:4). As the word of truth and the message of God's grace, it is in this gospel that God reveals the realities of eternity and thus the security of our heavenly hope. Nothing the false teachers offer can match this.

---

19. See 'faithful' in 4:7, 9.
20. For others who are 'beloved' in Paul's correspondence with these Colossian believers see 4:7, 9, 14; Phlm. 1, 16.

## ii Prayer for the Colossians' continued growth in the gospel (1:9–14)

*Context*

In these verses Paul moves from a summary of the content of his prayer: knowledge of God's will (1:9); to the purpose for praying this: to live a life worthy of the Lord and pleasing him (1:10a); to the means by which this can be done, using four participles: bearing fruit, growing, being strengthened and giving thanks (1:10b–12a). Then Paul rounds out the discussion with what the Father has done, probably providing further reasons for giving thanks. The greatness of Paul's vision of the Christian life shines through here, not only in the bold requests for the Colossian believers, but in the fullness of the ways in which he describes the requests. This can be seen in the concentrated use of the Greek word for 'all' (*pas* in Greek). The word 'all' is used with 'wisdom and understanding' (1:9), 'pleasing' (1:10; 'every way', NIV), 'good work' (1:10; 'every', NIV), 'power' (1:11) and 'endurance and patience' (1:10; 'great', NIV).

Specific terms are repeated from the preceding verses such as 'pray' (1:3, 9), 'thanks' (1:3, 12) to the 'Father' (1:3, 12), 'heard' (1:4, 9), 'know/understand' (1:6, 9, 10), 'bearing fruit' (1:6, 10), 'growing' (1:6, 10), as well as conceptual allusions to the future hope in the gospel (1:5, 12) and a brief elaboration on the good news (1:13–14). The many links with the preceding section show that Paul has in mind his thankfulness for what God has already done when he turns to pray for the outworking of this in the Colossians' lives.

These verses also anticipate themes to be developed in the body of the letter. This is especially seen in the way 1:14 begins with a relative pronoun ('in whom') that looks back to the reference to 'the Son' (1:13). Thus 'the Son' becomes the subject of the next main section (1:15). Paul's main prayer request for the Colossians to be filled with the knowledge of God's will through wisdom and understanding (1:9) foreshadows his later description of the gospel as the mystery that God has made known, and that is embodied in Christ, in whom are hidden all the treasures of wisdom and knowledge (1:25–27; 2:2–3). Likewise the references to redemption and the forgiveness of sins will also be developed in the body of the letter (1:21–22; 2:13–14). The purpose of Paul's prayer that they 'live a life' ('walk') worthy of the Lord (1:10) connects this prayer to the central purpose statement of the letter, that the Colossians continue to 'live' ('walk') in Christ (2:6–7). This section, therefore, is an important transition in this letter, showing what Paul prays for, why he prays this, and how the answer to this prayer will be seen in their lives.

*Comment*
**9.** As Paul said in verse 3, whenever he prays for the Colossian believers he gives thanks to God. Now Paul continues to unpack the content of his prayer for the Colossians, moving from thanksgiving to specific petition. Just as Jesus taught, Paul sees God as the giver of good gifts and so his *praying* is characterized by 'asking' (cf. Luke 11:9–13). As the opening phrase, *for this reason*, and the repetition of key phrases from 1:3–8 throughout 1:9–14 show, Paul's request is in keeping with what God has already done in the lives of the believers. It is because of the fruit of the gospel in their lives that Paul is spurred on to continual prayer for them. Paul's prayer for them is not, therefore, simply due to the threat of the false teachers.[21] Thus, although they already have 'fullness' (2:10) in Christ, in the sense that he is sufficient for all their spiritual needs before God, still Paul prays that God would 'fill' them with *the knowledge of his will*. When Paul said his apostleship was 'by the will of God' (1:1) he meant that it was God's sovereign purpose that was carried out in appointing him. When he later states that Epaphras prays that the Colossians 'may stand firm in all the will of God' (4:12) he means for them to live in accordance with what God has revealed in Christ.[22] In this context, because of the following purpose that Paul gives for this prayer (1:10a), God's 'will' is probably a reference to God's revealed purposes in Christ and the implications of the gospel for Christian living under the new covenant (see comments on 3:16). Thus, because this knowledge is gained *through all the wisdom and understanding that the Spirit gives* ('spiritual wisdom and understanding', ESV), the implication is that Paul refers to the knowledge of God's will that is available to them in the (Old Testament) Scriptures as the framework for understanding

---

21. Pao, p. 68.
22. Or that they may have assurance of God's sovereign purposes.

his saving purposes in the Messiah, but also to the application of this by the Spirit in light of the coming of Christ and as taught by his apostles. Similar language is found throughout the Old Testament, such as in Exodus 31:3 where Bezalel is equipped by God, Isaiah 11:2 where the descendant of David will be characterized by Spirit-given wisdom, knowledge and fear of the Lord, and many passages in the wisdom literature as a description of the person who fears the Lord (e.g. Prov. 1:7; 2:6).

This is the first reference to wisdom in Colossians and it is instructive to see how Paul uses the term in this letter. In this immediate context, *wisdom and understanding*, as we noted above, is the knowledge of God's revealed will in Christ, and is the continued outworking of what they had 'understood' and 'learned' in the gospel of Christ (1:6, 7; cf. 2:2). Indeed, Christ is the one 'in whom are hidden all the treasures of wisdom and knowledge' (2:3). Teaching one another in wisdom will be how the 'word of Christ' dwells richly among the Colossians (3:16) and seeking to point others to the gospel is how one 'walks in wisdom' among those outside the Christian community (4:5). In contrast to this emphasis on the gospel of Christ, the regulations of the false teachers only have the 'appearance of wisdom' (2:23). Thus, 'wisdom and understanding' for Paul is not abstract observations on life, but life seen through the scriptural lens of God's saving purposes in Christ, as explained by his apostles and applied and grasped by the Holy Spirit.

**10.** Having given the content of his prayer as a request for the knowledge of God's will, and the means by which this knowledge will be gained as wisdom and understanding given by the Spirit, Paul now specifies the purpose for this prayer for knowledge of God's will. The goal is so that the Colossians may live lives *worthy of the Lord and please him in every way*. The phrase *live a life* could be translated 'walk' (ESV, NASB; Greek *peripateō*) and recalls the Old Testament metaphor of 'walking' that refers to living in the ways of God, that is in obedience to him, in wisdom (e.g. Deut. 11:22; Prov. 6:22; 8:20).[23] Paul says that this will be so that they live

---

23. On the meaning of 'walk', translated as 'live a life' here in the NIV ('lead lives', NRSV) see also comments on 2:6 (cf. also 3:7; 4:5).

lives *worthy of the Lord*. In Colossians the 'Lord' is a reference to the Lord Jesus (1:1; 2:6; 3:17, 24). This phrase, therefore, confirms the above conclusion that Paul prays they would know how to live in the light of the gospel of Christ. This phrase also continues the salvation-historical understanding of 'God's will' noted above since to walk in God's ways now means to live a life *worthy of the Lord*. 'Worthy' means to live in such a way that one grasps the greatness of who Jesus is as 'Lord' (something that Paul will unpack in the rest of this chapter), such that this wonder shapes believers' lives and they reflect his likeness. Despite his greatness and our need of God's grace (1:6), astonishingly, Paul states that this knowledge means that believers can *please him in every way*.[24] There is both challenge and encouragement here. The challenge is that the orientation of believers' lives is to be pleasing the Lord, not pleasing the old self (3:9) or the false teachers (2:16, 18, 20). This amazing statement is also a great encouragement, however, to those who have grasped the greatness of the Lord Jesus. To know and to live in accordance with God's will as seen in the gracious message of the gospel is to know that he is pleased.

The four participles in the Greek text of 1:10b–12a which follow further unpack what it looks like to 'walk in a manner worthy of the Lord and pleasing to him'. It will involve 'bearing fruit', 'growing', 'being strengthened' and 'giving thanks'. The comprehensiveness of Paul's confidence is reinforced with the reference to *bearing fruit in every good work*. That Paul continues to have 1:3–8 in view is seen in the repetition of the words *bearing fruit* and *growing* from 1:6. There Paul was referring to the spread and acceptance of the gospel. Here he is referring to their daily lives growing in conformity to the gospel. *Good work* in the context of Colossians can be understood in contrast to the description of 'evil work' in 1:21 that characterized behaviour in alienation from God, and is defined further in the description of the 'clothing' believers 'put on' in 3:12–17 where Paul concludes with

---

24. The clause could be a second (parallel) purpose for being filled with the knowledge of God's will, or the goal of walking in a manner worthy of the Lord.

reference to every 'work' being done in the name of the Lord Jesus (3:17).[25]

Paul's reference to the *knowledge of God* can be understood in light of his preceding emphasis on 'knowledge' in this context. The verb *epiginōskō* ('to know') is used in 1:6, and the cognate noun *epignōsis* ('knowledge') is used in 1:9 and again here in 1:10. Thus, if responding to the gospel may be described as 'understanding' or 'knowing' the grace of God (1:6), and if on the basis of this Paul continues to ask that God fill them with the 'knowledge' of his will in the application of the gospel to their daily lives (1:9), the continuing outworking of this is growing in the 'knowledge of God'. This is the heart of the good news and the essence of the Christian life, knowing God himself (John 17:3).

**11.** How is such a high vision for the Christian life able to be attained and what does it look like? With the third participle in this sequence, 'being strengthened', and in a piling up of terms for power, Paul affirms that such lives are possible only through *being strengthened with all power according to his glorious might*. The NRSV captures the play on words in translating Paul's prayer that they may be 'made strong with all the strength that comes from his glorious power'. As Paul has shown in 1:8 (with reference to love) and 1:9 (with reference to wisdom and understanding), life in the new covenant for believers is a life that includes both the knowledge of God's will in light of the coming of Christ as well as the provision of his Spirit to enable new covenant obedience. The passive voice indicates that God is the one doing the strengthening, and the references to 'all' and 'glory' reinforce the fullness of his provision in keeping with his majesty. Thus, in contrast to the human-originated demands of the false teachers, Paul's prayer shows that God empowers his people to walk in his ways. What this looks like is not viewed in terms of spectacular demonstrations of power or momentary bursts of enthusiasm, but rather *endurance and patience*. The two terms are probably not meant to be firmly distinguished, but express the same general idea. *Endurance* is continued trust in

---

25. The same Greek word *ergon* is used in 1:10, 21; 3:17. BDAG defines *ergon* as 'deeds . . . exhibiting a consistent moral character', p. 390.

the Lord over the long haul through the ups and downs of living in a fallen world, especially in the face of trials, even while there remains a continual tendency to live in such a way that is not worthy of the Lord. Such endurance is the outworking of *patience* that learns to wait for the complete fulfilment of the Lord's purposes in the age to come.[26]

**12.** Paul now concludes his sequence of descriptors of those who know God's will in order to live lives worthy of and pleasing to the Lord. In a sequence of four participles, Paul says that this will involve 'bearing fruit' in every good work, 'growing' in the knowledge of God, 'being strengthened' with God's power to endure, and finally, *giving joyful thanks to the Father*.[27] Paul began his prayer with thankfulness to the Father because he is the source of their faith and love. Now he concludes his prayer with the observation that thankfulness is the characteristic not just of his own prayer but of all believers.[28] In this context, thankfulness will arise due to the recognition of God's power in the gospel and the fruit of the gospel in their lives, their deepening knowledge of him and his grace in the gospel, and his strengthening power that enables them to persevere. Indeed, the Father's saving work is the focus of 1:12b–13.

In the following description of the Father, therefore, Paul focuses on what the Father has done for believers: he has 'qualified' us, 'rescued' us and 'brought' us into the kingdom. Three great reasons for giving thanks to the Father! Verse 14 will add to this the blessings we have from being in the kingdom. The term *qualified* (only used in 2 Cor. 3:6 elsewhere in the New Testament) refers to the means by which believers can be sure they can look forward

---

26. Cf. the same word for 'patience' (*makrothumia*) in 3:12; Heb. 6:12; Jas 5:10.
27. Since each of the participles has a connecting prepositional phrase, it seems best to link the phrase 'with joy' at the end of 1:11 to 'giving thanks' in 1:12 (NIV, NRSV) rather than link it with 'endurance and patience' in 1:11 (ESV, NKJV).
28. On thankfulness elsewhere in Colossians, see comments on 1:3; 2:7; 3:17; 4:2.

to their *inheritance*. Their confidence comes not from their ability to endure or hold on, but from the authorization that comes from none other than the Father himself. The language of 'inheritance' and God's 'holy people' again indicates both continuity and discontinuity from Old Testament themes. 'Inheritance' is a term used for the promise of the land to the people of Israel (Exod. 6:8; Num. 26:55; Deut. 26:1). The term is used here to refer to the promise of God's presence in heaven (1:5). While the future orientation of 1:5 did not discount a present realization of that promise already in anticipation of that future reality, so here 'inheritance' points to the future reality that will be described as realized already in the next verse as a transfer into God's 'kingdom'. Such a promise is for God's *holy people* (see comments on 1:2 on 'holy'), that is, the people that God himself has set apart to belong to him through faith in the Lord Jesus. Similar language to that found here and the following verse is used in Acts 26:18. In the words of the Lord Jesus, Paul's ministry will involve people turning from 'darkness' to 'light' to receive 'forgiveness of sins' and an 'inheritance' among those who have been 'sanctified' (or made holy) by faith in him.[29] The reference to 'the light' contrasts with the 'dominion of darkness' in 1:13 (hence the NIV addition of the reference to 'kingdom'). Still, the references to knowledge, wisdom and understanding in the preceding verses may indicate that the description of believers as 'saints in light' (ESV, NASB; cf. NRSV) refers to their true understanding of God's grace in the gospel in contrast to those who, in darkness, rely on merely human tradition (cf. 2:8; Ps. 43:3).[30]

**13.** The Father's saving work and the inheritance of his people is further described with two parallel actions. On the one hand they are *rescued . . . from the dominion of darkness*. On the other hand they are also *brought . . . into the kingdom of the Son he loves*. With the term *rescued* ('delivered') Paul uses language that was used of God's rescue of individuals (e.g. 2 Sam. 22:18, 44, 49; and regularly in the psalms, e.g. Ps. 6:4; 7:1 [LXX 6:5; 7:2], as well as his rescue and

---

29. Thus it could be that Paul's explanation of God's saving purposes here has been shaped by Jesus himself.
30. Although some see 'light' as modifying 'inheritance' here, Harris, p. 31.

'redemption' (1:14) of Israel from Egypt (Exod. 6:6), and such language shaped the hope of Israel's prophets (Isa. 42:7, 16; Hos. 13:14).[31] In this context the term highlights the believers' helplessness to escape the wrath of God that sin deserves (3:6) and the term *dominion* further accentuates this helplessness with reference to the ruling power that dominated lives lived in separation from God. *Darkness* indicates that such a rule of sin apart from God's grace is ultimately the rule of Satan (cf. Ps. 107:14; see again Acts 26:18).

But, thanks be to the Father, he has rescued us from sin and Satan and graciously brought us into another realm and rule, the kingdom of his Son. This kingdom is also called the kingdom of God in 4:11 and refers to the saving rule of God over his people, long anticipated and brought into this world with the arrival of the Son (cf. Mark 1:15).[32] In keeping with Jesus' own teaching on both the inaugurated and the future reality of the kingdom, Paul teaches that believers currently enjoy the blessings of knowing God as Saviour (cf. 1:14), but will enter the fullness or consummation of his saving rule in the age to come (Acts 14:22), the hope of heaven (1:5).

The title *Son* may pick up on messianic hopes for the king in the line of David who would be God's 'son' in the sense that he would reflect God's rule (2 Sam. 7:14; Ps. 2:7; cf. Matt. 26:63; Acts 13:33). That Jesus as Son is 'beloved' by the Father recalls the Father's pronouncement at his baptism and entrance into public ministry (Matt. 3:17). Still, this context also focuses on the unique relationship the Father has with the Son (e.g. 1:3) who existed with him prior to creation (1:16–17; cf. John 1:1). It is the unique Son of the Father who came to be the royal son. The emphasis here is that this Son as *the Son he loves* assures believers that the Father's rescue of them and love for them does not falter, as if it were determined by their fruitful good work (1:10). On the contrary, this rescue is as secure as the Father's love for his own Son, who (unlike us) is untainted by sin.

---

31. Pao, p. 76.

32. On the 'realm transfer' involved see comments on 1:2.

**14.** Paul concludes his account of what the Father has done for his people with the blessings entailed in this rescue and transfer into the kingdom of his Son: it is in the Son that we have *redemption, forgiveness of sins*. The majesty of the Son will then be the focus of 1:15–20. The term *redemption* picks up on the use of the term 'rescue' in the previous verse and describes our salvation with the imagery of slavery and the purchase of slaves for their freedom. Ephesians 1:7 specifies that the price of this redemption was the sacrificial death ('the blood') of the Son.[33] Similarly, Galatians 3:13 states that Christ 'redeemed' us from the curse (i.e. the punishment) of the law, by becoming a curse in our place (i.e. by taking that punishment upon himself). This redemption, and the cause of this slavery, is further described with the phrase *forgiveness of sins* (see again Jesus' words in Acts 26:18). This points to the predicament which we needed to be freed from: 'our sins', that is, our rebellion against God and his good commands. Paul's salvation-historical framework is in view here with reference to the new covenant promise of forgiveness of sins, which, as Jesus said, was inaugurated with his death, and is received through repentance and faith (Jer. 31:34; Luke 22:20; 24:46–47).

Thus, although the details are not elaborated upon here (cf. 2:13–14), the close association of 'redemption' and 'forgiveness of sins' as descriptions of the blessings of the Father's 'rescue' indicates that he rescues sinners from the debt of unforgiven sin by his grace, through the death of his beloved Son, and enables them to turn to the Son he loves. The emphasis in the concluding verses of Paul's prayer, therefore, is on thankfulness to the Father for his work of salvation through the Son: he is the one who has 'qualified' us for the inheritance, he is the one who has 'delivered' us from the realm of darkness, he is the one who has 'brought' us into the saving rule of his beloved Son, and in his Son we have assurance of the sins forgiven. This is why grasping this gospel message is described as 'truly understanding God's grace' above (1:6). Amazingly, in this

---

33. There is a textual variant that shows some later scribes added that phrase here in Colossians (cf. NKJV), probably because of the influence of Ephesians 1:7.

context, 'giving thanks' to the Father for all of this is itself an answer to Paul's prayer and part of what it means to 'live a life worthy of the Lord and please him in every way' (1:10).

*Theology*
These verses continue the emphasis of the preceding verses on the initiative and grace of God. Just as Paul thanked God for the faith and love evident in the Colossians so he prays that God would continue to apply the gospel to their lives. God is the one who will enable them to grow in their knowledge of his will in wisdom and understanding. Likewise, God is the one who strengthens them to be able to live this way with endurance and patience. As Paul concludes his prayer with thanksgiving to the Father he again highlights the Father's initiative in salvation as reasons for this thanksgiving. It is the Father who 'rescued' and 'brought' us into the kingdom of his Son. The Son, likewise, is the one in whom we have redemption and forgiveness.

These verses also highlight the continuity and discontinuity between the Testaments. The language of 'inheritance', 'rescue' and 'redemption' alludes to the exodus events in which God rescued his people from slavery and brought them to the land to worship him. Yet Paul does not refer to a transfer from one geographical location to another here, for he is talking in new covenant terms of the 'forgiveness of sins'. The hoped-for eternal inheritance is the enjoyment of God in his presence. Thus permeating this section is the wonderful privilege of 'knowing God' by his grace. The reason for our need of rescue, redemption and forgiveness, together with the greatness of the Son through whom the Father accomplishes these blessings, will now be developed in the rest of the letter.

## B. The gospel centres on the Son's supremacy (1:15–20)

*Context*
This section is a continuation of the preceding verses as the opening word of 1:15 looks back to the reference to the Son in 1:13–14. Nevertheless, the concentrated focus on the Son in the following verses justifies treating this section as a discrete development in the letter. In its immediate setting the passage serves to highlight

the greatness of the Son into whose kingdom God's people have been brought, and provides further encouragement to give thanks to the Father. Since so much of the rest of the letter is oriented towards encouraging the Colossian believers not to depart from the sufficiency of Christ, however, it is not surprising that a number of terms and phrases are also picked up later in the letter. Some of these include the following: Christ's supremacy over every power and authority (1:16; 2:10b, 15); Christ as 'head' of the body, the church (1:18; 2:19; and 'head' over every power and authority, 2:10b); Christ's resurrection and its significance for those who belong to him (1:18; 2:12–13; 3:1–4); the 'fullness' of God 'dwelling' in Jesus (1:19; 2:9); the new humanity in Christ (1:18; 2:10–11); and the reconciliation that 'makes peace' between God and sinful humanity through the cross (1:20 and 1:21–22; 2:13–14).[34] Furthermore, Paul probably has his teaching on the supremacy of Christ in view later as he tells the Colossians that he 'proclaims him' (1:28), urges them to continue to live in him as their Lord (2:6), warns of teachings that do not depend on Christ (2:8) or that conflict with the reality that is found in Christ (2:17), declares that Christ is all and is in all (3:11) and encourages them to do everything in the name of the Lord Jesus (3:17).

As one of the highest mountain peaks of Christology, not only of Colossians but of all of Paul's letters, in showing the majesty of the Lord Jesus, this passage has also understandably attracted a lot of scholarly attention.[35] Three issues that have particularly attracted attention are: the structure of the passage, the style of the passage and whether or not the subject of the passage, Jesus, is described as wisdom personified. Since the literature on these topics is enormous, I will only summarize the main issues, indicate the approach I will be taking and provide pointers to further discussion.

First, the structure of the passage. The following is a very abbreviated outline of the passage to help identify the main Greek phrases in this discussion as well as where the main dividing lines are and why.

---

34. See the table in Gordley, *Hymn*, pp. 265–266.
35. See summary, ibid., pp. 5–18.

> ¹⁵He is (*hos estin*) the image . . .
>   ¹⁶For in/by him all things . . .
>   ¹⁷And he is (*kai autos estin*) before all things
>     and (*kai*) in him all things hold together
> ¹⁸And he is (*kai autos estin*) the head . . .
>   He is (*hos estin*) the beginning . . .
>   ¹⁹For in him . . .
>   ²⁰and through him to reconcile all things . . .

There are three main ways of dividing the passage:[36]

1. a two-part structure of 1:15–17 and 1:18–20;
2. a two-part structure of 1:15–18a and 1:18b–20 because of the similar *hos estin* (who/he is) in 1:15 and 18b; and
3. a three-part structure of 1:15–16, 17–18a, and 18b–20 because of the sequence of *kai* . . . *kai* . . . *kai* . . . ('and . . . and . . . and') in 1:17–18a.

I follow the first suggestion which broadly highlights the Son's supremacy over all creation (1:15–17) and the Son's supremacy over the new creation (1:18–20). In this breakdown, the relative clauses 'who/he is' in 1:15 and 18b introduce the following verses that further develop the statement that immediately precedes (i.e. 1:13–14; and 1:18a). Verse 17 is better understood as a summary of the implications of the preceding verses rather than the centre of the passage. Therefore, the three *kai* . . . *kai* . . . *kai* . . . phrases of 1:17–18a combine to conclude 1:15–16 (which 1:17 does) and introduce 1:18–20 (which 1:18a does).[37]

Second, the style of the passage has also been the subject of much debate, centring mainly around the question of whether or not this passage is a hymn. There are clear stylistic emphases in these verses that are not found in the preceding or following verses. The following table summarizes Moo's comparison of 1:15–20 with

---

36. See the summary in Harris, p. 38; more extensively, Gordley, *Hymn*, pp. 5–16.
37. McKnight, *Colossians*, p. 144.

a similar length of verses before (1:3–8 and 9–14) and after (1:21–23) this section.

Table 1: A comparison of 1: 15–20 with surrounding verses

|  | 1:3–8 | 1:9–14 | 1:15–20 | 1:21–23 |
| --- | --- | --- | --- | --- |
| adverbial participles | 6 | 6 | 1 | 4 |
| indicative verbs | 2 | 1 | 7 | 2 |
| pronouns | 9 | 4 | 0 | 2 |
| 1st/2nd person verbs | 6 | 4 | 0 | 3 |

In contrast to the complex sentences of the surrounding verses, these verses are characterized by a series of assertions about Christ.[38] Debate then surrounds what the significance of this shift in style might be. Does this shift in style mean that this is a hymn? If so, was this an established hymn that Paul adapts or was it written by Paul for this letter? Does the description of this passage as 'elevated prose' differ much from calling it a hymn? If this is a hymn, then is this what Paul alludes to later in the letter when he encourages the Colossians to 'sing . . . hymns and spiritual songs' (3:16)? Whether or not this was already written and adapted by Paul or written by Paul himself, it is clearly integrated into the argument of the letter. If an ancient hymn may be described in terms of its contents that primarily centre on 'praise of the divine in a descriptive or declarative style' then this passage could be called a hymn.[39] Apart from the insight it might give us into early Christian hymnody, however, once the obvious point about the place of the passage in the argument of the letter is granted, it does not

---

38. Moo, p. 108.
39. The definition provided by Gordley, *Hymn*, p. 32. Cf. Balchin, 'Colossians 1:15–20', pp. 65–94 for an earlier recognition of many of the following stylistic features and critique of the view that this is a hymn. For a more recent critique of the view that this is a hymn, with reference also to patristic reception history see Edsall and Strawbridge, 'Songs', pp. 290–311.

make much difference to the exegesis of the passage whether one calls it a hymn or elevated prose written before or by Paul.

Many interpreters, regardless of their view of the prehistory or genre of this passage, recognize the following literary features of the passage. There are parallel references, in the same sequence, in 1:15–17, 18–20, such as:

'who is' (1:15, 18)
'firstborn' (1:15, 18)
'for in him' (1:16, 19)
the 'heavens' and the 'earth' (1:16, 20)
'in', 'through' and 'for' (1:16, 20)

There are also literary devices such as isocolon (a similar number of syllables in pairs of lines) in 1:16, 17–18, 20; inclusio in 1:16 (*ektisthē ta panta . . . ta panta . . . ektistai*); antithesis (heaven and earth, things visible and things invisible); paronomasia (a play on similar words, *orata, aorata*); epanaphora (repetition at the beginning of successive clauses, *eite . . . eite . . . eite . . . eite*); and alliteration (. . . *ai, . . . ai, . . . ai*; especially 1:16).[40] The repetition of the word 'all' (*pas*) throughout the passage (eight times) serves both to link the various claims about Christ as well as emphasize the main point of the passage: the supremacy of Christ over all. As we noted above, what Paul says here in exaltation of the Lord Jesus is directly linked to the preceding reference to the kingdom of the Son and to what the rest of the letter says about Christ's sufficiency. Clearly it was the identity of the subject of these lines that led Paul to use such exalted language in this passage.

Third, much discussion has centred around the question of whether or not Jesus is described in language drawn from the wisdom tradition and in particular the personification of wisdom.[41] Stimuli for this suggestion are similarities in Proverbs 8:22–31 and texts in Jewish literature, especially Philo (and Wisdom; Sirach),

---

40. Witherington, p. 133.

41. See e.g. Dunn, pp. 88–94; McKnight, *Colossians*, pp. 138–143; Talbert, pp. 187–188; Beetham, *Echoes*, pp. 113–141.

that use terms such as 'image', 'firstborn', and 'beginning' for wisdom and that refer to the role of wisdom in creation and therefore the pre-existence of wisdom before creation (Philo, *Legum Alegoria* 1.43 calls wisdom 'beginning' and 'image'). Colossians also regularly refers to 'wisdom' (*sophia*; 1:9, 28; 2:3, 23; 3:16; 4:5). However, parallel terms are not necessarily evidence of direct dependence since common terms may be used in different ways. Although the majority of interpreters are in favour of these connections, I will briefly summarize Fee's objections.[42]

The term 'firstborn' (*prōtotokos*) is nowhere used for wisdom in Philo.[43] The 'image' in Wisdom 7:26 is developing the metaphor of a mirror and is not alluding to Genesis 1–2 as Paul is. In Colossians, the Son *is* before all things, not 'created' before all things, and he *is* the beginning, not just there 'at' the beginning (in contrast to wisdom in Sirach 1:4, 9; 24:9; Prov. 8:22–23; and wisdom is never

---

42. Fee, *Christology*, pp. 317–325, 595–619 (cf. also Ridderbos, *Paul*, pp. 78–80; McDonough, *Christ*, pp. 175–179; Bauckham, 'Confessing', pp. 157–161, 170–171).
43. The same can be said for the use of *prōtotokos* in Wisdom 18:3; Psalms of Solomon 13:9; 18:4 (the only uses in those books) which all refer to firstborn children. Some suggest a similarity with another term Philo uses, *prōtogonos*, Beale, p. 122. (Some cite Philo, *Quaestiones et Solutiones in Genesin* 4.97 but 'firstborn mother of all things' is not close to Paul and there is no Greek text to confirm the word Philo uses.) Beetham, *Echoes*, pp. 126–127, n. 61 suggests that since Philo uses *prōtogonos* with reference to 'word', and since word and wisdom overlap in Philo there is more to these than Fee allows. This might be so with *De Agricultura* 51 (though there *prōtogonos* modifies 'son'); *De Confusione Linguarum* 146; and *De Somniis* 1.215, but it doesn't appear to be so for *De Posteritate Cain* 1.63 and *De Fuga et Inventione* 208 (both with ref. to Israel as 'son'), and *De Confusione Linguarum* 63 (with ref. to a son imitating his father). Beetham also cites Philo, *Quis rerum divinarum heres sit*, 117–119 as using the same word, *prōtotokos*, as Colossians 1:15, 18 to describe the 'divine word'. However, the word there is a citation of Exodus 13:2 and parallels *prōtogenēs* to refer to firstborn in a literal sense of all that 'open the womb' in 117 before *prōtogenēs* is applied more broadly in 119.

said to be the 'goal' of creation). The references to 'wisdom' elsewhere in Colossians do undoubtedly draw on the wisdom tradition (and we could add to that the references to 'walking', see comments on 1:10; 2:6), yet they refer to believers acting 'wisely' rather than the personification of wisdom. Christ's possession of wisdom and knowledge in 2:3 does not mean that Christ is the 'Wisdom' figure (see comments on 2:3). In Colossians, creation accounts such as Genesis 1 better explain the use of terms such as 'image' and 'beginning'. 'Firstborn' (*prōtotokos*) picks up on what is said about the Davidic king in Psalm 89:27, especially since Colossians 1:15 looks back to the references to 'kingdom' and beloved 'Son' in 1:13–14.

Fee's observations should add caution to seeing personified wisdom as the main lens through which to understand Paul's description of Christ in this magnificent passage. Nevertheless, the combination of 'beginning' and 'image' with reference to wisdom and creation in Philo *Legum Alegoria* 1.43 is intriguing, as are the echoes of references to phrases used in Colossians 1 in Wisdom 1:7; 7:8, 21–22, 26, 27.[44] The wisdom tradition, therefore, is a possible background to what Paul says here, perhaps combined with creation allusions, as a way of describing the Son as Creator, yet distinguishable from the Father. In the foreground, however, are texts such as Genesis 1 and Psalm 89.[45] Even if there are potential echoes to personified wisdom here, what Paul says about Christ far exceeds what is said about wisdom in this literature: Christ is the Creator and goal of all creation. His pre-existence is assumed here because in the Creator–creation distinction, Christ is on the Creator side.[46]

### i. The Son's supremacy over creation (1:15–17)
#### Comment

**15.** Although conventions of English style require a new sentence here (as seen in most translations), Paul is continuing his description of the Father's Son. It is *the Son* in whom we have

---

44. Though see Bauckham, 'Confessing', p. 159 on the differences.
45. Beale, p. 121 uses the language of 'background' and 'foreground', though he sees more allusions to wisdom than I do here.
46. Cf. Bauckham, *Jesus*, pp. 26, 183–185; Hurtado, *Lord*, pp. 507–508.

redemption and the forgiveness of sins who is now described.[47] As noted above, Paul's apparent digression is a further development of reasons for giving thanks to the Father (which in turn is an explanation of what it means to live a life worthy of the Lord and please him in every way). God the Father has rescued us and brought us into the kingdom of his Son whom he loves. And what a kingdom this must be, just look at who this Son is! The focus is on the greatness of the Son into whose kingdom believers have been brought. When we look around us at anything and everything in creation, the Son is greater than all.

In the first phrase, *the image of the invisible God*, Paul speaks of the Son's relationship to the Father. In the second phrase, *the firstborn over all creation*, Paul speaks of the Son's relationship to creation. The use of the term 'image' in the context of this discussion of creation indicates that Genesis is in the background and that Paul probably alludes to Adam as the original representative of God and his rule over creation. Nevertheless, when combined with the description of God as 'invisible' the term 'image' has the idea of 'visible representation' that expresses the exact likeness of God's being and character. The following phrases make clear that Paul will describe the pre-existent state and creating activity of the Son. Yet the language of *image of the invisible God* also indicates that in this context Paul views the pre-existence of the Son in eternity past from the perspective of his earthly life and ministry. As Jesus said, 'Anyone who has seen me has seen the Father' (John 14:9). Even though Paul describes the Son's pre-existent state and relation to the Father in eternity past, he describes the Son as one who would come to reveal the Father and rescue his people. As Ridderbos emphasizes, for Paul, Christ is

> from before the foundation of the world and to all eternity God-for-us. It is not the Godhood of Christ in itself, but that he is God and God's Son for us ... He is God who became man and who was to become man.[48]

---

47. The relative pronoun of the Greek text is reflected in the KJV ('who is ...').
48. Ridderbos, *Paul*, p. 77

The pre-existent Son is the one who perfectly reveals what the Father is like, the Creator and Sustainer of all things.[49]

The description of the Son as *firstborn* has created difficulties for Bible readers because it sounds as though Jesus is created, even if being 'first' might sound significant. As many have pointed out, however, the language of 'kingdom' and 'firstborn', together with the repeated use of 'Christ/Messiah' in the preceding verses (1:1, 2, 3, 4, 7), probably means that the use of the term 'firstborn' recalls the description of the Davidic king in Psalm 89:27. There the phrase, 'the most exalted of the kings of the earth', that is parallel to 'firstborn', shows that the term 'firstborn' emphasizes the supremacy and priority in rank of the Davidic king, not literally that he was 'born first'.[50] David of course was neither the first king nor the oldest child. It is for this reason (and the reason given in the following verse) that the NIV correctly translates the genitive phrase that follows 'firstborn' as *over all creation*.[51] The following verse will confirm why the Son is supreme over all creation rather than being a part of creation. Thus this genitive phrase alludes to the claim that will be developed in the next verse, that the Son is on the Creator's side of the Creator–creation distinction.

**16.** The first word of this verse shows that what follows is an explanation of the previous statement that the Son is the 'firstborn over all creation'. The reason the Son is supreme over all creation is 'because' (*for*) the totality of creation only exists and has purpose with reference to him. In this regard, all creation came about and

---

49. It is even quite possible that since Paul says that the Son 'is' the image of the invisible God, whereas Genesis 1:27 states that God created humankind 'in' or 'according to' the image of God, Paul may intend that the Son is the original image that Adam was then created to reflect. See Beale's extensive discussion, pp. 80–91. I have focused instead on the description of God here as 'the invisible' God that the 'image' reveals.
50. The following verses also indicate a temporal priority as the creator of all things.
51. The translation of the genitive phrase 'of all creation' (ESV) may lead to the misunderstanding that Jesus is part of creation. The following verse would correct this misunderstanding.

exists 'in association with' Christ (*in him*).⁵² The supremacy of the Son over all creation is then reinforced with a further elaboration on *all things* as well as a final clarification. The emphasis is on Jesus' supremacy over the totality of creation. The repetition of the phrase *all things* (framing the verse), as well as the contrasting references to *in heaven and on earth* and the *visible and invisible* reinforce the idea that nothing is excluded. Even if we were to travel where no one else can go and even if we were to see what no one else can see, we would still not be able to discover anything that the Son is not supreme over.

To emphasize this even further Paul follows up with a fourfold piling up of terms for the most powerful in creation, perhaps as possible contenders to the Son's supremacy, 'whether thrones or powers or rulers or authorities'. It is possible that the four terms are merely a general reference to any rule or authority, whether human or angelic.⁵³ However, the use of similar terms in 2:15 indicates that Paul is further unpacking the *invisible* so that what Paul describes here are spiritual powers or angelic beings.⁵⁴ Just as today and throughout time, so also the Colossians may have thought that spiritual forces are powerful and are to be feared or appeased. Paul insists, however, that even the most powerful beings in the universe are only created beings and pale in comparison to the supremacy of the Son. Indeed Paul goes further, specifying that not only are all things created *through* the Son, they have been created *for him* (cf. 1 Cor. 8:6). These two prepositions 'through' and 'for' probably unpack the more general preposition 'in' and point to the beginning and end goal of creation.⁵⁵ This final phrase serves to show that the

---

52. Harris, p. 40. The agency of Christ in creation is included here, but is expressed more specifically at the end of the verse in the phrase 'through him'. Cf. also 1 Cor. 8:6.
53. See e.g. Luke 12:11; Titus 3:1 for references to human rulers. The 'authority' the false teachers ascribe to themselves in 2:8, 16, 18 should also be kept in mind here.
54. Cf. also 'dominion of darkness' in 1:13 (cf. also Rom. 8:38; Eph. 1:21; 2:2; 3:10; 6:12).
55. Moo, p. 124.

Son is at the centre of the universe. If all things are made *through him and for him* then all things must be done for his honour (3:17), all teaching that distracts and detracts from his sufficiency must be avoided (2:8) and those who are brought into his kingdom have received the most wonderful gift imaginable (1:12–14).

**17.** The comprehensive and repeated reference to *all things*, together with the repetition of a threefold 'and' (*kai*) in the Greek text of verses 17–18a, may suggest that this verse is the centre of this passage. The phrase 'who is' (NKJV; Gk. *hos estin*) that parallels 1:15 and 18b may also lend support to the view that a new section begins at 1:18b. However, the repetition of 'all things' from 1:16 suggests that Paul continues his focus on the Son's relationship to creation even as he transitions to a focus on the new creation in 1:18. Therefore this verse looks back to 1:15–16 and summarizes the main implications. By stating that the Son *is before all things*, Paul spells out an implication of the previous statements about the Son as the agent and goal of all creation: that is, his pre-existence with the Father before creation, and his pre-eminence over creation.[56] Paul summarizes his emphasis on the 'firstness' of the Son. Lest the Son's priority over creation be thought to refer only to the past act of creation, Paul clarifies that *in him all things hold together*. The verb translated as 'holds together' in this context includes a reference to 'the unity ('together') and cohesiveness . . . of the whole universe'.[57] The perfect tense draws attention to the continuing state of cohesion that the whole universe has. Thus Paul concludes this focus on the Son's relationship to creation with the astounding statement that the Son is the reason why anything in all creation continues to exist at all. In this context, the final phrase explains Paul's confidence that not only did all creation have its origin through Christ (1:15–16), Christ is also the end goal of all creation.

---

56. Cf. Harris, pp. 42–43. Thus the word 'before' in this context is understood to refer to temporal priority (as it usually does) as well as greatness with the meaning 'above all' (see BDAG, p. 864 meaning 3 which lists Jas 5:12; 1 Pet. 4:8; a similar argument of supremacy based on temporal priority is made in John 1:30).

57. Ibid., p. 43.

The point is that Christ himself is the means by which the end goal is reached. Thus Paul's point here is similar to his emphasis on the future hope that the gospel provides. Christ is the assurance that all things will reach that future goal. He is indeed the hope of glory!

### ii. *The Son's supremacy over the new creation (1:18–20)*

**18.** Paul continues his focus on the supremacy of the Son, turning now to the Son's supremacy over God's people of the new creation. The Son's relationship to the people of God is described in terms of a head's relationship to the body, which in this context highlights the Son's government and leadership of God's people. As noted above, most English translations smooth over the relative phrase 'who is the beginning' (NKJV) to begin a new phrase here. Noting the parallel with 1:15, however, helps to see that just as the relative phrase in 1:15 is designed to clarify the Son's relationship to the Father as Creator, the relative phrase here serves to clarify the Son's 'headship' of the church. The metaphor that Paul uses for the church – 'body' (*sōma*) – points to the unity and cohesiveness of the whole church in a way that is similar to 1 Corinthians 12:27–30. Likewise the use of the word 'church' (*ekklēsia*) refers not to a local congregation (as in 4:15, 16), but to all those who belong to Christ by faith. The emphasis in this context on Christ's 'supremacy' and lordship is applied to his role over the people who belong to him.[58] It is Christ himself (Gk. *autos*) who governs the people who gather to him. The description of the Son as *the beginning and the firstborn* again focuses on his priority and pre-eminence (his 'firstness').[59] In this context, because *firstborn* (see above on 1:15) is tied to the word *beginning* (again alluding to Gen. 1:1) and the phrase *from among the dead*, the term incorporates both priority in time as well as supremacy. Because the resurrection was an event reserved for the end of the age, in his resurrection Christ brings into this age

---

58. Thus the genitive 'of the body' means 'over the body' (a genitive of subordination, Campbell, p. 14; objective genitive or genitive of reference, Harris, p. 43).
59. Cf. the similar description of Reuben in Gen. 49:3 (Moo, p. 129).

that which was reserved for the end. He is the founder and leader of the new humanity and he brings those who have been rescued and reconciled with God (1:13, 22) on account of their faith in him (1:4, 23) with him into the new creation through his resurrection *from among the dead*. The description here is similar to the language of 'firstfruits' (1 Cor. 15:20) in that both 'firstness' and the 'guarantee' of more to follow is in view. By his defeat of death, Jesus has done what no one else is able to do for those who belong to him.

The final statement is a purpose clause (*so that*) showing why the Son is supreme over all creation and the new creation. This is *so that in everything he might have the supremacy*. The term 'supremacy' again emphasizes the 'firstness' of the Son that Paul has been developing throughout. Indeed some translations render the term as 'first place' (e.g. NRSV, CSB).[60] More specifically, the Son's supremacy or 'firstness' is emphasized as belonging to him alone ('he himself' NET; Gk. *autos*) and is universal (*in everything*). The Greek adjective *pas* ('all', 'everything') is used here for the sixth time in 1:15–18 and culminates the emphasis throughout these four verses on the unique and universal sovereignty of the Son. By repeatedly pointing to Christ's supremacy over 'all things' Paul aims to press home for the Colossians that Jesus Messiah is the one that believers must depend upon, not human rules or self-effort. Christ is our only hope for this life and the next. This is the all-sufficient Christ that is proclaimed in the gospel of Christ and not the self-oriented focus of the false teachers.

**19.** The opening word (*for*) shows that what follows is a further explanation of the Son's supremacy and again, as with 1:15, this has to do with the nature of his relationship with the Father. The reason why the Son has supremacy in all things is because he has the divine fullness. Although the Greek text does not explicitly use the name 'God', most translations recognize that the repetition of the phrase 'all the fullness' in 2:9 clarifies that God the Father 'in all his fullness' is the subject in this verse (and in 1:20 he is the one who reconciles and makes peace through the Son).[61] As

---

60. BDAG, p. 892.
61. Harris, p. 45. E.g. NIV, ESV ('God'); NKJV ('the Father').

Campbell notes, 'cognates of *plērōma* ['fullness'] are found in the OT (LXX) with reference to God filling heaven and earth (Ps. 72:19; Isa. 6:3; Jer. 23:24) and the temple (Ezek. 43:5; 44:4)'.[62] In fact the same language of God being 'pleased to dwell' in the temple is used in Psalm 68:16.[63] The combination of 'all' with the language of 'fullness' emphasizes the totality of the Son's deity; he is not lacking in any way. Thus this verse identifies the Son as fully God, hence his supremacy in everything, while also distinguishing between God the Son and God the Father.

**20.** This section began with reference to the Son's relationship to the Father. As the 'image' of the invisible God he perfectly reveals God as Creator and Ruler over all creation. The focus from 1:15, therefore, has been on the Son's relationship to all creation as the one in whom, through whom and for whom all things exist. In relation to creation, the Son is supreme. From 1:18 the focus has narrowed to his relationship to the people of the new creation. As head and founder of the church through his resurrection the Son is supreme there too. Furthermore this supremacy is because 'God in all his fullness was pleased to dwell' in Christ (1:19). And so, in 1:19 Paul returns to the Son's relationship to the Father and the Father remains the subject of the verbs in 1:20.[64]

With the mention of the need to *reconcile to himself all things* we are reminded that sin has caused a breach in the relationship between God and creation since humanity has rebelled against the Creator

---

62. Campbell, p. 16.
63. As many have noted. Cf. Moo, p. 131; Beale, pp. 108–109; Bauckham, 'Confessing', pp. 163–165.
64. The pronouns in this verse are notoriously tricky with some debate over the pronoun translated 'himself' in English translations (except e.g. NJB which has 'him'). Fee, *Christology*, pp. 308–312, argues that this pronoun is 'him' and that all things are reconciled to the Son (so also Moo, pp. 133–134). For arguments that the pronoun refers to God (and can be translated 'himself') see Harris, p. 46. Since the alienation is from God (1:21), the pronoun here is best understood as a reflexive 'himself' in keeping with the sense of the sentence from 1:19.

and creation has suffered for it (Rom. 1:18–32; 8:19–21). Thus we are taken back to where this excursus on the greatness of the Son began in 1:13–14 and the Father's provision of redemption and forgiveness of sins in him as the means by which the Father has 'qualified' his people to share in the inheritance that is his presence. This verse reiterates that the Son is the means (*through him*) by which God's purposes for the world are carried out. Continuing on from the previous verse, therefore, it is the Father that is the subject of the reconciling and peace-making activity. In keeping with the emphasis on 'all things', 'all' and 'everything' in the preceding verses, the object of this activity is again *all things*, emphasizing the totality of the Father's activity. This comprehensiveness is reinforced with the additional reference to *things on earth or things in heaven* which alludes to the scriptural hope for a new heaven and a new earth, that is, a new creation (Isa. 65:17; 66:22; 2 Pet. 3:13).

In the context of this letter to the Colossians, the comprehensiveness of the 'reconciling' or 'peace-making' activity could not mean that the salvation of every individual is in view. In the immediately following verses, this reconciliation is appropriated through persevering faith (1:23). Outside of the union with Christ that is appropriated through faith (2:12), the unbeliever faces wrath (3:6) rather than reconciliation. The universality of this reconciling or peace-making work described here then must mean that despite the continuing sin, rebellion and enmity of many (1:21) God's saving work is secure. He rescues his people from being the enemies of God that they were, and also disarms and defeats the enemies of his people (2:15). While rebellion persists for now, it does not succeed against God, and it will not ultimately prevail because 'the wrath of God is coming' (3:6). 'Reconciliation' in this sense includes that which is 'pacified'.[65]

The means by which God the Father reconciles is *through him*, and this is then clarified more specifically as *making peace through his blood, shed on the cross*. The pronoun referring to *his blood* ('the blood of his cross', NRSV, ESV) indicates that this is referring to the Son (specified in the NLT as 'Christ's blood'). This is the only reference

---

65. Pao, p. 103; Moo, pp. 136–137; Beale, p. 111.

to Christ's 'blood' in Colossians, but the association of the cross with sacrificial death is crucial to Paul's understanding of the accomplishment of Christ's death (see e.g. Rom. 3:25; 5:9; Gal. 3:13). Although this will be developed further in 1:21–22 and 2:13–15,[66] in this context Paul highlights the crucial role that the death of Jesus has in the Father's reconciling work. Thus, in summary, Paul began this section with the amazing claim that Jesus is the one who reveals the Father as the Creator and Sustainer of the entire universe. This is meant to assure the Colossians that the Jesus of the gospel message is supreme, nothing is outside his control. What then of the evident effects of sin in rebellious humanity and a fallen world? Paul concludes this section with a claim no less astonishing than how he began. The Son is also the Father's means by which the new creation will be brought into harmony with him. Jesus' resurrection marks the entrance of the new creation into this age. He is therefore the founder and ruler of the new humanity, the church. And Jesus' own death on a cross is the means by which sin and all its many effects throughout all of creation are dealt with. Thus this same Jesus is the one who is supreme, even over rebellious creatures and fallen creation, as the means by which the Father's comprehensive reconciling work is achieved.

*Theology*

It is hard to summarize the theological heights scaled in this passage without simply repeating all that is said here. As we have noted above, Paul's emphasis on 'all' places Christ on the side of the Creator and therefore 'above' all else. Nothing in all creation can compare with him nor compete with him. Pre-existence and what later became expressed in trinitarian terms is not argued for but presupposed. The Son is not the Father, yet he is identified with the Father.[67] They are united yet distinct. The Father and the Son create and reconcile, yet it is the Father through the Son who

---

66. The only other reference to the cross in the Greek text of Colossians is found in 2:14, where the disarming of the powers and authorities is the result (2:15).
67. See e.g. Bauckham, *Jesus*, p. 19.

creates and reconciles. The Son's incarnation is also presupposed. As evidenced in his earthly ministry, Christ reveals the Father, rules over creation, and has power over all (including spiritual forces). Yet it was his physical death on the cross and his resurrection from the dead that reconciles, defeats death and inaugurates the new creation. Christ's supremacy in creation and redemption, therefore, is meant in this context to encourage the Colossian believers. It is the sovereign Lord who is their redeemer. It is only through him that they can be reconciled to God (something Paul will take up in the following verses), and they can have confidence in him to bring all things to their intended conclusion, including their own salvation. Christ's person (who he is as God) and work (what he has accomplished in his death and resurrection) is portrayed in universal and cosmic terms in order to show the greatness of his kingdom, the saving rule of the Father's beloved Son, in whom we have redemption, the forgiveness of sins (1:13–14).

This passage also encourages believers not to fear that anything in creation can ultimately threaten the Father's good purposes. Furthermore, it is the Son, not elements in creation, who brings reconciliation with God. This means, looking ahead to the rest of the letter, that neither worship of angels, nor harsh treatment of the body, will help; such only detracts from the glory of the Son and neglects the Father's plan through him. Believers have 'fullness' in Christ. Paul's spotlight on the Son's supremacy in all things casts shade on any merely human-originated teachings the Colossians are hearing that seeks to add to or detract from his majesty.

## C. The gospel provides hope in the Son for the final judgment (1:21–23)

*Context*
As we noted in the introduction to 1:15–20, there is a noticeable shift in style in 1:21 from the preceding verses as Paul begins using again the pronoun 'you' (placed forward for emphasis in 1:21, and again in 1:22) and second person verbs ('if you continue' and 'which you heard' in 1:23). This passage, therefore, looks back to the preceding verses as Paul now applies the universal reconciling work of the Father through the Son to the Colossians. The passage

also looks further back to the introduction to the preceding section which spoke of our rescue, redemption and forgiveness in the Son (1:13–14). In these ways, the personal saving work of the Father through the Son frames the description of the supremacy of the Son over creation and the new creation. These verses further specify how we receive the blessing of the new creation. Thus the passage proceeds by highlighting our need for reconciliation (1:21), the means and purpose of this reconciliation (1:22) and the appropriation of this reconciliation (1:23). Both the purpose ('to present you . . .') and the appropriation ('not moved from the hope') look forward in confidence to the future judgment. The final verse, while looking back to the Colossians' reception of the gospel ('faith', 'hope', 'heard', 'gospel', the 'world', cf. 1:5–6), also transitions to a focus on Paul's ministry of proclaiming the gospel, which he will take up in the following verses.

*Comment*
**21.** The pronoun 'you' is placed at the beginning of this verse ('and you', NRSV, ESV) for emphasis and highlights the shift here from the universal sovereignty of the Son and the Father's comprehensive work of reconciliation through him to the specific application of this in the lives of the Colossian believers.[68] The specific application of this reconciling work of the Father must first be understood in terms of the need for this reconciliation. So this verse first describes those who are the object of the Father's reconciling work, before the following verse develops further the means and purpose of this work. Reconciliation was needed because the Colossian believers were *once . . . alienated from God*. Although the term 'alienated' (*apēllotriōmenous*) is found elsewhere in the New Testament only in Ephesians 2:14 and 4:18, it is used in the prophets to speak of the people of Israel who are separated from God and have turned to idols.[69] As indicated by these uses of the word in the Old Testament, this alienation is not merely neutral indifference;

---

68. The coordinating conjunction *kai* ('and') is omitted from the NIV, but this helps to show the link from the preceding section.
69. Cf. LXX Jer. 19:4; Ezek. 14:5, 7; Hos. 9:10.

rather, they were *enemies in your minds*, that is, they were actively 'hostile in mind' (NRSV, ESV).[70] Their previous hostility 'in mind' (i.e. in their thinking and reasoning) would have included an antagonism towards God's general revelation in creation and conscience (cf. Rom. 1:21–23, 32; 2:14–15). Paul again highlights the significance of the mind or 'mindset' (cf. Rom. 8:7) as he contrasts how they were alienated from God with how they received the gospel. Elsewhere, Paul thanks God that the Colossians had 'understood' God's grace in the gospel (1:6), and he continues to pray that they would be filled with the knowledge of God's will through wisdom and understanding (1:9), and warns them not to get taken captive through philosophy and empty deceit that depends on human teachings (2:8, 22). Indeed, he urges them to set their minds on things above rather than on earthly things (3:2).

This hostility in mind is given outward expression in *evil behaviour*. Although the Greek phrase could be understood to mean that the cause of this hostility in mind was their evil behaviour (NIV), the phrase more likely indicates the outworking of a mind hostile to God ('as expressed through your evil deeds', NET).[71] Thus it is not evil behaviour by itself that causes this alienation and hostility, such that better behaviour might be a possible remedy. Instead, this alienation from God pervades one's inner thinking in priorities, attitudes and evaluations. What is required to turn us from our hostility and rescue us from God's wrath must be truly radical, providing a way to deal with the consequences of such hostility and activity so as to be reconciled and right with God, and also a means by which this internal hostility is transformed. The latter is provided through the Spirit (1:8, 9) and the former is developed in the following verse.

**22.** Although the Colossian believers were *once* alienated (1:21), they are *now reconciled* (*pote . . . nuni*). This 'once . . . but now' description of the contrast between life outside of Christ and life with

---

70. Although being God's enemies includes the idea that God is at enmity with sinners (see e.g. Rom. 5:10 and the reference to wrath in 5:9), in this immediate context the emphasis is on the hostility of the Colossians against God (though see Col. 3:6).

71. The prepositional phrase is *en tois ergois tois ponērois* ('in evil works', cf. ASV).

Christ will come up again in Colossians (cf. 2:12, 13, 20; 3:7–10) and is a common feature of Paul's theology of the Christian life.[72] The amazing events of salvation history find their concrete application in particular lives at particular times when through the embrace of the gospel lives are transformed from alienation to reconciliation. The repetition of the word 'reconcile' from 1:20 confirms that Paul is applying the broader emphasis on God's activity in all of creation to the Colossians. Again, the subject of the reconciling activity is the Father, and the means by which he reconciles is through the death of Jesus.[73] The language of 'the blood of his cross' (RSV, ESV) in 1:20 is here replaced with 'his body of flesh by his death' (RSV, ESV). Both descriptions emphasize the physical death of Jesus.[74] Although the atoning significance of Jesus' death is not spelled out here in terms of how Jesus' death effects this reconciliation (see 2:13–15), the implication is that, at the Father's initiative, because of Jesus' death believers no longer face the consequences of their enmity and evil behaviour. Thus reconciliation with God has been accomplished because Jesus' sacrificial death has taken the judgment. He was 'alienated' in the place of those who belong to him so we could be reconciled.[75]

The emphasis on the Father's gracious initiative continues with a statement that highlights the purpose of the Father's reconciling activity through Jesus ('in order to', RSV, ESV), a purpose that is depicted with three overlapping descriptions: *holy . . . without blemish and free from accusation* ('holy, faultless, and blameless', CSB). The first term, 'holy', states positively that believers belong to God, set apart from evil and dedicated to him, with an emphasis on purity.[76]

---

72. See e.g. Rom. 6:22; 7:6; cf. also the discussion at Phlm. v. 11.
73. The debate about who the pronouns refer to in this verse continues from 1:21. For the view that the pronouns in 1:22 continue to refer to Christ see e.g. Pao, pp. 106–109; Fee, *Christology*, pp. 313–316.
74. The pronoun 'his' implies a reference to Jesus (specified in the NIV).
75. Beale, p. 114. On propitiation as the means of reconciliation see Porter, Καταλλάσσω, pp. 159–160.
76. Believers are described as 'holy' many times in Colossians (see 1:2, 4, 12, 26; 3:12). See also Eph. 1:4; 5:27.

The following terms, 'faultless and blameless', emphasize that there is no corresponding fault or sin that would give rise to a just accusation.[77] All of this does not mean present sinlessness, but rather a standing or position before God. The phrase *to present you . . . in his sight* shows that the future judgment is in view here, and amazingly this will be a judgment scene in which there is no judgment or guilty verdict.[78] Nevertheless, the image here of the presence of God (*in his sight*) should not be overlooked. This pictures the loving gaze of God upon believers as fully reconciled, at peace with and without any reason at all for displeasure. Thus this verse has transitioned from the past ('once alienated') to the present ('now reconciled') and to the future ('in order to present you'). This forms part of the future hope found in the gospel that Paul encourages the Colossians with (see 1:23). All this is for the one who trusts in God's provision in Christ. The nature of that trust is elaborated upon in the following verse.

**23.** Having moved from describing God's comprehensive reconciling activity to the specific application of that activity in the lives of the Colossians, Paul now clarifies the means by which this reconciliation is appropriated: faith. Paul has already spoken of their faith as something which he thanks God for (1:3–5) and as something that involves hearing and truly understanding God's grace (1:6). Having spoken of the Colossians in terms of 'once you were . . . but now', Paul now clarifies that such faith, if it is genuine faith, is not a mere passing interest in Jesus, nor can there be assurance of reconciliation on the basis of an earlier, but abandoned, response of faith. Thus the wording of the conditional phrase of this verse, *if you continue in your faith*, means that genuine faith

---

77. See Phil. 2:15 and Jude 24 ('without blemish'); 1 Cor. 1:8 ('free from accusation'). On the debate over whether this language is judicial or sacrificial see the brief summary in McKnight, *Colossians*, pp. 176–177.

78. Cf. the word *paristēmi* (to 'present') in Rom. 14:10 ('stand'); 2 Cor. 4:14; Eph. 5:27. See also Jude 24 ('before him') and on 1:28 below.

continues to depend on God's reconciling work through Jesus. In this sense it is *established and firm* (cf. 1:11; 2:5). Paul's use of building metaphors further emphasizes the enduring rather than temporary trust that is required. These terms also clarify that Paul refers to their personal faith rather than a more objective reference to 'the faith' (i.e. taking the definite article as *your* as in the NIV). Paul cannot mean by this that there could not be any periods of uncertainty or temptations to find satisfaction elsewhere, otherwise he would not urge the Colossians to be *strengthened in the faith* (2:7) or warn them not to be deceived (2:8). Nor does he mean that it is the strength of one's faith that guarantees salvation. This continuing faith is focused on *the hope held out in the gospel*. The heavenly security of the Colossians' hope, in the sense of what is hoped for, is what the Colossians heard about in the gospel and is the reason for their faith (1:5). In this context, this future hope that they have heard in the gospel picks up on the future orientation of the previous verse. That is, because the purpose of Jesus' death is to present those who belong to him as 'holy, faultless, and blameless' (CSB) at the judgment, therefore those who believe in him have the assurance that this good news brings.

Having mentioned the particularity that this hope is only articulated and known through the gospel message, Paul returns to the universality of this message. The comprehensive nature of God's reconciling activity through the Son (1:19–20), together with the need for faith to appropriate that reconciliation (1:23a), means that there is an urgency to make this good news known everywhere (see 1:6), so Paul refers to the worldwide proclamation of the gospel that had already taken place (cf. Rom. 15:19; Acts 2:9–11).[79] He uses extravagant language here, however, to reflect the universal claims and rule of Christ over all creation (1:16–20). Because it is only in this universally applicable gospel message that reconciliation with God and heavenly hope is found, Paul therefore views himself as one who is a *servant* of this gospel (see on 1:7 above). The alternative to this would be a message that can be altered, adapted or

---

79. The prepositional phrase *en pasē ktisei* is better understood as 'in all creation' (ESV, CSB).

manipulated by Paul to suit his own interests or in order to be more appealing to his audiences in the various locations around the world where it is proclaimed. The nature of the message is not at the mercy of Paul or his audiences. Rather, it is Paul who is a servant of the message, proclaiming the promises and warning of that message and conforming his life and ministry to this message of a sacrificial Saviour. With references to their 'faith', their heavenly 'hope', the Colossians' 'hearing' of the gospel, the worldwide proclamation of the gospel and the particular proclaimer of the gospel as a 'servant' (*diakonos*), Paul repeats terms and phrases from 1:4–7.[80] This section, therefore, links the Colossians' reception of the gospel to the supremacy of Christ and the grand purposes of God for the entire creation as a foundation for warning the Colossians not to be deceived and distracted from their faith in the Christ of the gospel. The transition to Paul's own role as a servant of the gospel then leads to an extended focus in the next section on what Paul proclaims, as well as to whom and why Paul proclaims this gospel.

*Theology*
This passage is important for understanding both the basis of Paul's appeal as well as his concern for the Colossians. The basis for his appeal is that the believers in Colossae have already moved from enmity to peace with God. Their 'once . . . but now' experience undercuts the appeal of the false teachers. What more can they offer? Furthermore, even if the false teachers are 'judging' them (2:16, 18), the Colossian believers can be assured of their appearance at God's judgment as 'holy, blameless and faultless' (1:22). This is the 'hope' held out in the gospel and this renders all other 'additions' not only as unnecessary but as the antithesis of this hope. For it is only by trusting in God's provision that this reconciliation is appropriated. And herein lies Paul's concern. This trust is continuing trust and the Colossians must continue to trust in Christ (1:5).

---

80. Cf. Moo, pp.145–146; Beale, pp. 118–119, sees this as an 'inclusio' around this section of the letter.

## D. The gospel of Christ is the centre of Paul's ministry (1:24 – 2:5)

Having referred to himself as a 'servant' of the gospel (1:23), Paul now elaborates on what this means. There is a noticeable shift to first-person verbs as Paul speaks more personally of his own ministry ('I rejoice', 'I fill up', 'I have become', etc) within God's sovereign purposes. In addition to the repetition of 'servant', references to Christ's sufferings (1:20, 22, 24) and the church (1:18, 24) also tie this section to the preceding verses.

The beginning of a new chapter at 2:1 should not detract from the fact that the verses in 1:24–29 and 2:1–5 are tightly connected. Paul repeats numerous terms and phrases that he uses in 1:24–29 (regarding his ministry in God's purposes in general) again in 2:1–5 (regarding his personal concern for the Colossians). These links include the following: rejoice (1:24; 2:5), flesh/body (1:24; 2:5), riches (1:27; 2:2), mystery/Christ (1:27; 2:2), and struggle (1:29; 2:1). In this section Paul's statements can be interpreted to move from rejoicing to a discussion of the mystery, and then to his struggle/toil and back to mystery and rejoicing, a chiastic pattern which places his struggle in his service for the gospel at the centre. It is difficult to be sure of this, but the repetition of these terms serves to directly link his commission more broadly with his concern for the Colossians more specifically.

The concluding reference to the Colossians' faith recalls the conclusion to the preceding section (1:23) and helps to show that the Colossians have not yet succumbed to the threat that Paul warns them about; they are instead continuing to hold to the gospel Paul proclaims. Nevertheless, the focus on Paul's personal concern for the Colossians in 2:1–5 prepares the way for his warnings in the next section. The gospel that Epaphras preached, and that magnifies Christ, is the gospel that Paul preaches. It is this gospel, not the rules of the false teachers, that the Colossians must hold on to.

### *i. Paul labours to proclaim Christ with the final judgment in view (1:24–29)*
*Context*
The Christ-centred gospel that the Colossian believers have received and that provides hope for the future and strength for the

present is the same gospel that Paul is commissioned by God to proclaim. Paul rejoices in the suffering that accompanies his proclamation of the gospel because the gospel is the fulfilment of God's promise for the nations to know his saving plan. Christ, the hope of glory, therefore, is who Paul proclaims.

*Comment*

**24.** Having unpacked the significance of God's saving rule through the Son, Paul now develops further his own part in the proclamation of this message of good news, having just alluded to this in 1:23. As Paul has already pointed out, the suffering of Christ is central in this saving mission. It is through Jesus' 'blood, shed on the cross' (1:20), the death of 'Christ's physical body' (1:22), that reconciliation comes. Likewise, it is through suffering, in keeping with this message of a suffering Saviour, that Paul, as an authorized representative of Christ, participates in the proclamation of this message. Not that this is something Paul resents. Rather, says Paul, *I rejoice in what I am suffering.* He rejoices in the high calling of representing Jesus. Paul notes that this is suffering *for you*, the Colossians. His following clarification that this is *for the sake of his body, which is the church*, indicates that he views this suffering for the Colossians as a subset or as included within his broader calling as an apostle.

This observation that Paul talks specifically of his role as an apostolic representative can help us unpack Paul's complex statement that he is filling up in his flesh *what is still lacking in regard to Christ's afflictions.* This statement is widely recognized as one of the most difficult phrases in this letter.[81] Some see it as indicating some lack in what Christ did on the cross, others see it as a reference to a way that Paul can reduce the amount of suffering the church will face in this era of 'messianic woes', still others see it as a general reference to the suffering all Christians will face. I understand this phrase in this immediate context to refer to Paul's proclamation of the gospel that is required for the achievement of Christ's death to be heard and received, so that the above-mentioned reconciliation can be received and experienced.

---

81. See Clark, *Completing*, pp. 150–157; White, 'Sufferings', pp. 181–198.

We can begin by recognizing what else Paul says about Christ's suffering in his letter to the Colossians.[82] As noted above, Christ's suffering on the cross is the means by which God accomplishes his reconciling work (1:19–20, 22). Furthermore, his death on the cross was the means by which 'the charge of our legal indebtedness, which stood against us and condemned us' (2:14) was erased. There is no hint of any deficiency in Christ's death or any indication that Paul or anyone else needs to, or is somehow able to, supplement what the cross accomplished in God's saving activity. What then can Paul mean when he says that he is filling up that which is still lacking?

As we noted above, the context speaks of Paul's proclamation of this saving work and the suffering that accompanies that proclamation. Thus when Paul says *I fill up in my flesh* he seems to be referring to this suffering in his physical body that accompanies his proclamation (cf. 2 Cor. 11:23–29). What then is *lacking*? In keeping with what is emphasized in this context, it must be the need for this suffering Messiah's saving activity on the cross to be proclaimed by Paul, his suffering servant. Paul has just said that this gospel must be heard and proclaimed in all creation (1:23). It is only when the Colossians 'heard and understood' that the gospel bore fruit among them (1:6, 23). This is why Paul will go on to say in the following verses that his task is to make known this mystery (1:27) and proclaim Christ to everyone (1:28), a task that requires intense labour and struggle (1:29; 2:1).

There is a possible parallel example of this way of speaking in Philippians 2:30 (see also 1 Cor. 16:17).[83] There Paul speaks of how Epaphroditus came to minister to Paul, on behalf of the Philippians. In this sense he came to 'fill up what was lacking' in their

---

82. Taking the genitive 'afflictions of Christ' as referring to Christ's own sufferings (though the word used for 'afflictions' [*thlipsis*] is never attributed to Christ's atoning work in the New Testament).
83. The Greek text of Phil. 2:30 and 1 Cor. 16:17 include the two terms 'fill' (though with the similar *anaplēroō* instead of *antanaplēroō*) and 'lack' that are also in Col. 1:24. As noted by Pao, p. 124.

service to Paul (cf. ESV); he came in place of, and as a representative of, the Philippian believers. Thus, similarly with regard to the need for the message of Christ's sufferings to be proclaimed, Paul 'fills' that need and does so as a suffering servant representing his suffering Saviour, for the establishment of the Saviour's people, *his body, which is the church*.

Paul's description of the people who belong to Christ as both *his body* and *the church* reflects the language he used in 1:18. In this context the terminology highlights the unity of the people Paul serves. Unlike the schismatics who are dividing Christ's people, Paul embraces the suffering associated with proclaiming Christ for the sake of Christ's people.

**25.** Paul states that he is a *servant* of the church (see 1:7, 23), using the same language he employed in 1:23 of his relationship to the proclamation of the gospel. Once again the language is important for understanding Paul's obligations. He is not committed to proclaiming the gospel so he can advance his own name or reputation among Christ's people or gain financially from Christ's people. Rather, he is committed to proclaiming the gospel so there will be a growing and healthy body of Christ's people, those who 'hear and understand' God's grace (1:6).

Furthermore, this task is not something that Paul has even initiated as it is *the commission God gave* to him. The term Paul uses for 'commission' (*oikonomia*) is used in contexts where the governance or management of a household or estate is in view (Luke 16:2–4). Paul uses the term to refer more comprehensively to God's overall saving plan (Eph. 1:10; 3:9; 1 Tim. 1:4), as well as more specifically of the task that he has been given within that plan (1 Cor. 9:17; Eph. 3:2). Thus the use of the term here highlights the place of Paul's ministry within God's sovereign purposes to rescue people from darkness and bring them into his saving rule (1:13–14), showing that the means by which God will accomplish his saving plan includes the proclamation of this good news so people can hear and respond.

What Paul has been commissioned to preach is further described as presenting to the Colossians *the word of God in its fullness*, and then, in the following verse, as God's *mystery*. The gospel then, is a message, the announcement of good news, and it is from God, since he is the one who reveals his saving plan and our hope for eternity (see 1:5). The phrase 'the word of God in its fullness' (NIV) could also be rendered 'to fulfil the word of God' (NKJV). For Paul to 'fulfil' the word of God could refer to the totality of the message that Paul is committed to (hence the NIV). However, the parallel with 1:24 might favour the view that Paul refers to his labour for everyone to hear this news (Rom. 15:19). 'Fulfil', therefore, refers to the purposes of God to bring reconciliation through a message of good news about the death of Christ; a message about a suffering Messiah that is mediated by suffering servants and must be proclaimed everywhere, and heard and 'understood' with genuine faith (1:5–6, 23).

**26–27.** Paul further describes this gospel message as a *mystery*.[84] As the following description (and Paul's treatment of this term elsewhere) shows, Paul's use of the term *mystery* does not mean 'mysterious' or 'indecipherable'. Nor does Paul derive the term from the mystery religions in which a 'secret' is only known by selected initiates. As Paul indicates here and elsewhere, this term refers to God's saving plan (or aspects of it) as something that was *hidden for ages and generations* but has *now* been revealed in the arrival and saving death and resurrection of Christ and his saving rule.[85] The use of the term to refer to God's plan and saving rule goes back to Daniel (2:18–47) and Jesus (Mark 4:11). Elsewhere, Paul states that this mystery is 'now revealed and made known through the prophetic writings' (Rom. 16:26) which means there is a sense that God's saving plan was both hidden and yet always there in the Scriptures. The coming of Jesus Messiah in salvation history makes known God's saving plan and shows how God's patterns and promises throughout Scripture of both a reigning king and a suffering servant, one from the line of David and yet

---

84. The word 'mystery' in 1:26 is in apposition to 'the word of God' in 1:25. Thus the gospel message is here directly linked to the anticipation of this message in the (Old Testament) Scriptures. The word 'mystery' also occurs in 1:27; 2:2; 4:3 (see below). Cf. 1 Cor. 2:7; Eph. 1:9; 3:3, 4, 9; 5:32; 6:19.
85. See Beale and Gladd, *Hidden*.

also the coming of God himself, can all come to pass in the one person.[86]

Thus Paul casts his eye across the whole of history and sees that by God's grace those who belong to Christ live in the era of the outworking of God's saving plan for the world, long awaited but now fulfilled in Christ and announced in the gospel. Paul can hardly contain himself as he bursts with wonder expressing the significance of the momentous truth that this gospel is. Once focused on the people of Israel, God's saving plan is now *made known among the Gentiles*. In keeping with the character of God, this saving plan is not haphazard but *God has chosen to make known* this mystery; nor is it minor or miserly but this mystery is God's *glorious riches*.[87] It is both *Christ in you* now, and also *the hope of glory* for the future (with Christ, 3:4). Thus Gentiles, long outside of God's covenantal people, can now in the new covenant enjoy his presence through Christ, and can look forward to his presence in heaven because of Christ (cf. 1:5). Although Paul often describes a believer in Jesus as someone who is 'in Christ' (see 1:2), he also, less often, describes the closeness of a Christian's relationship with Christ as 'Christ in you'.[88] In a nutshell, the nature and content of this mystery can simply be summarized as *Christ* (2:2; 4:3).

**28.** In the final two verses of the chapter Paul summarizes succinctly his driving passion and goal in ministry. What does it mean for him to carry out the commission God gave him to (1) proclaim this mystery, (2) for the sake of Christ's people, (3) in the midst of hardship? We should note the striking shift from the repeated first person singular verbs and pronouns that began this section ('I' in 1:24–25) to the first person plural pronoun that is used in this verse ('we'). Although he has been highlighting the

---

86. See Carson, 'Mystery', pp. 390–436.
87. The word 'glory' here is evocative of God's own majesty. On 'riches' see Rom. 2:4; 9:23; 11:33; Eph. 1:7, 18; 2:7; 3:8, 16; Phil. 4:19.
88. The same phrase, for example, is used in Rom. 8:9–10 (cf. also 2 Cor. 13:5) where Paul speaks interchangeably of the Spirit 'in you' and Christ 'in you'.

centrality of Christ in his own commission in the preceding verses, perhaps Paul shifts to the plural here to show that this Christ-centred focus is characteristic of all who know Christ. Some suggest that Paul perhaps includes Timothy with himself in view of 1:1. However, the addition of the pronoun 'we' that follows on from the immediately preceding 'in you' (plural) of 1:27 may indicate a more general use of 'we'. Perhaps the repeated 'everyone' in this verse (mentioned below) also highlights this broader application.[89] In what follows, however, I will keep the focus on what this says about Paul since 1:29 will return to the first person singular.

First, Paul emphasizes that it is Christ that he proclaims. The relative pronoun 'whom' (*hon*) that is used in the Greek text is placed forward for emphasis. Since Christ is the embodiment of God's saving plans and the one who provides redemption and forgiveness of sins now (1:14) and a secure hope for the future (1:27), he is the one Paul centres his proclamation around. Paul's proclamation also includes both *admonishing and teaching*. Thus it becomes clear that for Paul, the task of proclaiming Christ is not reduced only to evangelizing non-believers. It includes the whole task of proclaiming Christ so those who do not know will hear and believe in Christ, as well as the continued proclamation of Christ to believers so they will continue to grow in their confidence in Christ and reflect the character of Christ in their lives. Thus, although they overlap in meaning, the two terms *admonishing* and *teaching* may cover the tasks of both warning (cf. ESV) about distractions from Christ's sufficiency, sinful actions and ungodly attitudes as well as positive instruction about Christ's sufficiency, Christlike actions and godly attitudes. The significance of Christ is such that he is the hope of everyone in every culture in every place, and so Paul again emphasizes that he proclaims Christ to everyone (cf. 1:23). Nevertheless, he does this *with all wisdom* (cf. 1:9). In this context, Paul may be referring to the application of the fullness of Christ to the wide variety of settings and complexities that require varied combinations of 'admonishing and teaching'.

---

89. Pao, pp. 131–132 makes similar observations.

Second, Paul states that his goal in all of this is to *present everyone fully mature in Christ*. Paul's goal corresponds with God's purpose in 1:22 'to present you holy in his sight, without blemish and free from accusation.' The same term 'present' (*paristēmi*) occurs in both verses and therefore indicates that an eschatological verdict is in view here.[90] The means by which this takes place is through proclaiming the sufficiency of Christ. Thus Paul's ministry centres on Christ and his sufficiency as the only hope for assurance before the final judgment. The phrase 'every person' is repeated three times in the Greek text of this verse, occurring after the words 'admonishing', 'teaching' and 'present'. On the one hand, in light of the reference to Gentiles in 1:27 this would refer to all people generally, Jews and Gentiles, in keeping with Paul's emphasis on the universal sovereignty of Christ and the worldwide proclamation of the gospel in this letter. On the other hand, this refers even more specifically to individuals, such that Paul regards the sufficiency of Christ as applicable to the sins and weaknesses of every individual. Therefore, since this is referring to an eschatological verdict, and since this goal will take place because Christ is proclaimed, the phrase *fully mature in Christ* probably means that each person is 'complete' (NASB) because they belong to Christ.[91] In contrast to the hopeless rules of the false teachers, this is Paul's hope for the Colossian believers, his goal in ministry and the reason for proclaiming Christ.

**29.** Paul's reference to his labour and struggle, returning to the first person singular 'I' of 1:24–25, perhaps includes what he had just said about the afflictions that come with being Christ's representative (1:24). Paul uses the term *kopiaō* ('to exert oneself . . . work hard', BDAG, p. 558; 'labour', NKJV) often in contexts that describe ministry work.[92] The other term that Paul uses here, *agōnizomai* ('strive', NKJV; 'struggle', ESV, BDAG, p. 17), further describes this labour and so the two terms are translated as *strenuously contend* in

---

90. Campbell, p. 26.

91. Cassirer, 'in virtue of his union with Christ' (p. 370).

92. Rom. 16:6, 12; 1 Cor. 15:10; 16:16; Gal. 4:11; Phil. 2:16; 1 Thess. 5:12; 1 Tim. 4:10; 5:17.

the NIV.[93] The two terms are also found together in 1 Timothy 4:10 where the context also refers to false teaching. The 'labour' or 'toil' (ESV) of ministry is carried out with much struggle, whether this be perseverance in the midst of persecution and opposition, continued responses to the distractions of false teachers, disheartening departures of former believers or fellow ministry partners, the challenges of living as weak creatures in a fallen world, and of course the continuing temptations within. How is Paul, how is anyone, able to persevere in the face of such struggle? The answer, says Paul, comes from outside of us. Not only is Christ the one who provides forgiveness now and a secure hope for the judgment, he also provides the energy for service. The NKJV highlights Paul's play on words: 'according to his working [*energeia*] which works [*energeō*] in me mightily'. The emphasis is on the power of Christ to sustain his people in their service for him (cf. 1:11). The combination of human effort by divine enabling is found regularly in Paul and elsewhere in Scripture (cf. 1 Cor. 15:10; Phil. 2:12–13). Intense labour and provision for persevering in ministry should not be misapplied to mean that serving Christ ignores wisdom to re-evaluate the viability of a particular course of action, or the accompanying need to rest or seek the advice and assistance of others. All of these, together with prayer and dependence on Christ, may be seen as the help that Christ gives, enabling his people to serve him wisely.

*Theology*

Although Paul focuses on his own ministry, he does so in the context of God's grand plans and these should not be missed here. In these verses we learn more about the significance of God's saving plans. The language of 'mystery' draws attention to the longevity of God's purposes. He promises and plans over the course of ages and generations. This again points to the continuity and discontinuity between the Testaments and serves to highlight the momentous significance of the time Paul calls 'now'. It is 'now' that these saving plans have been made known in all their fullness,

---

93. The verb *agōnizomai* is used in Col. 4:12 of Epaphras (the only two uses in Colossians).

because the Messiah has come. So the mystery is essentially a person, Christ. Just as he is the goal of creation, he is also the goal of salvation history. The preaching of this mystery is also not outside God's purposes. He has commissioned Paul to make this momentous news known to the nations, and enables him to persevere in this task. Now all the nations are joining in this saving plan of God's. Suffering is an accompanying feature of this proclamation (1:24, 29) just as it was at the heart of Christ's own ministry (1:24). Paul's part then in God's purposes is to proclaim the suffering Messiah, as his suffering servant, so others may come to know the Messiah and be complete in him. Christ is the centre of God's saving plans, the hope of glory, the reason why believers will be 'complete' at the judgment, and the means by which the hard work of this proclamation is carried out.

## ii. Paul labours to see the Colossians remain firm in Christ (2:1–5)

*Context*

We have already noted the links to the preceding verses in the introduction to 1:24 – 2:5. The specific link between 1:29 and 2:1 connects these sections with reference to Paul's 'striving' in gospel ministry. Thus Paul moves from a broader reference to his commission in God's saving plan in the preceding section, to his concern for the Colossians in particular in this section. There is a possibility of another chiastic structure here as Paul refers to his concern for the Colossians (2:1, 5), his hoped-for response from the readers (2:2, 4), and his focus on Christ, the mystery in the centre of these verses (2:3). For the first time in this letter Paul indicates that there is a potential threat to the Colossians' understanding of Christ (2:4) which will be taken up in greater detail in the following section.

*Comment*

1. As seen in his repeated use of 'you' and in the opening word 'for' (NRSV, ESV; omitted in NIV), Paul now turns from what he has said about his ministry generally to apply this to the specifics of the believers at Colossae. By repeating similar words, Paul shows that just as he *strenuously contends* (1:29; 'struggling', ESV) to proclaim the

gospel in ministry generally, so too is he *contending* (2:1; 'great struggle', ESV) for the believers at Colossae and nearby Laodicea.[94] Indeed Paul is engaged in this struggle even for those whom he has not met *personally* ('face to face', NRSV, ESV). In light of the shift from Paul's general and universal ministry in 1:24–29 to 'you' (Colossian and Laodicean believers) more specifically, this phrase probably refers to those Paul had not met personally in this region of the Lycus valley (including the believers in Hierapolis; 4:13), rather than people everywhere that he had not met.[95] This takes us back to Paul's proclamation of the gospel in suffering to carry out God's plan for the gospel of reconciliation to be proclaimed everywhere (1:21–23, 24–27). With this reference to 'contending' specifically for the Colossians (and those nearby) Paul foreshadows a reference more specifically to the false teachings he is concerned about.

**2.** In a tightly packed series of purpose clauses Paul unpacks his goal for all believers, and the reason why he labours for them. The following layout may help to see Paul's goal(s) more clearly:

> that their hearts may be encouraged
> having been united in love
> that they may have all the riches of full assurance that comes from understanding
> that they may have (or that comes from) knowledge of God's 'mystery', Christ

The connection between the verb 'encouraged' and the participle 'being united' is probably temporal, so the action of being *united in love* precedes the action of being *encouraged in heart* (Campbell, p. 28), even if the effect is still essentially two distinct goals of Paul (NIV; Harris, p. 73). The Colossians' love for one another is something that Paul has mentioned a number of times in the opening verses of the letter (1:4, 5, 8), and the many ways in which their love for one another is to be expressed will be the focus of 3:12–14. In contrast to the false teachers who were separating the Colossian

---

94. On Laodicea see 4:13, 15, 16.
95. Harris, p. 72.

believers on the basis of their rules, the Colossian believers are 'knit together in love' (ESV). To be *united in love* is an outgrowth of their common understanding of the gospel of grace that Paul labours so much for them to know and grasp.

This bond in love for one another out of their unity in Christ will then serve to give the Colossians great *encouragement in their hearts*. The term 'heart' refers to the inner person's thinking, emotions and decision-making centre and is used elsewhere in Colossians 3:15, 16, 22; and 4:8. In 4:8 Paul again expresses his goal that the Colossians be 'encouraged in heart', this time through sending Tychicus to them to bring them news of Paul's ministry. To better understand what Paul would like for the Colossians here it may help to think of the opposite. Those who have been in a congregation characterized by division, where one group seeks to disrupt or divide or lead away some of the congregation over some new side issue or sophisticated-sounding departure from the faith know how heartbreaking that can be. The pain of broken relationships is compounded by the concern for the spiritual wellbeing of those who are enamoured with something new, tangential to, or different from the gospel. Thus for the Colossians to be *encouraged in heart* means that Paul wants them to know the soul-strengthening joy that comes from being part of a community who, because of their common commitment to the gospel of grace, are bound together in a genuine and gracious concern for one another's good.[96]

Paul's goal in labouring for the gospel is also so that believers may have *the full riches of complete understanding*. The complex Greek phrase underlying the NIV's *complete understanding* means that Paul aims for them to have the 'full assurance' that comes from 'understanding' the gospel (cf. ESV; see comments on 1:6).[97] Thus once

---

96. McKnight, p. 207, notes how 'Paul often wants the churches to be encouraged' and cites 1 Thess. 3:2; 4:18; 5:11, 14; 1 Cor. 14:31; Rom. 12:8; Titus 1:9; 2:15. Note also Rom. 1:12.

97. The word translated 'full assurance' above (*plērophorias*) in this context is more likely to refer to 'assurance' (as in 1 Thess. 1:5; Heb. 10:22) than merely 'fullness' (as in Heb. 6:11). Cf. BDAG, p. 827 ('complete certainty').

again Paul is concerned with the Colossians' thinking and notes the rational coherence of the gospel message as something that can and must be understood. Yet this understanding, rather than an end in itself, or as a purely theoretical activity, is associated with or leads to 'full assurance'. 'Assurance', a consistent concern of Paul's in Colossians, is a confident conviction of the truth of the gospel such that no other diversion from Christ's sufficiency unsettles or distracts. It is evidenced in his emphasis on the security of their hope (1:5, 23), his prayer for them to grow in the knowledge of God being strengthened for endurance and patience (1:9–11), his emphasis on the greatness of the Son over all (1:15–20), his warnings not to be distracted from Christ (2:4), and his exhortations to remain with Christ (2:6–7). This 'full assurance' is so precious that it is further described as *the full riches*. The term 'riches' highlights the abundance or wealth that one has with this assurance, but the additional adjective 'full' or 'all' emphasizes the completeness of this even more, such is the blessing of this assurance that comes from knowing Christ and his sufficiency.

A final purpose clause completes this verse with a summary that points to the foundational basis for all of the above: *that they may know the mystery of God, namely Christ*. As we noted in 1:27, Paul's use of the term 'mystery' refers to the long-awaited saving plan of God now clearly made known in Christ. The designation *of God* could indicate that this saving plan belongs to God ('God's mystery', NRSV, ESV), or, more likely, that it comes from God since he is the one who has made it known (1:27). As noted in 1:27, a shorthand way of condensing the meaning of this momentous plan of God into one word, or rather one person, is to say *Christ*. Thus, when Paul states his final goal as *in order that they may know the mystery of God, namely, Christ*, it is likely that 'know' does not merely mean to understand the details of how God's plan, an open secret in the Old Testament, has now come to fruition in Christ. It must include this, but more. To *know Christ* must include a trust or confidence in him that includes a personal relationship that he, the sovereign Creator and Sustainer of the universe, is one's Saviour and Lord (cf. 2:6). The term for 'knowledge' (*epignōsis*) is used elsewhere in Colossians in contexts where Paul hopes the believers will continue to grow in their knowledge of God (1:9, 10; 3:10).[98]

**3.** Paul completes his thought here from the previous verse. Having just culminated his compact declaration of purpose with a summary reference to knowing Christ, Paul can't help but highlight again the sufficiency of Christ. He is the one *in whom are hidden all the treasures of wisdom and knowledge*. In other words, with the temptations the Colossians are facing to supplement Christ with additional, human-originated rules and teachings (see the next verse, and 2:8, 16, 18, 20–22), Paul reiterates that there is no need to supplement Christ with anything; he is all one needs to know and to please God. 'Wisdom' accompanies the understanding, articulation and application of the gospel in Colossians. It was first mentioned in 1:9 as that which the Spirit provides in enabling believers to be filled with the knowledge of God's will, in order to live life worthy of and pleasing to the Lord (see comments on 1:9 above). Wisdom is the means by which Paul proclaims Christ in 1:28 with the various warnings and instructions that are required for the varied people he encounters. Similarly, wisdom is needed for believers as they warn and teach one another with the word of Christ in song (3:16). By contrast, the additional regulations of the false teachers only have an appearance of wisdom and ultimately have no value (2:23). 'Knowledge' likewise in Colossians is associated with knowing God and his will (1:9, 10). For Christ to be the one *in whom are hidden all the treasures of wisdom and knowledge*, then, does not mean that they are hidden in the sense of being inaccessible. Rather it is that they are found or 'stored up' in him, in his person and in him alone.[99] 'All' in this context means 'without exception'.[100] To know Christ is to know the Creator's will and purposes for the universe, for history, for eternity, for

---

98. *Epignōsis* can be used for a 'knowledge directed toward (*epi*) a particular object that, if expressed, is indicated by the objective genitive' (Harris, p. 27; the object is the genitive phrase, *tou mystēriou tou theou, Christou*). The broader term *gnōsis* is used in the following verse (its only use in Colossians).
99. BDAG, p. 456.
100. Harris, p. 75.

humankind and for oneself. That *wisdom and knowledge* are *treasures* that are *hidden* means that these are of 'exceptional value and kept safe'.[101] Proverbs 2:3–7 declares that the Lord is the one who gives the treasures of wisdom, knowledge and understanding, and 'stores' success for the upright. The specific combination of these same words suggests that Proverbs 2:3–7 may well be in view here. Paul, therefore, is not just saying that Christ embodies wisdom; Christ is 'the Lord' who is the source of these![102] At this point we might wonder why the Colossians would want to follow teachings that would move them away from Christ. It is to this that Paul finally turns in the next verse.

**4.** Now for the first time in this letter, Paul hints that there may be other voices in the background seeking to undermine the Colossians' confidence in Christ. Although this will be developed further in the next section (esp. 2:8, 16, 18–19, 20–23), Paul indicates here that there are other teachers who could attempt to influence the Colossians. Paul's opening *I tell you this* probably looks back to what he has been saying about the focus of his ministry in proclaiming the sufficiency of Christ. Whereas Paul proclaims a Christ-centred message of good news, there are others who want to teach the Colossian believers something else. The reference to *no one*, together with similar indicators in 2:8 (*no one*), 16 and 18 (*anyone*),[103] suggest that there are real people in view here. What they are teaching is not explained except that rather than being easily dismissed or brushed off, it consists of *fine-sounding arguments*. *Fine-sounding* means that this is 'plausible, but false, speech resulting from the use of well-constructed, probable arguments – "convincing speech, plausible language"' (L&N 33.31; 'persuasive speech' BDAG, p. 812). These arguments 'sound reasonable' (CSB), so the teachers *may deceive* the Colossians. So, far from rebuking the Colossians for their gullibility or foolishness, Paul recognizes the challenge that this teaching

---

101. L&N 65.10 (*thēsauros*, 'treasures').
102. While most commentators note the link to Prov. 2, few note the connection to Yahweh here. See also Isa. 33:5–6 (McKnight, p. 212); Rom. 11:33.
103. The Greek text of 2:18 has the same word as here for 'no one'.

brings. The false teachers may or may not mean well, but their teaching deceives. Furthermore, it appears that this teaching has not yet taken hold of the Colossians. It may do, but it hasn't yet. As Paul has been demonstrating throughout the letter, he is not opposed to reasonable and persuasive arguments, and he assumes that the Colossians can follow and respond to his own detailed argumentation. He insists that the gospel itself has content about God's plans and the person of Christ that requires a logical and reasoned response (1:5–7). This false teaching, however, opposes the reality that the Creator of the world is revealed in Christ and that all one needs is to know Christ, relying on him alone for forgiveness and reconciliation. Therefore, although the teaching sounds reasonable and persuasive, if adopted, it would lead to spiritual harm.

**5.** Paul concludes this brief focus on his concerns and goals in ministry with a final rationale for why he is saying these things. The reason he is emphasizing Christ's sufficiency in order to help keep them from being taken in by inadequate substitutes (2:4) is because (*For*) even though he is *absent from* them *in body*, nevertheless he is *present with* them *in spirit*. The expression 'in body' means that he is not present with them physically. There is debate, however, about what Paul means when he says he is with them *in spirit*. Of the range of options for the meaning of this phrase, the paraphrase of the NLT, 'my heart is with you' perhaps comes closest. Although some see a reference to the Holy Spirit, the contrast with 'body' (Greek *sarx*, 'flesh') suggests that the focus is on how he is still 'with them' despite being physically absent. Since the following phrase, *and delight to see*, expresses a little further how it is that Paul is 'with them', the overall meaning here is one of support for them. His warnings from afar should not be interpreted as a sign of displeasure or emotional absence. On the contrary, he is 'with' them, 'delighting to see' the order of their lives and the firmness of their faith in Christ. Paul 'sees' these things in the sense that he has heard of them from Epaphras, and has much reason for thankfulness for them (cf. 1:4, 7–8, 9).[104]

---

104. The NIV (and most EVV) correctly translates the two participles 'rejoicing' and 'seeing' as a hendiadys (expressing the same idea with two words connected by 'and', Harris, pp. 79, 262).

What Paul is delighted to see in the Colossians is *how disciplined you are and how firm your faith in Christ is*. This, combined with the statements above about what he has heard about them from Epaphras, shows that Paul does not view the Colossians as already deceived or taken in by the false teaching he has just alluded to (and will unpack in the following verses). The Colossians have not departed from Christ, nor are they even at this point on shaky ground. The 'discipline' that Paul refers to is a reference to the way their lives are ordered around or in line with Christ. They are not 'all over the place' in their understanding of the gospel and the implications of the gospel. On the contrary, their faith is in Christ, and firm. That is, it is neither misplaced, nor is it unsure. This is the only occurrence of the term for 'firm' in the NT (*stereōma*). In the LXX the word can refer to the 'firmament' or something that was solid, to God as the 'rock' for believers, and to the strength of an army.[105] At this point the Colossians do not appear to be wavering or doubting and Paul is delighted in this. They are still relying upon and trusting in Christ. He writes to them from afar, therefore, as one who 'has their back' so to speak, supporting them, and watching out that no one harms them with destructive but deceptive lies. Having affirmed this, Paul will state the central point of the letter in the following verses.

*Theology*

In this and the preceding section we see Paul's pastoral theology, his heart as a pastor. For Paul this flows from his convictions about Jesus, salvation and the final judgment. We have seen so far that it is his view of Christ that shapes the content of his preaching (1:28; 2:2–3). It is because of what Christ has done that Paul knows that those who belong to Christ are 'complete' and can face the judgment (1:22, 28) and so have 'full assurance' or 'complete understanding' in him (2:2). Paul's view of faith, that genuine faith continues to trust and grow in trust, means that his ministry includes warning and teaching (1:28), so he warns of fine-sounding arguments that detract from faith in Christ (2:4). All of this

---

105. Cf. Gen. 1:6; Ps. 18:2 (LXX 17:3); 1 Maccabees 9:14.

demonstrates Paul's love of people. This can be seen in the number of the pronouns 'you' and 'they' throughout 2:1–5. These, combined with the high number of first-person references ('I') and explicit statements of Paul's purposes in ministry – his struggle for them, his desire that they be encouraged and grow deeper in their knowledge of Christ, his concern that they not be deceived, and his delight that they have firm faith – all provide a window into the pastoral heart of Paul. Far from being emotionally absent, or a merely 'bookish' debater, or worse, manipulative, Paul loves the people in the congregations in Colossae and Laodicea and wants them to know and to grow in Christ.

## 3. THE SUPREMACY OF CHRIST IN THE CHRISTIAN LIFE (2:6 – 4:6)

Although there are implied exhortations throughout the letter, there is a noticeable shift in style and content from 2:6 with the first imperative in Colossians (the second imperative is a corresponding prohibition in 2:8). This first imperative in the letter is followed by a further twenty-nine commands (including prohibitions) from 2:8 to 4:6.[1] The exhortation in 2:6–7 brings all that Paul has said so far to bear as he zeroes in on his main aim in this letter: that the Colossian believers not waiver from their trust in the supremacy and sufficiency of Jesus. The gospel that Epaphras preached, that centres on Christ, and that Paul proclaims, should continue to shape their lives. The subheadings and corresponding summaries for each subheading below will highlight the progression of thought. Broadly speaking, the hint in 2:4 that there are other teachings that would distract the Colossians away from Christ's

---

[1]. This number is made of twenty-three specific imperatives in the Greek text of 2:8–4:6 as well as implied commands in 3:13 (×2), 14, 17; 4:3, 6.

sufficiency is developed further in the rest of chapter 2. In contrast to the gospel, the false teachings are merely human and this-worldly, turning attention away from Christ's sufficiency to rules and regulations which do not offer a solution to the problem of the penalty and the power of sin. It is only in Christ that believers have full forgiveness and new life. The believer's new life in Christ, by God's grace, affects every relationship in the daily realities of life: church, family, work, with fellow believers and with those who do not know Christ.

## A. The heart of the matter: continue to be centred on Christ (2:6–7)

*Context*
Paul's double use of 'just as' looks back to what he has said already about their reception of the gospel that Paul proclaims (1:5–7; 1:24–2:5). His summary description of what they received, 'Jesus Christ as Lord', looks back to all he has said about Jesus as the ruler of creation and redemption (1:15–20) and the embodiment of God's saving plan, as God's mystery (1:25–27; 2:2–3). The main imperative ('walk', ESV, NASB; 'live' NIV; 2:6) urges a continuation of this trajectory. The majesty of Christ and his sufficiency must continue to be the centre of the Colossians life and trust. Then four participles emphasize what the continuation of this trajectory in line with this foundational conviction looks like (rooted, built up, strengthened and thankful). Thus these verses offer a condensed summary of Paul's main concern in this letter.

*Comment*
**6.** Having outlined the majesty of Christ and affirmed the genuineness of the Colossians' faith in him (see 2:5), with the words, *So then, just as . . .* , Paul builds on this as the foundation for what he wants them to continue to do. Their faith in Christ is now described as 'receiving' or 'accepting' (NLT) Christ, indicating the positive and personal embrace of the Lord Jesus and the teaching about him. Some see a reference only to the traditions that they had been taught about Jesus. But Paul specifies that what they had *received* was *Christ Jesus* himself. To do this is, of course, inseparable from

receiving the teaching about him that they 'understood' and 'learned' (1:6, 7). The combination of all three words – Jesus, Christ and Lord – is seen elsewhere in this letter only in 1:3 (see the various combinations listed there), and this particular construction is unique in Paul's letters. The NIV's translation, *Christ Jesus as Lord* could also be translated as *Christ Jesus the Lord* (NRSV, NASB, ESV).[2] The former could be understood in terms of a focus on their personal reception of Jesus 'as Lord' whereas the latter could be understood in terms of the identity of Jesus as taught to them, 'the Lord'. Either way, the construction emphasizes the authority and lordship of Jesus the Messiah. In light of the way this term, *kyrios* ('Lord'), is used in the LXX, and the way the New Testament uses Old Testament texts with the word *kyrios* (e.g. Rom. 10:9–13; 1 Pet. 3:15), the claim that Jesus is 'the Lord' means that he is identified with Yahweh, the one true God.[3] Paul is saying that the Colossians started the Christian life in this way: with a trust in Jesus as the promised Messiah in fulfilment of God's promises, relying upon him alone as the ruling Lord of creation and salvation (see 1:4). This then is the way they are to continue in their Christian lives (see 1:23).

The NIV's *continue to live your lives in him* helps to explain more word-for-word translations such as 'walk in him' (NRSV, NASB, ESV). As we noted in our comments on 1:10, the use of the imagery of 'walking' is a common biblical metaphor for how people conduct or go about their lives and it recalls Old Testament teaching about walking in wisdom and in the ways of God and in obedience to him (e.g. Deut. 11:22; Prov. 6:22; 8:20). That this is to be done *in him* highlights the authority of the Lord Jesus as the one who is to determine the direction of their lives.[4] Although positive instruction has been implied all the way through Colossians, this command to continue to 'live' or 'walk' in Christ is the first imperative in the letter. This verse, therefore, succinctly expresses the goal of the whole letter. It highlights the Colossians' original reception

---

2. See Harris, p. 80 for other variations.
3. Beale, p. 171 and n. 7.
4. Harris, p. 80; Campbell, p. 32. Cf. 'walk' in 1:10; 3:7; 4:5.

of Christ, it focuses on the significance of his majesty and it centres on Paul's key concern that the Colossians not be diverted from Christ and his sufficiency for Christian living. Jesus, the Messiah and Lord, is the one upon whom their lives depend. Paul essentially says, 'Keep looking to him alone!' Correspondingly, the second imperative in the letter occurs in the warning of verse 8.

**7.** Paul then adds four participles that show what 'walking' or 'living' based on their foundational acceptance of and dependence upon Christ's authority looks like. These participles are: rooted, built up, strengthened and overflowing in thankfulness. If we compare this with Paul's prayer in 1:10b–12a we can immediately see the similarities and how Paul's prayer both anticipates his aims in the letter and also grounds these aims in God's work of grace applying the gospel to their lives. The first two terms form a pair and once again combine agricultural and building metaphors that emphasize the importance of continuing the trajectory that the foundation sets.[5] To be *rooted . . . in him* highlights the strength that, like deep roots to a big tree, the authority of Christ is able to supply to the Christian continuing to live in Christ. The term itself looks to an action that has already taken place (i.e. 'taken root') and the passive voice points to an action accomplished by God (as with each of the first three terms here). To be *built up in him* focuses more on the continuing process of the work that has already begun. The implication is that this will continue to build upon and follow the trajectory set by a foundational conviction of Christ's authority and gracious provision for forgiveness and reconciliation.

The third participle, *strengthened (in the faith)* or 'firm' (NET), picks up on Paul's goal of full assurance for the Colossians (see 2:2) and refers to a conviction of the validity of the faith, that it is confirmed as true. In this sense although there is some discussion as to whether the object of what is strengthened is 'the faith' (NIV, ESV) or 'your faith' (NET, NASB), it is difficult to separate the two here. The additional qualifier, *as you were taught*, looks back to what has

---

5. See Pao, pp. 156–157, and Beale, p. 173 for the suggestion that these metaphors were associated with the temple.

been said so far in 2:6–7 and emphasizes again the theme of these two verses, that their original 'receiving' of the truth about Jesus is the way in which they are to continue in their Christian lives. Jesus' sovereignty and sufficiency is to remain in their focus.

The fourth and final participial phrase, *overflowing with thankfulness* also builds on the foundational theme of Christ's sufficiency. Just as Paul has already affirmed in 1:12, thankfulness is the appropriate response to all that God has done for believers in Christ. Paul's return to the theme of thankfulness as one of the key descriptors of what it looks like to *continue to live . . . lives in him* is a reminder to believers that ultimately it is God's work for us, not what we do, that defines who we are. *Thankfulness* arises from a recognition of Christ's lordship as the Creator and Sustainer of all things (1:16–17). Thankfulness is also the antidote to the false teachings since the reminder of God's gracious work in Christ and the sovereignty and sufficiency of Christ for believers helps to put the claims of others as to what our own accomplishments or activity might achieve into perspective. It is this human-derived and human-oriented teaching that Paul turns to next.

*Theology*
This shift in focus, signalled by the first imperative in Colossians, from foundational teaching with implied exhortation to more specific exhortation (with the following twenty-nine imperatives) that accompanies continued teaching, exemplifies a broader pattern in Paul's teaching that moves from the indicative (what God has done in Christ) to the imperative (how we are to respond and live in light of what he has done), with the former being the basis for the latter.[6] The principle of 'inseparable but distinguishable' is helpful here, as it is in many areas of Christian theology. Paul would never say God's grace leaves a person unchanged, yet he would never make continuing change the basis for knowing God's grace. These verses in particular look back to the foundational acceptance of Christ's sovereignty and sufficiency in his person and work as the key to what gives shape to the Christian life. Growth is not found

---

6. Moo, p. 176.

in 'progressing' beyond Christ but in continued reliance upon him, looking to him in thankfulness for his provision.

## B. Threats to Christ-centred living from the false teachers (2:8–23)

### i. Fullness is found in Christ (2:8–15)
*Context*
Having hinted that there are others in the background who might seek to deceive the Colossians (2:4), Paul now begins to warn the believers about the false teachers more directly. However, the warning of 2:8 is not developed in more detail until 2:16–23 and especially 2:20–23 where he repeats the description of the teaching as the 'elementary principles of the world' (NASB). Before he develops this warning more directly, in 2:9–15 Paul elaborates on his reference to 'Christ' at the end of 2:8. Thus the accomplishment of Christ in providing 'fullness' for those who belong to him by faith (outlined in 2:9–15) is set in contrast to the 'empty' teaching of the false teachers with their demands. In doing so, Paul also develops further some of the earlier statements of Christ's accomplishments. The reference to 'fullness' picks up and develops 1:19; the reference to the 'cross' and Christ's death looks back to 1:20–22; the importance of Christ's resurrection has already been noted in 1:18; and the reference to 'forgiveness' picks up and develops the earlier reference in 1:14.

*Comment*
**8.** The shift from the first imperative in the letter in 2:6 to the second imperative, here a prohibition (*see to it that no one . . .*), serves to highlight the flip side to Paul's positive exhortations to continue to 'live' or 'walk' in Christ; that is, the warning against depending on something other than Christ. Paul's allusion in 2:4 to persuasive or 'fine-sounding' arguments that could 'deceive' the Colossians hinted at the danger posed by false teachers. Now Paul develops this warning further. The repetition of the words *no one* from 2:4 shows that there are probably specific individuals in view. Paul highlights the potential danger with the warning that those who propound the teaching he will refer to could *take you captive*. The

'captivity' imagery points to the power of this teaching and pictures one being carried off as a captive in war and controlled such that error rather than truth is now ruling. Even if the specifics are not spelled out, Paul's descriptions of the teaching that is being propounded is our closest clue to what the danger facing the Colossians was.

This captivity would come *through hollow and deceptive philosophy*. The term 'philosophy', if one goes simply by the etymology of the individual parts of the word, could mean something general like 'love of wisdom'. The term covered a wide range of uses, from Josephus' description of the different groups within Judaism such as Pharisees, Sadducees and Essenes (*Antiquities* 18.11), as well as to particular teachings such as those from Pythagoras and Thales (Josephus, *Against Apion* 1.14).[7] By 'philosophy' Paul does not mean to oppose a 'love of wisdom', as his references to wisdom in this letter demonstrate (cf. 1:9, 28; 2:3). For Paul, true wisdom comes from knowing God and his purposes in Christ for a sinful world alienated from God. What Paul is concerned about is a certain kind of 'wisdom' that he develops in the following descriptions. It is a 'wisdom', or understanding of the world and how it works, that is *hollow and deceptive*. It is 'hollow' in the sense that it is empty or devoid of anything that has spiritual value, probably to be contrasted with the language of 'fullness' in the next verse.[8] It is also 'deceptive' in that it claims to offer spiritual insight while leading people away from the truth of the gospel (see 1:5–6).

Paul then completes this description with three parallel phrases best seen in the ESV and NRSV's threefold 'according to'. The idea is that what follows is the guiding standard that determines the focus and make up of this erroneous teaching. The NIV's equivalent phrase, 'which depends on', and the CSB's 'based on' shows that what follows is the foundation that determines the content of this

---

7. See Pao, p. 159; Moo, p. 185–186, for these and other references. See also the use of the word in 4 Maccabees 1:1; 5:11, 22; 7:9, 21 (5:7, 35; 7:7; 8:1) for what has been called a Judaeo-Stoicism.

8. BDAG, p. 539.

*hollow and deceptive philosophy*. The following layout highlights the parallel phrases describing this 'philosophy'. This teaching is:

> according to the tradition 'of men'
> according to the 'elementals' of the world
> not according to Christ

First, this teaching *depends on human tradition*. By *tradition* Paul means that this has been passed along and handed down by others, something that is not a problem in and of itself (see e.g. 1 Cor. 11:2; 2 Thess. 3:6). The important qualifier is *human*. Jesus offered the same criticism against the hypocrisy of the Pharisees who elevated their own rules over God's commands, focusing on external matters rather than those of the heart (Mark 7:6–8; see on Col. 2:22).[9] In this context, *human tradition* is contrasted with the gospel which is the word of God, revealed by God and embodied in Christ (1:25–27). This teaching therefore does not come with God's approval, cannot help with knowing God and does not offer any insight into God's purposes and plans for the world. Any claim it makes about eternity and God's will must by definition lead away from God.

Second, this teaching *depends on . . . the elemental spiritual forces of this world*. This brings us to one of the most debated phrases in the letter to the Colossians. In the New Testament the Greek phrase *ta stoicheia tou kosmou* occurs both here and at 2:20 in Colossians, as well as in Galatians 4:3. The term *stoicheia* also occurs in Galatians 4:9; 2 Peter 3:10, 12 and Hebrews 5:12. In the Septuagint the term is found in 4 Maccabees 12:13; Wisdom 7:17 and 19:18. In this verse it has been given the following English translations grouped into three general types: 1. 'elemental spirits of the universe' (NRSV), 'elemental spirits of the world' (ESV, NET), 'spiritual powers of this world' (NLT), 'elemental spiritual forces of this world' (NIV); 2. 'elements of the world' (CSB); and 3. 'rudiments of the world' (KJV), 'basic principles of the world' (NKJV), 'basic principles of this world' (NIV84), 'elementary principles of the world' (NASB, LSB).

---

9. The same phrase 'human tradition' (*tēn paradosin tōn anthrōpōn*) is used in Mark 7:8 and Col. 2:8.

The term *stoicheia* refers to a basic element of something, for example to the letters of the alphabet from which words are formulated, or musical notes from which music is composed.[10] Three general interpretations of the expression in verse 8 are related to this basic idea. I will defend the third view.

1. The spirits or demons of the world (this is the view of most recent translations).[11] This meaning is probably not found elsewhere in the New Testament (though perhaps Gal. 4:9), nor is this the meaning of the three occurrences of the term in the Septuagint. Indeed, this usage does not appear to be present in ancient literature until the post-New Testament *Testament of Solomon* 8:2; 18:1–2. Proponents of this view argue that the phrase in 2:8 is equivalent to the reference to 'every power and authority' in 2:10 and the 'powers and authorities' in 2:15. It may also relate to the 'worship of angels' in 2:18. However, as Witherington observes, 'this would have to be the first place in all of Greek literature that *stoicheia* meant "spirits" or "beings."'[12]
2. The basic elements of the material world. This is the meaning of the term in 4 Maccabees 12:13 and Wisdom 7:17 as well as in the New Testament in 2 Peter 3:10, 12. This usage does not seem to fit this context where the content of teaching is being referred to rather than physical elements like earth, sky, fire and water. Many, however, argue that a spiritualizing of the elements is in view here such that the elements of the world are either being worshipped or treated as gods and therefore in place of Christ.[13] Thus this modification blends this view with the previous one and is probably behind the first and second group of translations above.

---

10. BDAG, 946; cf. Wisdom 19:18.
11. Pao, pp. 160–161.
12. Witherington, p. 154. I am indebted here to Witherington's succinct summary on pp. 154–155.
13. Moo, pp. 187–192; Beale, pp. 240–245, on 2:20 Beale describes these elements as part of the 'old world' that believers have died to in order to belong to the new creation.

3. The term was widely used for basic teachings, rules or principles, on a range of topics from geometry to diet.[14] This is the way the phrase is used elsewhere in the New Testament. In Hebrews 5:12 *stoicheia* is qualified with a reference to the introductory teaching of God's word. In Galatians 4:3 (and perhaps 4:9, in light of 4:10) *ta stoicheia tou kosmou* refers to the teaching that held sway until the age of maturity that came with Christ.[15] Are there any clues in this context that this phrase should be understood as a reference to some kind of teaching? In this verse, as noted above, the phrase is the second of three *kata* phrases. The third phrase, 'not according to Christ', forms a contrast, so the first of these, 'according to human tradition', appears to be a parallel expression with this second phrase. Thus, the focus here seems to be on 'human' or 'worldly' teaching rather than spiritual beings.

But what kind of teaching is this? Is it Jewish? Is it mystical? Is it Hellenistic? Or is it a combination of these and more? Paul is yet to unpack the content of this teaching, but unfortunately for commentators he does not identify the source of this teaching with specificity. We only get glimpses of what it might be with the presence of tantalizing hints. One such hint is probably found in verse 20 where *ta stoicheia tou kosmou* is parallel with a continued living in the world according to its rules. The kinds of rules Paul

---

14. Cf. Aristotle, *Politics* 1309b16; Plato, *Laws* 7.790C; Xenophon, *Memorabilia* 2.1.1; Philo, *De Opificio Mundi* 126. Cited by Witherington, p. 155 n. 12. For the following defence of this view, in addition to Witherington, see Hendriksen's extensive footnote on pp. 135–137 n. 83. Hendriksen also notes early church support from Clement of Alexandria (*Stromata*, 6.8) and Tertullian (*Against Marcion*, 5.19). See also Thompson, pp. 52–54.
15. Cf. also the cognate verb *stoicheō* for 'walking' according to a set of rules or standard in Acts 21:24 (the law); Rom. 4:12 (Abraham's pattern of faith); Gal. 5:25 (the pattern set by the Spirit), 6:16 (the rule/standard set in 6:15); Phil. 3:16.

has in mind are then stated in the following verses as various commands not to touch or taste and are then described again as 'merely human commands and teachings' (2:22). Thus, in summary, in this context, the phrase *ta stoicheia tou kosmou* seems to be another similar description of what Paul has just called *human tradition*. It is this-worldly, human-originated teaching. We must await further detail in 2:16–18, but for now this phrase adds the nuance that such teaching is basic or fundamental to the false teachers who want to explain the world apart from Christ. Indeed, Paul's final comment on this *hollow and deceptive philosophy* is that it is not 'according to' or 'does not depend on' Christ. Paul draws again on what he has said already about 'the word of God'. God's saving plan is revealed and embodied in Christ who came to redeem and rescue sinners by his death on the cross (1:25–27). In the following verses, Paul unpacks the significance of the fullness of Christ and his accomplishments on the cross in order to highlight once again the contrast between the hope of the gospel and the ineffectiveness of the false teaching.

**9.** With the word *for*, Paul provides the first of two reasons that accentuate the difference between who Christ is and what he has done in contrast to the false teaching and its demands. The first reason concerns who Christ is. The phrase *all the fullness* is used again (cf. 1:19), this time with the added specification *of the Deity* that confirms Paul means all the fullness of who God is. 'The entire fullness of God's nature' (CSB) captures the idea. As in 1:19, the combination of 'all' and 'fullness' makes a staggering claim about Jesus and about how God is to be understood as completely and exclusively seen in him, even as there is distinction in view between these two persons of the Godhead.[16] However, just as Paul has repeatedly highlighted the physical historical person of Jesus and his revelation of God in his earthly ministry (1:22), so here Paul specifies that this fullness of God *dwells* in the person of Jesus *bodily*. As Paul's previous references to Christ's physical body indicate (1:20, 22, 24), Paul's teaching is not centred around an abstract ideal or general religious principles.[17] In contrast to the

---

16. McKnight, p. 229.
17. Note the contrasting harsh treatment of human 'bodies' in 2:23.

'empty' or 'hollow and deceptive' human speculations basic to a merely this-worldly understanding, all the 'fullness' of God and his purposes are only understood in the historical and physical person of Jesus, 'the image of the invisible God' who reveals God (1:15).

**10.** The second reason Paul gives that highlights the difference between Christ and what he has done in contrast to the demands of the false teaching, continues the language of 'fullness' from the preceding verse. If Christ is the 'fullness' of God, then those who belong to Christ, those who are 'in Christ' *have been brought to fullness*. The NIV captures the significance of the perfect tense of the verb 'filled' that Paul uses here ('you have been filled', ESV). The perfect tense emphasizes the state of fullness, thus 'filled to the full' is the idea. The passive voice indicates that God has brought this fullness. In other words, there is nothing lacking spiritually for the person who trusts in and belongs to Christ; because Christ is 'fully' God, to know him is to know God. The additional requirements advocated by human-derived instructions, which are 'hollow' anyway, cannot add to one's redemption and reconciliation in Christ, or to one's knowledge of God. In order to reinforce the point that there is no lack in Christ and there is no need to look elsewhere, Paul concludes this sentence with a reminder of Christ's supremacy over all. As he has already emphasized in Colossians 1, Christ is the Creator of 'rulers' and 'authorities' (see 1:16), and thus has authority over *every power and authority* as their *head*. In adding that he is their 'head' in this context Paul does not mean they are part of his body (as the metaphor is used in 1:18), but that these spiritual rulers and authorities (see 1:16) do not have authority over Christ or those who belong to Christ. Paul's use of the word *every* once again highlights the universal and unrivalled authority of Christ.

**11.** The following verses will continue to unpack what it means to have 'fullness' in Christ by developing further what Christ has achieved in his death and resurrection for those who belong to him. The first description of people who belong to Christ is that they *were also circumcised*. In its Old Testament usage, this word referred to the physical act that symbolized belonging to the people of God (Gen. 17:11). As Paul will clarify in the description that follows, he refers here to a spiritual action carried out by God (the verb is in the passive voice) that describes what it means to belong to God's new covenant people. This is something God promised to do for Israel's descendants (Deut. 30:6), and it ultimately became part of the new covenant hope for a new heart (Ezek. 36:26–28).

The word underlying the phrase *not performed by human hands* (*acheiropoiēton*) reinforces the idea that this is an action performed by God and is eternal, as seen in the two other places in the New Testament where the term occurs (Mark 14:58 and 2 Cor. 5:1). A similar negation in Hebrews 9:11 is explained there as meaning 'not part of this creation'. It is possible that the term may imply a critique of idolatry among the Colossians (cf. Isa. 31:7; Acts 17:24). The focus here, however, is once again on the contrast between that which is merely human, depends on human activity, and is ultimately temporary and ineffective to change hearts (2:8; cf. 2:22), and that which is accomplished for us spiritually by God through Christ. This seems to be the way Paul develops his meaning in the following phrases, which continue to explain how this spiritual circumcision came about. I will lay out the phrases visually with a more word-for-word translation along with the NIV to help us follow Paul's flow of thought:

> you were circumcised, with a circumcision not made
>> by human hands
> in the putting off of the body of flesh (*your whole self ruled by the flesh was put off*)
> in the circumcision of Christ (*when you were circumcised by Christ*)

The main interpretive decision concerns the second and third lines. It seems likely that they are parallel and refer to the same event. Although there are variations, the main question is, do these phrases refer to what has happened to the person who is 'in Christ' or do these phrases refer to Christ himself, and his death? The NIV's *your whole self ruled by the flesh* translates the Greek phrase *tou sōmatos tēs sarkos* which, as indicated above, some other translations render more word-for-word as 'the body of the flesh' (NRSV, NASB, ESV; cf. CSB). Because a similar Greek phrase is used in 1:22 to refer to Christ's physical body and death, some have argued that this also refers to Christ's death, in this case as the means by which the spiritual circumcision was accomplished (and thus as a parallel expression to the following phrase, *by Christ*, which is also interpreted as a reference to Christ's death, see more below).[18] In 1:22, however, there is an important modifying pronoun, 'his', that clearly indicates that Christ is being referred to. Furthermore, it isn't clear what it means for 'the body of flesh' to be 'removed' (NASB; *put off*, NIV). This would be a unique way of speaking of death.[19] In 2:13 *the uncircumcision of your flesh* is clearly talking about the state of the believer 'before' coming to Christ, and this seems to be deliberately recalling the similar phrase here.[20] Likewise, the similar language in 3:9 of having 'put off the old self' (ESV) is closer to what is being referred to here than 1:22. The NIV's translation, therefore, helps to show that Paul refers to the removal of who we were outside of Christ, 'ruled by' the sinful tendencies of the flesh.

The final phrase of this verse is also debated. The NIV's *when you were circumcised by Christ* translates the genitive that other translations leave as 'of Christ' (NRSV, NASB, ESV, CSB). What then is the 'circumcision of Christ'? Once again, as above, some see this as a reference to the death of Christ and therefore as a parallel to 'the body of flesh' as the time when Christ was 'circumcised'. The reference to Christ's death in 1:22 is again viewed as providing support.[21] However, the repeated references to 'circumcision' and 'uncircumcised' throughout these verses all refer to individuals who were outside of Christ but who are recipients of his saving activity. The opening statement of this verse that '*you* were ... circumcised' confirms that the 'circumcision of Christ' is best understood as 'the circumcision done by Christ' (NET). The phrases, therefore, are parallel descriptions of what has happened to the

---

18. E.g. Pao, pp. 165–166; Beale, pp. 188–190.
19. This is the only place in the Greek Old and New Testaments where the noun *apekdusis* ('removal/stripping off') occurs. The cognate verb *apekduomai* ('strip off/disarm') is also rare, occurring only in Col. 2:15 and 3:9.
20. Moo, p. 199.
21. The genitive 'of Christ' is understood in this view as an objective genitive referring to the 'circumcision' that Christ received.

person who belongs to Christ (rather than parallel descriptions of Christ's death). Thus Paul speaks here of a spiritual circumcision by Christ that brings us into the people of God. It is true that Christ does this by his death on the cross and his resurrection, but that will become the focus of 2:14–15. For now, in 2:11–13 Paul focuses on the blessing of belonging to Christ in contrast to the emptiness of merely human tradition. Before leaving this verse we might wonder: why does Paul mention circumcision here? Circumcision appears to enter into Paul's discussion unexpectedly. Many have concluded that Paul discusses circumcision because this must have been a major focus of the false teachers. Yet Paul does not directly counter a wrong view of circumcision here. The word 'flesh' does, however, reoccur in Paul's direct critique of the false teaching. In 2:23 Paul concludes that their human commands cannot restrain 'the flesh' (cf. also 2:18, their 'fleshly minds'). Paul, therefore counters a useless focus on attempts to restrain the flesh with the biblical-theological and new covenant teaching on what Christ has already done to 'remove the body of flesh'.[22]

**12.** The opening phrase of this verse, *having been buried with him in baptism*, modifies and is contemporaneous with the opening phrase of the previous verse, *in him you were also circumcised*. Paul, therefore, further explains that this circumcision is a spiritual circumcision that takes place when one belongs to Christ.[23] The reference to being *buried* and *raised* refers to the death of the old self

---

22. Moo, pp. 196–197.
23. A continuing debate concerns whether or not baptism in the New Testament replaces circumcision in the Old Testament, with implications for whether or not infants should also be baptized even though none are explicitly said to be baptized in the New Testament. This verse may not be as directly related to that debate as first appears, however, since, as we argue above, 'baptism' here is linked with conversion ('faith') and paralleled with spiritual circumcision. The debate over infant baptism is better focused on the significance of the new covenant and who is in that covenant. See the exchange in Salter, 'Baptism', pp. 15–29, Gibson, 'Sacramental', pp. 191–208, Salter, 'Response', pp. 209–210.

and the new life one has in Christ. Being buried *with him* and raised *with him* shows that the believer participates in and benefits from the accomplishments of Christ's actions, his life, death and resurrection, paralleling the 'in him' opening of 2:11. His death, bearing judgment, becomes ours. His resurrection life, showing that the penalty of death no longer holds sway, likewise becomes ours.

How and when does this identification with Christ take place? Paul's clarification that this takes place *through your faith in the working of God, who raised him from the dead* shows that he is talking about the time when the accomplishments of Jesus' death and resurrection were appropriated by those who entrust themselves to Christ, believing that his death and resurrection are the means and demonstration of God's saving power. Since this takes place *through your faith* (see 1:4), baptism here is best understood as referring to the water baptism that is associated with conversion elsewhere in the New Testament (see e.g. Acts 2:38; 8:35–36; 10:47; 16:14–15, 30–34; 18:8).[24] Broader New Testament teaching clarifies that it is faith, relying on God's work in Christ, not works, that save, and that baptism in itself does not save since it is an outward expression of this inward reality.[25] Nevertheless, as noted above, baptism is associated with conversion. The object of faith is *the working of God* which may be a deliberate contrast with the emphasis of the false teachers on human rules and practices (2:20–23). What matters is relying on (i.e. 'faith', 'trust') what God has done in Christ, rather than any of the rules or obligations imposed on the Colossians by the false teachers. Thus, in summary, this spiritual circumcision – the removal of the old self and transfer from death to life and into the people of God through belonging to Christ – takes place at one's conversion, when faith is placed in the risen Christ, as one's baptism shows.

**13.** In 2:13–15 Paul clarifies even further how God's saving purposes in Christ's death on the cross bring life to believers. First, combining the references to 'death' (2:12) and 'uncircumcision' (2:11) in the preceding verses, Paul again highlights our plight outside of

---

24. Cf. Rom. 6:1–4.
25. Compare, e.g. Rom. 4:1–5 and Simon in Acts 8:13, 20–21.

Christ. Being *dead in your sins* refers to the sentence of spiritual death, that is alienation from God, that one is under because of sin (though physical death follows).[26] Thus sin, and the penalty for sin, must be dealt with for this change to take place. Paul will unpack how this was done in the following verse. As noted in 2:11, *the uncircumcision of your flesh* highlights the spiritual reality that the old self, outside of Christ, is not among the people of God, and is governed by sin. This is the plight of all humanity, as Paul says in Romans, because we belong to Adam (Rom. 5:12–19; 7:5). In spite of all this, God, in his grace, *made you alive with Christ*. The condition of death clearly means that the escape from this condition can't be accomplished by individuals themselves. Thus it is the 'working of God' who raised Christ from the dead (2:12) who likewise raised us from spiritual death on the basis of Christ's resurrection.[27]

Although the NIV begins a new sentence with *He forgave us*, the term 'forgiving' here is linked to being 'made alive' and is the first of two terms that explain the way in which God has made us alive (by forgiving us).[28] The second term, in 2:14, will further elaborate on this forgiveness. As Paul has implied in the preceding reference to sin, and as he has stated in 1:14, central to our redemption, reconciliation and (here) new life is the final and complete dealing with sin. The term Paul uses may be more accurately translated as 'graciously forgiven' (LSB). The idea is that we have been pardoned by grace (*charizomai*). The recipient of this gracious action is 'us', as we are the ones who have wronged God.[29] We are forgiven of *all*

---

26. The preposition 'in' (Greek *en*) is probably causal here (Harris, p. 95).
27. The parallel with 2:12 ('raised with him through your faith . . .') indicates that the appropriation of Christ's resurrection life and means of forgiveness takes place when one relies upon God's work in faith.
28. The participle 'forgiving' could be temporal ('when he forgave', NRSV), or perhaps causal ('for he forgave', NLT); Harris, p. 96.
29. There is no significance to the shift from 'you' in 2:10–13a to 'us' in 2:13b as if (according to some) the preceding verses (and the immediately preceding verb) were referring to Gentiles only and then Paul turns to speak of 'us' Jews or Jews and Gentiles together only from 2:13b (and in the shift from 'made alive' to 'forgave').

*our sins*. Every misstep and variation from God's good will is no longer stacked against those who belong to Christ. The emphasis on 'all' should be remembered when agonizing over the conditional meaning of texts such as 1:23. It is not by exerting persevering effort that forgiveness is received, such that we could never know if enough had been done, or if some sins required more from us. Rather, the emphasis is on totality, *all our sins*. How we are forgiven is further developed in the following verse.

**14.** This full and tightly packed verse is abounding in images that communicate the effectiveness of Jesus' death for those who trust in him. Because Paul uses a number of less common terms it may help to lay out the flow of thought with the following rendering, noting some of the Greek words referred to below.

> 2:13 made alive
> > by forgiving
>
> 2:14 by cancelling/erasing (*exaleipsas*)
> > the hand-written document (*cheirographon*)
> > > which with (or because of) commandments (*dogmasin*)
> > > > was against us
> > > > and opposed to us
> >
> > he has taken it away
> > > by nailing it to the cross

First, unpacking the references to sin from the previous verse, Paul speaks of *the charge of our legal indebtedness*. This translation covers two terms in the Greek text. The first is *cheirographon* and refers to a 'hand-written document'.[30] The second term is *dogmata* and this further qualifies this handwritten item as a document with 'requirements' or 'commandments' ('obligations', CSB). This second term, *dogmata* ('commandments'), is used elsewhere by Paul only in Ephesians 2:15 and its usage there may help to explain the less clear preceding term *cheirographon* ('hand-written document') here. The whole phrase in Ephesians 2:15 placed together with the phrase here will help to highlight the parallel.

---

30. BDAG, p. 1083.

Ephesians 2:15  the law of commandments with regulations
(*ton nomon tōn entolōn en dogmasin*)
Colossians 2:14  the 'handwritten' document with regulations
(*cheirographon tois dogmasin*)

What then does this 'hand-written document' refer to in this context? Many point to the use of this word in extrabiblical writings for an 'IOU' and so it is often referred to as a 'certificate of debt' (e.g. CSB, NASB).[31] Its wider use for hand-written documents such as receipts, contracts of sale or employment, and authorization of stewards, however, suggests that although it may be used to refer to certificates of debt, the term does not by itself *mean* certificate of debt.[32] The use of the term 'regulations' (*dogmata*) in Ephesians to refer to the law suggests a reference to the law may also be in view here. The immediately preceding reference to circumcision (2:11) means that the old covenant has been alluded to already in this context. Since Paul will say this handwritten document has 'regulations' and is 'against us' it is unlikely to be a document written by us.[33] The term *dogmata* is also used elsewhere in the New Testament to refer to decrees of Caesar (Luke 2:1; Acts 17:7), so it could also allude more broadly to all of the commands of God that humanity is obligated to (cf. also Rom. 1:32; 2:14–15; Moo, pp. 210–211). Even so, as Paul says in Romans 3:19, what the law says silences every mouth and renders the whole world accountable to God.

The reference to this hand-written document with regulations is followed by two more phrases that describe it: this document *stood against us and condemned us.* The last term may be translated as 'opposed to us' (CSB) and thus by repetition emphasizes hostility

---

31. See e.g. Beale, pp. 197, 209–210.
32. See Grindheim, 'Law', p. 104 for papyri references and this conclusion.
33. Some say that the certificate of debt is against us 'because'
    of the regulations/commandments (of God). Grindheim, 'Law',
    p. 105 suggests that the reference to 'hand-written' 'regulations/
    commandments' may allude to the giving of the law on tablets since
    they were described as written by 'the finger of God' (Exod. 31:18;
    Deut. 9:10).

with the added peril of penalty.[34] This hand-written document with regulations, therefore, is a graphic image of the predicament we are in as sinners, with a documented record of the requirements that we have failed to meet and that stand against us by not rendering to our Creator and sovereign Lord the obedience that is owed to his commandments.

Even though 2:13–14a describe our predicament in great detail, Paul's emphasis is on what God has done with this document. He has *cancelled the charge*. The NIV's translation of this participle as *having cancelled* interprets this as temporal in relation to the preceding reference to gracious forgiveness. However, the participle probably shows the means of forgiveness, how God forgave, and thus the translation 'by cancelling' (RSV, ESV) may express this better. This term (*exaleipsas*) can refer more generally to removing something 'so as to leave no trace'.[35] With documents, as here, the term can mean to 'cause to disappear by wiping' (hence 'erased', CSB).[36] The same term is used in Revelation 7:17 and 21:4 where God wipes away every tear (cf. also Acts 3:19; Rev. 3:5). In this context, it is a further explanation of the gracious forgiveness God grants, the record against us is wiped, and this in turn is a further explanation of the way in which we are made alive when we were dead in our sins.

To further emphasize the totality of our forgiveness, Paul adds that this document has been *taken . . . away*. Not only has the document been completely cleaned of all charges, it has been removed entirely. The condemnation that this certificate declares and holds against us because of our disobedience is no longer there! How can this be so? The answer is given in the last phrase, he has taken it away by *nailing it to the cross*. Thus this tightly packed verse shows how God's gracious forgiveness is tied to Jesus' death. The penalty that we were under, being 'dead' because of our sins and disobedience to God's law, was removed. The phrase 'nailing it to the cross' shows that the charges and the consequent penalty have been borne by Jesus for us in his death, enabling us to be 'made alive'

---

34. Harris, p. 96.
35. BDAG, p. 344.
36. Ibid.

and graciously forgiven (2:13). This verse develops what was only alluded to earlier in the letter: redemption and forgiveness of sins (1:14), making peace through his blood (1:20), reconciliation by Christ's physical body through death (1:22), and ultimately presented holy, without blemish and free from accusation (1:22). This is, in broader theological terms, a 'penal substitutionary' explanation of the significance of Jesus' death. As Paul declares in Galatians 3:13, 'Christ redeemed us from the curse of the law by becoming a curse for us'.

**15.** The consequence of this accomplishment through the cross is that God has made *the powers and authorities . . . a public spectacle* since he has *disarmed them*. As noted above in 2:10 and especially 1:16, the 'powers and authorities' that Paul refers to are probably spiritual powers or angelic beings. The reference to 'disarmed' indicates that these powers are demonic powers that would belong to Satan's rule, the 'dominion of darkness' (1:13). If, as we suggested regarding 1:16, the Colossians, like many today, thought that spiritual forces were powerful and to be feared or appeased, they can take comfort from knowing that not only do they pale in comparison to the supremacy of the Son, they no longer have power over those who belong to the Son.[37] To be *disarmed* means to have power removed, and may better be translated as 'stripped of power' (cf. NJB).[38] What was this power that they had that is now removed? In this context, it must relate to the penalty of death because of our sin and disobedience to the demands of the law. As the 'accuser', Satan points to our sin and holds this against us as those who do not deserve God's love (Rev. 12:10). Apart from God's loving forgiveness, Satan holds this power over us. Yet by nailing what condemned us to the cross, God has removed the basis for this power because Jesus has taken the punishment for us. In this sense

---

37. As noted in comments on 1:16, the same terms ('rulers and authorities') refer to human rulers in Luke 12:11. Perhaps Paul has the judgments/condemnations of the false teachers in view here too (2:16, 18).

38. As noted above on 2:11, the verb (*apekduomai*) refers to taking off or removing 'the old self' like clothes in 3:9. Here it has the metaphorical sense 'strip of/remove power', hence 'disarm'.

then it is a *public spectacle, triumphing over them* like a 'triumphal procession' (NJB) that publicly and demonstrably shows that Satan's powers have been defeated and no longer have any sway.[39] The NIV's final description that this was done *by the cross* interprets a pronoun in the Greek text as referring back to 'the cross' in the previous verse. The pronoun, however, could also be translated as 'in him' (RSV, ESV) and indeed this is the meaning of this form elsewhere in Colossians (cf. 1:16, 17, 19; 2:6, 7, 9, 10). In this immediate context, from 2:10, Paul has been saying that believers have fullness, spiritual circumcision, burial and new life in Christ. Thus the flow of argument lends support to the meaning 'in him'. Of course, Paul has just specified that it was Christ's death on the cross that has removed the charge and penalty against us, rendering Satan's power ineffective. So it was in Christ, and through his death on the cross, that the rulers and authorities have been stripped of their power. Translating the pronoun as 'in him' also allows for the broader emphasis in these verses on Jesus' death and resurrection with perhaps the resurrection in particular serving as the public demonstration of that defeat.

*Theology*
This passage has as much densely packed theology as any other in Colossians. What Paul says about Jesus looks back to what he said in 1:15–20, affirming the full deity of Christ as well as the significance of his death and resurrection. Because of Christ's person (the fullness of the Deity) and work (taking the penalty for our disobedience) the one who belongs to him by faith need not fear either the influence of the invisible rulers and authorities, or the judgment of the false teachers that he will refer to in the following section. In broader theological terms, the *Christus Victor* explanation of the significance of Christ's death in 2:15 relates to the 'penal substitutionary' explanation in the previous verse (2:14) as cause ('penal substitution' enabling forgiveness of sins) and effect (stripping the

---

39. See, for example, the only other use of the verb *thriumbeuō* in the New Testament in 2 Cor. 2:14 where a triumphal procession is in view.

powers of power). Furthermore, in effecting a transfer from death to new life through Christ, God has accomplished a spiritual transformation in putting off the flesh that the regulations of the false teachers are unable to do.

### ii. The regulations of the false teaching offer no spiritual good (2:16–23)
*Context*
Having zeroed in on the spiritual fullness that Christ provides to all who belong to him by faith, Paul now develops in more detail the danger that he has alluded to in 2:4. The opening word 'therefore' signals another development in his argument (also in 2:6 and 3:1; Pao, p. 181). Following the elaboration of the concluding phrase of 2:8 ('on Christ') in 2:9–15, Paul now develops the general warning of 2:8 in 2:16–23 with more detail about the demands of the teachers but with the wording of 2:8 still in view: the empty and vain characteristics in 2:18, the contrast with Christ in 2:19, and the human worldly elements in 2:20, 22. The central feature of this section is the two prohibitions of 2:16–17 (not judged) and 2:18–19 (not condemned), with 2:20–23 further specifying the regulations that false teachers were imposing and further defining these regulations as merely human and related to the transitory orientation of this world. These final verses (2:20–23) are also transitional as the issue of the ineffectiveness of these regulations and the significant change that a believer has undergone prepares for the focused attention on the believer's new life in the following section.

*Comment*
**16.** With the opening word *therefore* Paul transitions to a more sustained warning against teaching that offers an alternative to the sufficiency of Christ, a warning that runs through to the end of this chapter. The significance of the word *therefore* should not be overlooked as it is an important link between what Paul has just said and the following exhortations. It is in light of the spiritual fullness that believers have in Christ (new life, forgiveness of sins, no longer facing the accusation from the failed demands of the law) that Paul addresses issues of judgment and condemnation from

others in 2:16, 18. With the second prohibition in the letter, Paul will now elaborate on the warning he gave in 2:8 (and hinted at in 2:4). Thus it is likely that we are given a window into some of the content of the false teaching he warned about in 2:8, the human-oriented and human-derived deceptive teaching that does not depend on Christ.

As in 2:8, the warning not to let *anyone* act in the ways discussed suggests that there were indeed some people who were seeking to influence the Colossian believers with their teaching. In particular, the Colossians must not let anyone *judge* them about the five following matters. The language of *judge* and *disqualify* (2:18) implies that at least part of the problem was that the Colossians were being told they were inadequate or lacked something that the false teachers were requiring. Thus *judge* has the sense of 'pass an unfavorable judgment upon, criticize, find fault with, condemn'.[40] There is a sense of course in which they cannot prevent the false teachers from acting in this way. By exhorting the Colossians to *not let anyone judge you*, Paul probably means that they should refuse to take on board or accept their condemnation of their status before God. The reason this judgment does not count is because in Christ believers are 'free from accusation' (1:22).

What is it then that the false teachers were passing judgment on (ESV)? The combination of *what you eat or drink, or with regard to a religious festival, a New Moon celebration or a Sabbath day*, seems to assume practices found in the Old Testament. Certainly the final three terms referring to a feast, New Moon and Sabbath are all prominent terms in the Old Testament. The term for feast or festival is the most general one, but is often used to refer to the Passover and the Feast of Unleavened Bread (cf. Luke 22:1). Instructions about 'New Moon' sacrifices are given in Numbers 28:11–15. All three terms are mentioned together in 1 Chronicles 23:31; 2 Chronicles 2:4; 31:3; Ezekiel 45:17; Hosea 2:11 (LXX Hos. 2:13). The New Moon and the Sabbath are mentioned together in 2 Kings 4:23, and Amos 8:5 as times of sacrifice and abstinence

---

40. BDAG, p. 567.

from other work.[41] Thus the opening pair, 'what you eat or drink' most likely also refers to Old Testament food laws, with the additional reference to 'drinking' either a natural complement to restrictions revolving around meals (to 'eat and drink' is a common combination in Scripture, e.g. Gen. 26:30; Exod. 24:11; 1 Kings 4:20; Luke 13:26; Acts 10:41), a reference to instructions about drink offerings and drinking restrictions for special circumstances (cf. Lev. 11:34; Num. 6:3; cf. also Rom. 14:17; 1 Tim. 5:23; Heb. 9:10), or a broader application of laws either to avoid idolatry or some aspect of the surrounding culture (e.g. Dan. 1:10; Acts 15:19–20).

Paul's statement, together with the following salvation-historical contrast that points to fulfilment in Christ, shows that the false teachers included some kind of emphasis on Old Testament law keeping as a means of passing judgment on others. The earlier emphasis on human tradition and human-oriented teaching, however, indicates that more than a salvation-historical error of focus is involved. The teachers are using the Old Testament for their own ends to advance their own status, and probably with their own additional emphases and applications. Later verses in this section (2:21–23) indicate that there was an extra edge of harshness in abstinence and the treatment of the body that went along with this condemning approach to the Colossian believers. Since the contrast here and in 2:8, 21–23 is between human-originated rules and the fullness that a believer has in Christ, the issue is unlikely to be merely one of Jewish exclusiveness in excluding Gentiles from the people of God. The issue is empty and useless regulations versus Christ. If the impetus, however, for their harsh teaching has come from the Old Testament, then an understanding of the fundamental relationship between the Old Testament and Christ is required to cut the false teaching off at its root, and that is what Paul turns to next.

---

41. Cf. also Isa. 1:13, 14; Ps. 81:3 ('new moon' and 'feast'); Ezek. 46:1, 3 ('Sabbath' and 'New Moon'). Elsewhere in the LXX all three are found together in 1 Esdras 5:51; Judith 8:6; 1 Maccabees 10:34.

**17.** *These*, says Paul, referring to the observance of the preceding rules or feasts, are merely *a shadow of the things that were to come*. A number of significant implications follow from this. These Old Testament requirements cannot be the basis for measuring godliness, status or even how one best serves God. They are temporary. Nevertheless, they are also anticipatory, they pointed ahead to something that was to come. The participle translated as *the things that were to come* is often used in the New Testament with an eschatological sense (e.g. Acts 26:22). An almost identical point is made in Hebrews 10:1 that 'the law is only a shadow of the good things that are coming'. As a *shadow* they also are not unrelated or unconnected to what is *to come*, they reflect the shape and contours of that *reality*. The contrast to the shadow and what is to come is *the reality*, that *is found in Christ*.[42] Thus Paul cuts the claims of the false teachers off at the root: since the Colossian believers have Christ they therefore have even more than what the teachers were saying they needed. The Greek word *sōma* that the NIV translates as *reality* usually refers to 'bodies' of various kinds (cf. KJV). Elsewhere in Colossians the word has been used to refer to physical bodies (2:23; cf. 2:11); Christ's own physical body (1:22; cf. 2:9), and his 'body', the church (1:18, 24; 2:19; 3:15). In this context, when contrasted with a shadow, the meaning of *sōma* is 'substance' (NRSV, ESV) and hence the NIV's 'reality'.[43]

Paul makes the salvation-historical point that Christ is the goal of all of these apparently disparate requirements and feasts in the Old Testament. Picking up on 2:8b ('rather than on Christ'), Paul's point is Christological (about Jesus), not ecclesiological (about defining who the people of God are). Now that Christ has come, he shows what they were meant for and he fulfils them. Matters of unclean and clean are solved in Christ who cleanses us. Feasts that celebrate God's provision are fulfilled in Christ, in whom we have redemption and forgiveness. Observance of specific days and feasts related to the enjoyment of God's presence and provision are

---

42. The genitive 'of Christ' (NKJV) is likely to be possessive, hence 'belongs to Christ' (ESV).
43. BDAG, p. 984; LSJ, p. 1749.

fulfilled when one comes to Christ, in whom 'all the fullness of the Deity lives in bodily form'.[44] Therefore, instead of being condemned for not observing these practices, the one who has come to Christ is the one who has realized the aim and purpose of all of them simply because that person belongs to Christ. To insist on keeping such practices now would denigrate Christ and place one at odds with God and his purposes rather than place that person in a position of superiority over others.

**18.** With the second prohibition of this section (see 2:16) Paul continues to warn against teachers (*Do not let anyone . . .*) who impose human-oriented requirements on believers that detract from the sufficiency they have in Christ. This tightly compact verse is another one of the most debated verses in Colossians. To assist us in following my explanations below I will outline the overall flow of thought, anticipating conclusions that will be clarified below:

>
> Do not let anyone pass judgment on you
> > who delights in
> > > their false humility
> > > their worship of angels
> >
> > who goes on about what they think they see
> > > being puffed up with idle notions by their unspiritual minds
>
> 2:19a who does not hold to the head . . .

The false teachers are seeking to *disqualify* the Colossians. This translation (also NRSV, ESV) has been said to reflect the activity of presiding over others like an umpire who renders a verdict that deprives someone of a prize.[45] Although this could be read as though Paul is warning the Colossians that they were in danger of

---

44. Thus the reference to the Sabbath in 2:16 is in keeping with what Paul says in Romans 14:5. Although the principle of rest, evidencing trust in God to provide and an awareness of our own frailty, is essential to living in God's world, believers are no longer directly under the Mosaic covenant's obligation to set aside the seventh day.
45. Dunn, p. 177; Harris, p. 106; Campbell, p. 43.

missing out on their salvation, this word picks up and repeats the similar warning in 2:16 (see comments above). Thus the false teachers are seeking to 'pass judgment' (NET) and 'condemn' (CSB) the Colossians as lacking what they deemed as significant for spiritual status. In this renewed warning Paul describes the false teachers themselves rather than their teachings.[46] The phrase (*thelōn en*), common in the LXX, refers to 'taking pleasure in' something, so the translation 'delight in' captures the idea rather than 'insist on' (ESV, NRSV).[47]

They *delight in false humility and the worship of angels*. The same term Paul uses for 'humility' occurs again in 2:23 and 3:12. 'Humility' is a characteristic that Paul commends as part of the clothing that God's people wear (3:12). In this context, however, with the additional qualifications given in 2:23, the emphasis may be on harsh practices that give the appearance of humiliation, thus the NIV's *false humility*, or more specifically the CSB's 'ascetic practices' (cf. ESV), which perhaps accompanied claims to restrain the 'flesh' (2:23). The *worship of angels* has been understood in two main ways. Some see this as a reference to worship carried out by angels, and interpret this in light of the following reference to seeing visions. Thus, on this view, what the false teachers were emphasizing was their own ecstatic or visionary experiences of seeing angels worshipping God in the heavenly realms.[48] However, just as 'humility' is further defined in 2:23, so too is 'worship'. There 'worship' is described as 'self-imposed worship' and clearly refers to activity carried out by

---

46. The participles here are understood as attributive, modifying the opening subject 'anyone' (*mēdeis*), and specified in the NIV (and NET) with 'who'; Campbell, p. 43. It is also possible that the participles express the means by which they were condemning ('by delighting', CSB, NASB).

47. Dunn, p. 178; BDAG, p. 448.

48. E.g. Dunn, pp. 180–182; McKnight, pp. 274–277; see more extensively Smith, *Heavenly*, pp. 119–130. Grammatically, this view interprets the genitive 'of angels' as a subjective genitive (i.e. in which the word following is the subject, carrying out the action; in this case 'worship of angels' = angels worshipping).

people rather than angels (see comments on 2:23 below). Furthermore, Arnold has demonstrated that there is a lack of evidence for the term for 'worship' being followed by a subjective genitive.[49] Thus what could be in view here is some kind of invocation of angels (perhaps for protection), or veneration or honouring of angels, rather than Christ, who is the Creator of all things, visible and invisible (see the warnings in Rev. 19:10; 22:8–9).[50] The false teachers' fascination with angels may lie behind the emphasis elsewhere in Colossians on Christ's superiority over all spiritual beings.[51]

The false teachers are then described with three further phrases (paraphrased as the following): 'going into . . .', 'being puffed up with . . .', and 'not holding to . . .' (2:19a). The first phrase begins with a term, 'to enter into' (*embateuō*), found only here in the New Testament and the meaning here is also the subject of much debate. In the Septuagint the term can refer to entering into or taking possession of land, or to going into details in relating an account.[52] Due to wider usage outside of the Septuagint for entering into a sanctuary or a vision many have seen this as a technical term referring to the visionary experience of one who 'enters the sanctuary which he saw in ecstasy'.[53] Proponents of this view argue

---

49. Arnold, *Syncretism*, pp. 90–93. BDAG, p. 459 states that with *thrēskeia* 'the being who is worshipped is given in the objective genitive' (cited also by Arnold, p. 93). See also W. Radl, *EDNT*, II, pp. 154–155.
50. Grammatically, this view interprets the genitive 'of angels' as an objective genitive (i.e. in which the word following is the object of the action; in this case 'worship of angels' = people worshipping angels). See Arnold, *Syncretism*, pp. 101–102; and the texts for worship cited in BDAG, p. 459. See also Beale, p. 226.
51. Moo, p. 227.
52. For entering into land see LXX Joshua 19:49, 51; 1 Maccabees 12:25; 13:20; 14:31; 15:40. For going into details see LXX 2 Maccabees 2:30.
53. L&N 53.15. Cf. CSB 'claiming access to a visionary realm'. Cf. Pao, p. 190; Beale, extensively (and summarizing Arnold, *Syncretism*) pp. 228–237, 253–257 focuses on 'entering into a sanctuary' as the meaning and therefore sees temple allusions in Colossians as refuting these claims.

that such an experience includes ascetic practices as preparation for a visionary experience that includes seeing angels worshipping. However, the surrounding participle phrases 'delighting in' and 'being puffed up' suggest that something like 'going on about' is likely here; the three expressions highlight the false teachers' view of their own superiority. If the earlier activity in this verse is a means of condemning the Colossian believers, 'by delighting in', the parallel here may suggest that this activity is likewise a means of condemning, this time by lengthy explanation (rather than just 'accessing a temple/visionary realm', otherwise the word 'claiming' needs to be added, as with the CSB). Similarly, the parallel with 'being puffed up with' that follows this phrase may also tip the scales to understanding the phrase as a reference to what the false teachers are doing in 'judging' or 'condemning' the Colossian believers. Hence the NIV's translation, *Such a person goes into great detail* . . . and the ESV's translation 'going on in detail' are likely closer to the mark.[54]

They are going on in detail about *what they have seen*. The additional description *that they are puffed up with idle notions by their unspiritual mind* means that what they are going on about might more accurately be translated as what they have 'supposedly seen' (NET).[55] In other words, the false teachers are people who emphasize the lack that ordinary believers have, in part by emphasizing without any basis in reality but with great imagination what their own proud minds create. Due to the very nature of what it means to be a false teacher, claiming to have come up with something 'new and improved' over and against what believers had thought the gospel was saying, claiming to have something additional to the regular gospel that regular believers have always understood, it is not surprising that pride is involved, even if it is cloaked in false humility. This is particularly so when human effort in observing

---

54. See Harris, p. 108; Moo, pp. 227–229. 'That person goes on at great lengths' (NET); 'dwelling on' (NRSV).

55. 'Unspiritual mind' translates 'fleshly mind' (NASB) where 'flesh' is used in the wider Pauline sense of humanity apart from and opposed to God.

rules of human origin is thought to be essential to one's status before God.

**19.** The third and final description of these false teachers in 2:18–19 is that they are 'not holding fast to the Head' (NRSV, ESV). This is something that Paul comes back to again and again. Just as he had said that the false teaching depended upon human tradition rather than Christ (2:8), so here he observes that the teachers themselves only go on about what their own minds create rather than what God has revealed in Christ (1:26–27). These teachers are not simply genuine believers who have misunderstood, misapplied or mistakenly grasped some aspect of gospel truth. Rather, these teachers are propagating a human-oriented and human-originated teaching that they have created themselves and that is not of Christ. With the use of 'head' imagery Paul returns to the metaphor he has used already for Christ in 1:18 and 2:10. In 1:18 Paul emphasized that Christ was the founder and leader of the new humanity, the people of God. In 2:10 Paul highlighted Christ's authority over every power and authority. In this third and final use of the term in Colossians Paul describes the relationship between the false teachers and Christ. The NIV's *lost connection with the head* may suggest that the teachers were once connected to the head. Most translations, however, simply say that they are 'not connected' (NLT; cf. NJB) or 'not holding fast' (ESV, NRSV, NKJV; cf. NASB) to the head. On the one hand, Paul says that the false teachers have rejected Christ's authority and gospel, setting up themselves as judges of spiritual matters and emphasizing their own teaching.[56] On the other hand, Paul adds that there must be a vital connection between Christ and his people if there is to be genuine life. The life, growth and unity of the church is determined by Christ. It is *supported and held together* by belonging to Christ.

Thus, once again, Paul contrasts the gospel of Christ that unites all of God's people with the schisms that the false teachers generate with their teaching that detracts from and diminishes Christ and divides God's people into 'haves' and 'have nots' (see 1:6). Furthermore, Paul highlights again that it is only God who enables the

---

56. Cf. Harris, pp. 109–110.

growth of his people, by his grace, and through the gospel of Christ (cf. 1:6, 10). Although this growth in the wider context of Colossians would include an increasing number of people who come to know God's revelation in Christ (1:6; 4:3–6), the focus in this context is on believers as individuals and together growing in their grasp of God's will in Christ (cf. 1:10). By highlighting the necessity of this connection, Paul shows not only that the false teachers, being apart from Christ, do not know him, and have no life of their own, but also that their teaching cannot impart or sustain the spiritual life and growth of the Colossian believers, because they are severed from Christ (2:23). Instead, these teachers are parasitic on the livelihood of the church, destroying and distracting believers from their trust in Christ and diverting attention away from proclaiming this gospel to others.[57]

**20–21.** Some see a new section here with the reference to having *died with Christ* being picked up again in 3:1–3. It is preferable to see this section as Paul's final refutation of the false teaching before he concentrates on what the Colossian believers should instead be focusing on. Before we unpack Paul's argument, note first that the debated phrase *ta stoicheia tou kosmou* that lies behind the NIV's *elemental spiritual forces of this world* appears again. At 2:8 we concluded that a translation such as 'elementary principles of the world' (NASB) or 'basic principles of this world' (NIV84) reflects the wider usage of the phrase outside the New Testament, elsewhere in the New Testament, and also the surrounding descriptions here in Colossians 2 of these 'elementals' as merely human teachings.[58] This verse seems to confirm this understanding of the phrase since Paul further describes these 'elementary principles of this world' as *rules* or 'regulations' (NRSV, ESV) that belong to this world. The following verse (2:21) details what some of these rules are.

The Colossian believers have *died with Christ to* these 'elementary principles of the world'. Elsewhere, Paul says that believers have

---

57. Pao, p. 192.

58. As noted in 2:8, others see this as a reference to spiritual forces or elements of the physical world that are associated with spiritual powers. In that case, Paul is saying that believers are free from those powers.

died to sin (Rom. 6:2) and to the law (Rom. 7:6; Gal. 2:19), meaning that there has been a fundamental break to the weakness of our condition under law. This fundamental break comes when one belongs to Christ by faith. Although what Paul means by having *died with Christ* will be unpacked further in the following chapter, his initial argument here is that believers have broken with their past captivity to and condemnation by merely human and this-worldly rules and traditions when, by faith, they belong to Christ and receive the benefits of his substitutionary death which ended the condemnation pronounced by the law on sinners. These rules and regulations, therefore, have no claim on the Colossian believers since they have *died with Christ*. When Paul asks *why, as though you still belonged to the world, do you submit to its rules?* he assumes that such a break has taken place.

Whereas the 'world' in 1:6 is the sphere in which the gospel bears fruit and grows, the 'world' in 2:8 and here in 2:20 refers to a 'this-worldly' and 'merely human' determination of reality apart from God. Those who belong to Christ are no longer obligated to follow the futile attempts of 'the world' to determine the ultimate reality of one's standing with God. Before unpacking the significance of this for the new position of the person in Christ, Paul focuses on the worldly rules of the teachers and to which the Colossian believers have died. The specific rules that Paul cites – *Do not handle! Do not taste! Do not touch!* – are likely to be examples of the wider burden of rules the teachers were trying to impose on the Colossian believers. They may be Paul's succinct summary to highlight the constant demands of these teachers: 'Don't . . . don't . . . don't . . .'. The prohibition against 'taste' likely reflects the judgment mentioned in 2:16 concerning what they eat or drink. The other prohibitions not to 'handle' and 'touch' may overlap with 'taste' making the three terms about touching things of this world in general, or about food, perhaps in descending order (eat, taste, touch).[59] Or Paul refers to a combination of moral and dietary restrictions (cf. 1 Cor. 7:1 [NRSV]; 2 Cor. 6:17). Either way, we get a glimpse of what it might have been like for the Colossian

---

59. BDAG, p. 126.

believers to face the condemning teaching of the false teachers and to be told of their lack and how much they need the 'help' of the additions that the teachers brought. It is reminiscent of the burdens Jesus said the Pharisees would load up on people without lifting a finger to help (Matt. 23:4–5). Paul has so far responded by highlighting the glory of Christ, the blessing of the gospel and the character of the false teachers. In the final two verses of this chapter Paul exposes the ineffectiveness of their teachings.

**22.** The first deficiency of the rules from the 'elemental teachings' of these teachers that Paul highlights is their limited temporal focus. What is *destined to perish* could be the material objects of the preceding rules (referring to their limited physical focus), or the regulations themselves (referring to their this-worldly limited duration and focus). Either way, Paul implies a contrast between the gospel and the ineffectiveness of the false teachings because they will not prepare those under its regulations for the final judgment in contrast to the eternal and abiding truth of the gospel which provides the hope of heaven (cf. 1:5, 12, 22, 27–28). Such regulations are *based on merely human commands and teachings*. With this, Paul returns to a theme that he has been highlighting throughout this section. In 2:8 Paul said that this teaching is in accordance with 'human tradition' and the 'basic elements of this world'. In 2:18 he described the teachers as proudly going on about 'idle notions' derived from their 'unspiritual minds'. In 2:20 Paul said that these regulations held those who belong to 'this world' in sway and again were the 'basic elements of this world'. Now Paul says again that these are *based on* (or as in 2:8, 'according to') *merely human commands and teachings*. This last phrase alludes to the language of Isaiah 29:13 which Jesus used in Mark 7:6–8 in condemning the 'worship', hypocrisy and legalism of the Pharisees who were more concerned about external matters of food than their hearts, which were far from God. They had abandoned the commands of God and were 'holding' onto 'human tradition' (see above on 2:8).[60]

---

60. Beale, p. 248 (with reference to Col. 2:8). Interestingly, the same verb 'holding' is also used in Mark 7:8 (cf. 7:3, 4) and the negation in Col. 2:19.

Whereas the teachings of the false teachers are of merely human origin and are this-worldly only, the gospel, which is embodied in Christ, is the revelation of God, and is therefore powerful to effect God's gracious work of heart transformation and eternal salvation.

**23.** The beginning of Paul's statement about these regulations in 2:23 parallels the opening of 2:22 ('such regulations have . . .'), which in turn develops 2:20–21. Paul draws together in a final 'bottom-line' summary much of what he has been saying about this teaching throughout this section. *Such regulations*, says Paul, looking back to 2:21, *indeed have an appearance of wisdom* or perhaps more accurately, have 'a reputation for wisdom' (CSB).[61] As Paul said in 2:4, this false teaching is not necessarily nonsensical at face value. Such teaching consists of 'fine-sounding arguments' (2:4) in the sense that it can be persuasive and is deceptive (even if the teachers appear to have good intentions). The sense here is that these regulations are thought to help people's lives. Such regulations could have this reputation due to their severity. Those who were persuaded by this teaching may have thought that these rules were for spiritually advanced or serious-minded people because of how involved and committed one had to be to take on board such harsh activities. True wisdom for living, as Paul has highlighted throughout this letter, can only flow from knowing the one in whom 'all the treasures of wisdom and knowledge' are found (2:3). Knowing Christ is possible only through the gospel, God's revelation of his will and of what he has done for sinners through Christ (1:5–7, 9–10, 21–23, 27). In contrast to 'faith in the working of God' (2:12), the regulations of the false teachers emphasize what each individual person must do: *self-imposed worship . . . false humility and . . . harsh treatment of the body*. The first two items pick up on the description in 2:18 where false humility and worship (of angels) were combined. Here the worship is described as 'self-imposed' or 'self-made' (ESV), highlighting again the human origins of the false teaching (2:8,

---

61. The Greek word underlying the NIV's 'appearance' and the CSB's 'reputation' is *logos* ('word of wisdom' LSB).

20, 22).⁶² This description perhaps picks up on the critique by Isaiah and Jesus of false, human-originated worship oriented around external rules. This is a self-directed and self-created kind of religion in contrast to the kind of worship revealed by the sovereign Lord who is to be worshipped. The last item clarifies that some kind of asceticism is involved in which there is 'severe self-control, suggesting an ascetic and unsparing' approach.⁶³ This is evident in the series of restrictions listed in 2:21, and probably 2:16 as well.

Although the false teachings have the reputation for wisdom, they actually *lack any value in restraining sensual indulgence*. The phrase translated as *sensual indulgence* refers more generally to the 'indulgence of the flesh' (ESV) and picks up on the reference to the 'flesh' in 2:18 as that characteristic of human weakness which is apart from and opposed to God (cf. e.g. Rom. 7:5; 8:5–6). Thus not only are the teachers themselves characterized by 'flesh' in this sense (2:18), they also offer no help to others in escaping 'flesh'. These additional self-made rules, no matter how severe, appear to be for the wise and serious-minded, but in reality there is nothing to them; they have no value at all. They cannot help stop the flesh – humanity in weakness apart from God – from continuing along its path of satisfying itself apart from God. Thus they leave the person harmed, helpless and hopeless. People who belong to Christ, however, are not left on their own needing to appropriate endless humanly invented instructions that only serve to keep them apart from God. Nothing less than death and new life is needed and it is to that reality that Paul turns next.

*Theology*
Having focused on the person and work of Christ, in this section Paul treats the threat to the Colossians finding sufficiency in

---

62. The word *ethelothrēskia* emphasizes that this worship is 'by his own volition' and is a 'self-made' or 'do-it-yourself religion' (BDAG, p. 276). MM, p. 181 suggests this may be a term coined by Paul (cf. LSJ, p. 479).
63. L&N 88.90.

Christ: the identity and requirements of the false teachers. When we see the opposing message that the Colossians were facing, the gospel that Paul proclaims shines even brighter. Thus the false teachers who assume a position of authority rendering judgment contrast with the message Paul proclaims that leads to being presented holy, blameless and without accusation (1:22). The false teachers focus on themselves, talking endlessly about what they think they have seen, whereas Paul proclaims Christ (1:28). The false teachers emphasize self-effort and regulations in order to avoid judgment, whereas the gospel is about what Christ has done and this is received by 'faith in the working of God' (2:12, 13–14). The false teaching is made up of merely human commands and teaching, whereas the gospel is God's revelation of grace in Christ (1:6, 25–27). The false teachers think that harsh treatment of the body helps spiritually, whereas the gospel announces what Christ has done in his body on the cross and breaks our captivity to this-worldly rules (1:22; 2:20). 'Fullness' is truly found in Christ.

## C. Living a Christ-centred life (3:1 – 4:6)

After having one general imperative in 2:6 and three prohibitions in 2:8, 16, 18, imperatives become the focus from 3:1. Building on what he has said in 2:20 (and 2:12), Paul now unpacks the implications of Christ's supremacy for the Christian life (signalled by the word 'then' in 3:1, Greek *oun*). Broadly speaking, in contrast to the focus of the false teachers, which was 'self', Paul exhorts the Colossians to focus on Christ. In contrast to the external, temporary and human-derived rules, Paul directs their attention to the reality of who believers are in Christ as the foundation for how they are to live. In contrast to the schisms created by varying levels of adherence to the rules of the false teachers and their accompanying condemnations, the gospel draws God's people together. Consequently much of what Paul says here revolves around the impact that the new life in Christ has on the believer's everyday relationships. Not surprisingly, the believer's new life in Christ is to reflect the character of Christ.

## i. Heavenly thinking (3:1–4)

### Context

The word 'Christ' appears four times in these opening verses of chapter 3 as Paul builds on the Christology of chapters 1–2 as well as his description of the fullness believers have in Christ in 2:9–15. As the use of the word 'therefore' (Greek *oun*) in 3:5 indicates, these verses are also closely connected to 3:5 – 4:6. The two imperatives of 3:1–2 direct believers to Christ and his accomplishments for those who now belong to him as the basis for what Paul says about what this change will look like in their lives.

### Comment

**1–2.** Having emphasized the glory of Christ and the blessings of the gospel of Christ, Paul turns from his immediately preceding emphasis on the false teachings threatening the Colossian believers and directs them to where their focus should be, namely Christ. The basis of the imperatives in this section is the reality that just as 'you have died with Christ' (2:20), so also *you have been raised with Christ*. The structure of the opening phrase is the same in 2:20 and 3:1 and is rightly translated in the NIV with *since, then*. The passive voice of the verb 'raised' points to God's action for the believers. Since the Colossians came to Christ they now belong to him and the benefits of his death and resurrection are applied to them. His death becomes their death: their severance from who they were outside of Christ and their break from rules that provide no help (2:20). Since they have also been raised with Christ, the resurrection power that raised Christ from the dead has also given believers new spiritual life since they belong to him (2:12). Since this is true of all believers, the reality of who they are has changed. They no longer belong to or are obligated to the 'flesh' (i.e. who they were before coming to Christ). Picking up on the reality of this new resurrection life that he has mentioned earlier in 2:12, and building upon the implications of 2:20, Paul now uses spatial language to emphasize this change. Christ's resurrection and ascension mean the inauguration of his kingdom in the present (1:13) in anticipation of the consummation, the hope of glory (1:27; 3:4). Jesus rules from his place of authority and power, *seated at the right hand of God* (cf. Acts 2:33–34). Paul alludes to Psalm 110:1 and the inauguration of Christ's kingdom (1:13). The believer, therefore, as one who belongs to Christ, also ought to continue to 'seek' that which is in keeping with *where Christ is*, that is, *the things above*.[64] In the context of Colossians, this is a reference to 'heaven' where the believer's hope is secure (1:5) and where their 'Lord' is (4:1). We will come back to the meaning of 'things above' after looking at 3:2.

The exhortation of 3:1 is then repeated with a slight variation and an additional contrast in 3:2. The slight variation in 3:2 is the exhortation to *set your minds on things above*, which is not likely to be that different to the exhortation in 3:1 to 'seek' (NRSV, ESV) the things above. If anything, 'seek' is more general and refers to one's overarching purpose and goal worked out in actions that reveal one's fundamental direction in life. The more specific exhortation to *set your minds on things above* picks up on the many references to knowledge, understanding and thinking that occur throughout this letter. Whereas the Colossians were at one time 'enemies in their minds' (1:21), they came to 'understand God's grace' in the gospel, having 'learned it from Epaphras' (1:6–7). Paul prays for the Colossians' 'knowledge' of God's will and spiritual 'understanding' (1:9–10), and he labours so that they would have the 'full assurance' that comes from 'complete understanding', or the 'knowledge' of Christ, God's mystery revealed (2:2). Paul's contrasting phrase, *not on earthly things*, refers to that which is derived from and dependent upon the 'elementary principles of this world' with its human-oriented and this-worldly teaching that deceives and leads away from the sufficiency of Christ that the gospel teaches (2:4, 8, 18–19, 20–23). The *things above*, therefore, relate to God's eternal and saving purposes in what Christ has done. Since Christ has taken the penalty that we were under and removed the accusations against us, he has triumphed over the accuser, and now is risen and reigning, having inaugurated his saving rule. Thus Paul urges the Colossians not to be taken in by this-worldly human-oriented

---

64. The NIV's 'set your hearts' (3:1) may inadvertently imply a contrast between 'hearts' and 'minds' (3:2). The Greek text of 3:1 is better translated as simply 'seek' (ESV).

priorities but to orient their thinking around the accomplishments and the present reign of Christ as proclaimed in the gospel.

**3.** The reason Paul gives for believers directing their thinking to the accomplishments and present reign of Christ is because (*for*) *you died and your life is now hidden with Christ in God*. Paul now combines what he said in 2:12, 20; and 3:1. It is the indicative – the reality of what is already true for all believers – that is the basis for the exhortation to respond in this way. Paul does not (yet) say that believers too must die to or put to death anything. Rather he restates here what is spiritually true for all believers because they belong to Christ: they have already died and they have already risen to new life. That is, the saving benefits of Christ's actions and accomplishments are theirs already. This is the basis for the exhortation to focus on, be governed by and set their minds on these things.

The additional point that *your life is now hidden with Christ* emphasizes the security each individual believer now has.[65] The addition of *in God* serves to reinforce this security in light of the close association of Christ with God the Father in this letter (1:15–20, esp. 1:19; 2:9) and the way in which the saving purposes of the Father have been accomplished through Christ (1:13–14). Thus, because of Christ's resurrection and ascension to reign at the right hand of the Father, the person who belongs to Christ can be assured that the salvation ('life') they have in Christ is as secure as Christ's resurrection life and his relationship with God the Father (cf. 1:19; 2:9). Just as their hope is stored up in heaven (1:5), so too their relationship with God is hidden in the sense that it is secure and kept safe.[66] Just as all the treasures of wisdom and knowledge are bound up with Christ (2:3), so too is the believer's new life (2:13). This then is the reason why Paul can confidently exhort the Colossians. Even though they still live in a world in which strength to have endurance and patience is needed from God (1:12), they can in fact set their minds on Christ's saving rule because of the reality

---

65. The singular noun 'life' is distributive with the plural pronoun 'your' (Harris, p. 121).
66. BDAG, p. 571.

of the life-giving change that has most assuredly already taken place. The close connection with the language of 'revealed' in the next verse, together with the language of 'hidden . . . but now made known' in 1:26–27 for God's saving purposes, lends support to another feature of this 'hiddenness'. The reality of the believer's new life is 'hidden' in the sense that it is yet to be fully seen. The believer must live in anticipation of the future unveiling of this reality (1:5, 23, 27), and yet display the reality of this new life in everyday relationships (3:10 – 4:1).

**4.** Paul completes the sequence of salvation-historical events, implied in the allusion to Psalm 110:1 and Christ's present reign in 3:1, with the language of *when . . . then*. The inauguration of Christ's kingdom through his life, death, resurrection and ascension is brought to consummation with his return. Christ is first said to be *your life*.[67] Here Paul reaffirms in a more emphatic way that the believer's life is bound up with Christ's resurrection life and is as secure as saying that Christ *is your life*. The additional point that Paul makes here is that just as the events of Christ's death and resurrection are applied to those who belong to him, so too does the event of Christ's return affect the believer. Even though the security of this new life is hidden now, one day it will be made absolutely clear. That day will be *when Christ . . . appears*. This is the future hope that Paul has referred to numerous times in this letter. It is the hope that is stored up in heaven (1:5), the hope of glory (1:27). It is the anticipation of being presented before the throne of God holy, without blemish and free from accusation, complete in Christ (1:22, 28). It is based on the Father's 'qualification' of the believer to share in that inheritance (1:12; 3:24). It is the certainty that when Christ 'appears' then you too (those who belong to Christ) will 'appear' *with him in glory*. 'Glory' refers to the full manifestation of Christ's majesty when he will be seen for all he is at the consummation of history and the entrance of eternity at his second coming. This is the ultimate hope of the believer. Final transformation will be complete and the presence of God will be enjoyed for ever.

---

67. Some translations (e.g. NASB, NKJV) have 'our life' but the second person pronoun 'your' has earlier and wide manuscript support.

*Theology*
Paul develops the significance of the believers' identification with Christ. Because of Christ's supremacy, those who belong to him enjoy the blessings of all that he has accomplished. Because believers belong to him they are therefore to set their priorities by Christ's resurrection and eternal reign as he carries out the Father's saving purposes in contrast to that which is merely this-worldly or 'earthly'. In temporal terms, his death, resurrection and return all directly impact his people as they have consequently died to their past life outside of Christ, risen to new spiritual resurrection life and look forward to the full disclosure of this when the majesty of Christ is seen at his return. In a nutshell, Christ is our life! Everything hinges on our identification with Christ.

### ii. Putting off the practices of the 'old self' (3:5–11)
*Context*
Following the general imperatives based on the reality of the believer's death and resurrection with Christ in 3:1–2, Paul now develops in more detail one side of that twofold reality: the consequences of our death. Thus these verses build on the statement of reality in 3:3 that believers have already died with Christ. The section is driven by two main imperatives in 3:5 ('put to death') and 3:8 ('rid yourselves') and a further summarizing imperative in 3:9 ('do not lie'). Each of the first two imperatives are followed by a more specific list of five sins in 3:5 and 8. Following the imperative of 3:5 two supporting reasons are provided in 3:6–7. Following the third imperative in 3:9a two further supporting reasons are given in 3:9b–10. The final verse of this section concludes by noting that the powerful renewing work of God in the 'new self' is at work in all those who belong to Christ, in contrast to the inadequacy of the harsh rules the false teachers were enforcing. Throughout this section Paul develops the significance of what he has already said in the letter about the 'once . . . but now' transformation that takes place for a believer (cf. 1:21–22) based on the believer's identification with Christ (cf. 2:11–13).

*Comment*
**5.** It is in light of who believers are already by belonging to Christ that Paul turns now to urge believers to reflect that reality

in their lives. The word *therefore* looks back to the reality he has highlighted in 3:1–4. It is only because of the reality that believers have already died with Christ (2:12, 20; 3:3) that Paul can now say *put to death, therefore, whatever belongs to your earthly nature*. It is the 'indicative' that is the basis and prerequisite for Paul's 'imperative'. The reference to one's *earthly nature* picks up on the contrast between 'things above' and 'things on the earth' in 3:2. Therefore, the 'members which are on the earth' (NKJV) refer to whatever part of us (mind, affections, body) that we use to give life to that which is contrary to God's purposes for us in Christ (cf. Rom. 6:19b), the this-worldly framework to which we have died. To put them *to death* is to recognize that that is no longer who we are and thus we should actively seek to starve those things of attention and life. Because we have already 'died to the elemental principles of the world' (NASB) when we were incorporated in Jesus' death on the cross, a fundamental break has already occurred and new life has already been granted, enabling such a death to be put into effect. However, our appearance in glory is yet to come, and change from long-held practices, although possible, can also take time and require help. If this were automatic Paul would not need to follow 3:1–4 with the more specific exhortations of these verses.

The following list of sins is a general summary of the kinds of sins associated with behaviour that is outside God's purpose for our lives and the life that rejects Christ.[68] The lists here and in 3:8–9 centre around the various harmful ways people relate to one another even if the focus here is primarily sexual immorality, whereas the list in 3:8–9 is more generally interpersonal. The first term in the list, *porneia*, is a general reference to any form of *sexual immorality* and likely sets the stage for the following vices.[69] Likewise, *impurity* can refer to anything that is 'unclean' (NKJV) but in the context of moral impurity it is associated with sexual sin in general.[70] The same can

---

68. Similar 'vice lists' are found in Rom. 1:28–31; 13:13; 1 Cor. 5:9–11; 6:9–10; 2 Cor. 12:20–21; Gal. 5:19–21; Eph. 4:25–32; 5:3–7.
69. See e.g. Lev. 18 (McKnight, *Colossians*, p. 304).
70. L&N 88.261.

be said of *lust*. The term itself, *pathos*, can refer generally to 'strong desire' or 'passion' (ESV). But in contexts where sexual immorality is in view, the term refers to immoral desires. The modifying description of *desire* as *evil* means that the opposite of 'good' desires are in view, with the sense being 'improper' rather than 'proper'.[71] Finally, *greed* concludes this list along with the explanation that greed is *idolatry*. The association of greed with the preceding list at first glance seems out of place. However, like the prohibition against coveting in the Ten Commandments, 'covetousness' here as an increasing desire for more and more probably looks back to the preceding list as the underlying motivation for all of them. In this sense the root of these is a 'refusal to submit to the lordship of Christ'.[72] Furthermore, idolatry is often associated with sexual immorality in Scripture (e.g. Rom. 1:21–25). Indeed idolatry is viewed as the fundamental sin in Romans 1, from which other immorality follows. Jesus warned against greed as that which threatens to take the place of God (Luke 12:15, 21; cf. Ps. 119:36) and likened money to an idol that one is devoted to and serves (Luke 16:13; cf. 1 Tim. 6:10–11). The same link between a covetous person and idolatry is made by Paul in Ephesians 5:5. Thus, having just mentioned lust and evil desires, Paul probably refers to greed as a summary desire that encompasses the all-consuming desire for something one does not have but wrongly believes will grant satisfaction apart from God. As such, it is the epitome of idolatry.[73]

**6.** The contrast between the sinfulness of humanity and the holiness of God is starkly stated here by Paul. It is *because* of sin that *the wrath of God is coming*. In saying this, Paul indicates that God's wrath is not arbitrary. If there were no sins such as those he has just listed then likewise there would be no wrath. Wrath, however, is an expression of God's perfect holiness which is essential to his being. Although God's wrath currently remains on those who reject the

---

71. Cf. e.g. Rom. 1:24, 26.
72. This observation of the link to the Ten Commandments is from Pao, pp. 220–221.
73. See Rosner, *Greed*.

Son (John 3:36), and his wrath is currently against the godlessness and wickedness of humanity (Rom. 1:18), there is also a 'day of wrath' yet to come when God's righteous judgment will be revealed (Rom. 2:5). The fact that such wrath *is coming* points to a certain judgment in which all wrongdoing, injustice and rebellion against God and his perfect ways will be met with just punishment. In a similar statement in Ephesians 5:6 Paul makes clear that such wrath comes on 'those who are disobedient', that is, those who are outside of Christ.[74] This, of course, is why Paul spoke so rapturously of God's reconciling work in Christ. Alienation from God and enmity with him has been replaced with reconciliation and peace with God (1:21–22). The written code that stood against us has been removed with forgiveness of sins through Christ who took our penalty in his death on the cross (2:13–14). *Wrath*, therefore, is the fundamental problem facing humanity and the reason for our need of redemption, forgiveness, reconciliation (1:13–14, 21–22; 2:13–15). This wrath has been removed for those who trust in the Lord Jesus. It is the abhorrence of such things to the God who has reconciled believers that Paul highlights. It is this same abhorrence towards sin and gratitude for God's grace that Paul is hoping for from the Colossian believers.

7. Paul's 'once . . . but now' contrast of 1:21–22 is brought out again here as he transitions to another list of sins in 3:8–9. They were 'once' alienated from God with their enmity exhibited in their evil behaviour (1:21). Likewise here, they were 'once' under the prospect of God's wrath, living in evil desires and idolatry. The emphasis on their former way of life is emphasized with the repetition of 'once' and 'when' at the centre of the Greek text of the verse. These were the ways in which the Colossian believers *used to walk* ('once walked' ESV), this was the life they *once lived* ('when you

---

74. The same phrase is missing from some early manuscripts in Col. 3:6 (included in e.g. CSB, NRSV, NASB). A decision about its inclusion here is difficult, but its addition by a scribe conforming it to Eph. 5:6 is easier to explain than its accidental omission. No theological point is lost if the phrase is not original since the context implies the meaning of the phrase here anyway.

were living', NRSV, ESV).[75] The term 'living' looks back to 2:20 where Paul spoke of adhering to the principles of this world 'as if you were living in the world' (NASB). Ironically, they were 'living' like this when they were (spiritually) 'dead in their sins' (2:13). This preceded their reception of spiritual life through 'faith in the power of God' (2:12). This verse may therefore indicate that the list of sins in 3:5 may be a general summary of sins that are characteristic of Gentile pagan lives rather than the current practices of the Colossians (but see below).

**8.** *But now* highlights the contrast to how they 'once' lived and indicates that the following list of sins may be Paul's immediate concern for the Colossians. The focus here is more particularly on interpersonal or relational animosity among them which could be traced to the effects of the false teachers. If some teachers were 'condemning' them or saying they are 'disqualified' for not adhering to their self-oriented and humanly derived rules and teachings, then it is not too difficult to see how the Colossian believers could be separated into the 'haves' and 'have nots' with subsequent interpersonal animosity. The imperative *you must also rid yourselves* parallels the imperative *put to death* that begins 3:5. Furthermore, Paul's reference to *all such things* is comprehensive, and would not exclude any of the preceding even if his focus here is on the following.

The first two items, *anger* and *rage*, are frequently paired together and are not likely to be sharply distinguished. While there is appropriate anger against sin and injustice that wants to see justice done (Eph. 4:26), the anger and rage in view in this context is the sinful uncontrolled emotional opposition to someone (or something). *Malice* may be the continuing outworking of the preceding anger and refers to a 'mean-spirited or vicious attitude or disposition' to someone (BDAG, p. 500). The final two items focus more on the outworking of this animosity in speech. *Slander* refers to 'speech that denigrates or defames' (BDAG, p. 178) and involves speaking against someone 'in such a way as to harm or injure his or her reputation' (L&N 33.400). In the context of this letter, 'slander'

---

75. On the imagery of 'walking' see comments on 2:6.

involves falsehood and malice rather than truth and warning or Paul would not describe the false teachers the way he does in 2:18–19. The final expression, *filthy language from your lips*, refers to that which is 'obscene' (ESV) or 'vulgar' speech (L&N 33.33). However, 'obscene expressions would also be used to flavor derogatory remarks' (BDAG, p. 29) and this may be in view here, especially since 'slander' was just referred to in this immediate context. Thus 'abusive language' (NRSV, NET, cf. also NASB) more broadly may be in view here.

**9a.** The final prohibition, *do not lie to each other*, completes both the sequence of sins related to interpersonal animosity as well as the immediately preceding sequence of sins of speech. To lie is to speak a falsehood with the intent to mislead or deceive and thus it would be 'to that person's detriment' who is lied to (BDAG, p. 1097). Falsehood also runs counter to the gospel which is 'the word of truth' (1:5 ESV), the message of God's grace which they understood 'in truth' (1:6). Falsehood is characteristic of the false teaching which is 'hollow and deceptive' (2:8). Thus, while it may not seem as immediately harmful compared to rage or even abusive language, the harmful effects of lying to one another also evidence hostility and destroys relationships and the open-hearted trust required for those relationships to deepen and flourish. In 3:12–17 Paul will contrast these behaviours of animosity with descriptions of love for one another. In 3:16 in particular Paul zeroes in on how the word of Christ is to affect our speech with one another, in stark contrast to the speech described in 3:8–9a.

**9b–10.** The second half of 3:9 and the beginning of 3:10 once again ground the preceding exhortations in the reality of who the believer is in Christ (*since you have*). This time Paul uses the imagery of clothing to describe the radical change that has already taken place for the believer (*taken off . . . put on*).[76] The similar wording in the Greek text of 3:9 and 10 is reflected in the RSV/ESV's 'put off and put on' ('stripped off . . . and clothed', NRSV). Paul regularly uses clothing imagery in his description of the Christian life. The word

---

76. The verb for 'put off' was used in 2:15 for God having 'stripped' the powers and authorities of their power.

he uses here ('put on') is used for the actual putting on of clothes (e.g. Luke 8:27; 12:22; 15:22), but is also used metaphorically, as here. It is used both for what has already taken place (Gal. 3:27; Col. 3:10) and also for what Paul exhorts believers to do (Rom. 13:14; Eph. 4:24; Col. 3:12; for armour, Rom. 13:12; Eph. 6:11, 14; 1 Thess. 5:8). In this context, once again, Paul does not (yet; see 3:12) say that they must 'put off' and 'put on', but rather that they already have done this and that this is the basis for the preceding prohibitions. What has already happened may be clarified after we see what it is that has been 'put off' and what has already been 'put on'.

Paul says that what has been removed is 'your old self', and this has been replaced with the 'new self'. Some translations (NKJV, NET) render the reference to *anthrōpos* as 'the old man' and 'the new man'. What then does this old and new self or man refer to? Paul refers here, in similar language to Romans 5–6, to who we were outside of Christ and who we are once we belong to Christ. The 'old self' is who we were when we belonged only to Adam. The 'new self' is the new person we are now that we belong to Christ. Just as the benefits of Christ's death and resurrection are applied to us such that we can be said to have died to that predicament and now have new life, moving from death to life in our relationship with God (2:12, 20; 3:1, 3), so also we can say that because we belong to Christ we are also a new person. Salvation-historically we no longer belong to Adam and the sinfulness that characterizes all humanity under judgment. Rather, we belong to Christ, who by his resurrection brings a new beginning and is the head of a new humanity (1:18). Even though belonging to a new humanity is in view here, the phrase 'old self' and 'new self' refers to the individual person and behaviours here and isn't in the first place referring to the 'new humanity' more broadly. Thus the *old self with its practices* (3:9b) refers to who we once were when we lived at enmity with God in our evil behaviour (1:21). The *new self* (3:10a) is new because we now belong to Christ. To belong to Christ means that, like death, and like clothing that has been removed and replaced, what characterized us when we were in rebellion to God no longer exists. Instead, like new life, and like a new covering of clothes, we have a new beginning, a 'change' and a new 'look' that will reflect Christ and his character.

Indeed, it is the character of renewal that Paul concludes this verse with. Although the removal of the old and the replacement with the new has already taken place, Paul adds that this *new* self is being *renewed*. The implication is once again that what is true of us before God is also being worked out in our life. The implication is also that this change is not reflected immediately or all at once in our lives. The passive voice implies that it is God who is doing the renewing work. This new self is *being renewed in knowledge*, which again picks up on Paul's prayer for the Colossians to be 'growing in the knowledge of God' (1:10). As we noted in 3:2, the true knowledge of the gospel of grace is the antidote to the harmful effects of the empty and deceptive lies of the false teachers. It is this knowledge that the Colossian believers are to set their minds on and it is this knowledge that they are being renewed in. In this context the 'knowledge' is 'according to the image of your Creator' (CSB). The wording of 'according to' (*in*, NIV) means 'in conformity with', 'after the pattern of'.[77] The *image* refers to Christ as the one who is the image of the invisible God, the one who perfectly and visibly reflects God's character (1:15). The *Creator* refers to God as the one who has created the 'new self' and is also renewing it.[78] Thus to summarize the remarkable assurance that Paul provides here: the person who belongs to Christ belongs to his new humanity, having already 'put on' or become a new person. This new person has been created by God, and is in fact being renewed more and more by God to reflect the character of Christ which leads ultimately to the fuller knowledge of God that Paul also prays for.

**11.** It is not exactly clear what *here* (NIV) refers to at the beginning of this verse. The reference clearly looks back to what has just been said, but it could be looking back to a new humanity in a collective sense, or the new self that is being renewed, or to Christ as 'the

---

77. Harris, p. 133.
78. This last phrase can be translated 'according to the image of the One who created him' (LSB). The pronoun 'him' looks back to the 'new self/man' (and rules out a simple identification of the 'new man' as Christ).

image' (NJB).⁷⁹ It is possible that a new humanity is partly in view in 3:10 and the following collection of categories also lends support to this idea of a new humanity united in Christ. Nevertheless, since the new person has been the focus of the preceding verse as that which has been 'put on' (in contrast to the 'old self' and its practices, specified in 3:8–9a), that which is being renewed according to the image of Christ, and that which has been created by God, it seems slightly preferable to see a continued reference to the renewal of the new person here too ('a renewal in which', NASB, LSB; 'in that renewal there is', NRSV). The following declaration that *there is no . . .* followed by various categories of people does not mean that these categories disappear entirely (cf. 3:22 – 4:1; 4:11) but there is 'no distinction between' these groups in terms of their reception of this new and renewed person (cf. NASB, NJB). The picture here recalls the allusions to the unity of God's people already in 1:4 and 7 and the reconciliation described in 1:20–22.

The following categories list eight possible groups linked into four (mostly) contrasting pairs. Similar statements of the significance of identity in Christ for the position and unity of believers who come from typical divisions are found in Galatians 3:28 and 1 Corinthians 12:13. In this list the first two pairs categorize people from a Jewish perspective into Jews and non-Jews: *Gentile or Jew, circumcised or uncircumcised.* The third pair, *barbarian, Scythian,* extends the description of Gentiles. 'Barbarian' is a reference to non-Greeks with an implication of being uncultured ('barbarian' is an onomatopoeic word reflecting what the speech of non-Greeks sounded like to Greeks when they spoke, 'bar bar bar').⁸⁰ A Scythian came from the region of the Black Sea and was 'frequently viewed as the epitome of unrefinement or savagery'.⁸¹ Thus Paul extends the

---

79. Cf. Harris, p. 133.
80. Cf. Rom. 1:14; 1 Cor. 14:11. Cf. also the negative use of the general term 'barbarous' in the LXX in 2 Maccabees 2:21; 4:25; 5:22; 10:4; 3 Maccabees 3:24; Ezek. 21:36 (English 21:31).
81. BDAG, p. 932; cited by Moo, p. 271. Cf. the negative portrayal of Scythians in the LXX in 2 Maccabees 4:47; 3 Maccabees 7:5; 4 Maccabees 10:7 (also cited by BDAG).

description of Gentiles from uncircumcised (from a Jewish perspective) to barbarian (from a Greek perspective) to Scythian (a further extension of barbarian).

The final pair, *slave or free*, becomes especially significant both later in this chapter as Paul speaks of slaves and masters as having a common 'master/Lord' in heaven (3:24–4:1), and also in Philemon where Paul speaks of Onesimus and Philemon as beloved and as brothers in the Lord (esp. Philemon 16). This is in part, therefore, Paul's answer to the futility of the harsh rules of the false teachers (2:23). God works renewal in all those who belong to Christ, even to the barbarian and Scythian! In contrast to these various ways of looking at the 'haves' and 'have nots', Paul says that this new self and consequent renewal to the likeness of Christ is for all. Indeed, *Christ is all, and is in all.* That is, just as Christ is our life, so also he is the ultimate determiner of what is new; he is 'all that matters' (NLT). The reason why these distinctions no longer exist is because he 'is in' each one who belongs to this new humanity. Thus Paul's strong incentive to loving harmony rather than interpersonal hostility is Christ-centred. We should no longer compete for status characterized by selfishness and disregard for others in order to advance ourselves. In coming to Christ we have put off that old self and have been clothed with a newness created by God that will reflect the likeness of Christ, the one who determines our new identity and whose character we are being renewed to reflect. This common reception of God's work in us by Christ enables us to build up the new humanity that we now are part of. It is to this that Paul now turns.

*Theology*
This section continues the indicative–imperative teaching that Paul introduced in 3:1–4. Paul adds to that his 'once . . . but now' understanding of the significance of conversion. This is particularly emphasized in 3:7 and 9b–10. In these verses we can see that in Paul's understanding of conversion he expects there to have been a change in the person's life. This change is not what saves, as his earlier references to 'faith' (1:4; 2:12) and Christ's work on the cross in order to provide forgiveness of sins have indicated (1:14, 22; 2:13–14). Yet because one receives new life because of this

forgiveness (2:13), and because the believer is identified with Christ's death and resurrection, Paul expects that there will be a change that accompanies this work of God's grace. Thus Paul expects those who have come to Christ to be able to look back to a time 'before' that was their 'old self'. This is the basis for turning from the selfish and abusive behaviour listed here: that behaviour is characteristic of an 'old self', not one that now belongs to Christ and that is being renewed. What of those who do not have a dramatic 'conversion story' or who came to faith in Christ at a young age? Paul would say: praise God for his kindness to you! These characteristics still describe what you could have been, and could be, outside of Christ and should still be 'taken off' like old clothes that don't fit who you are in Christ. The emphasis in the final verses on the renewing work of God in all those who belong to Christ prepares for the focus in the following section on what believers are to 'put on'.

### *iii. Putting on the practices of the 'new self' (3:12–17)*
*Context*

Just as the previous verses focused on the consequences of having already 'put off' the old self, so these verses focus on the consequences of having already 'put on' the new self (3:10). This 'new self' is being renewed according to the image of Christ and so it is not surprising that the practices listed here reflect his character as the image of God. There is further correspondence with the preceding section in that just as five sins were listed with the imperatives of 3:5 and 8, so are there five practices listed in 3:12. Just as the preceding sins focused on interpersonal and relational harm, these focus on their opposite, the outworking of love (3:14). Paul's reference to the oneness of the body (3:15) looks back to 3:11 and is a consequence of 1:18. The focus on speech in 3:16–17 likewise contrasts with the speech of 3:8–9a. Paul again provides the basis (indicative) for the exhortations (imperative) first (3:12a). The passage concludes with exhortations that provide the means by which the preceding can be carried out (3:15–16). Paul's final summary command in 3:17 referring to 'whatever we do' is also a transition to the following instructions (with references to the 'Lord' permeating the following instructions and the repetition in

3:23 of the phrase 'whatever you do'). The concluding emphasis on Christ in 3:16–17 (i.e. 'peace of Christ', 'word of Christ', 'name of the Lord Jesus') recall the general imperatives of 3:1–2 and frame the Christological focus of this section.

*Comment*
**12.** After the initial exhortations to focus on 'things above' rather than 'earthly things' in 3:1–4, Paul focused more specifically on the thinking and behaviour that characterized the person outside of Christ. Now Paul exhorts the Colossians to reflect the character of Christ to whom they now belong. Just as the Colossians were to 'put to death' what characterized their behaviour before they belonged to Christ on the basis of having already 'died with Christ' (cf. 2:20 and 3:5), so too Paul exhorts them to 'put on' (ESV; *clothe yourselves*, NIV) the new clothing that reflects the character of Christ on the basis of (*therefore*) having already 'taken off' the old self and 'put on' the new self that is being renewed to be like Christ (cf. 3:10).[82]

Before getting to these specific items of clothing, Paul will once again ground his exhortation in the reality of who the Colossians are already with three descriptions of their relationship to God. They are *God's chosen people, holy and dearly loved*. If ever believers are tempted to think that their performance, even of the harshest rules (2:20–23), could be the basis of their status before God, then these three descriptors would disavow them of such misplaced confidence. Each term is a common way of describing God's people throughout Scripture, both for Israel in the Old Testament and for all who belong to the Messiah by faith in the New Testament. *God's chosen people* points to God's initiative and grace such that the distinction between God's people and the rest of humanity rests not on some superior quality only found in believers, as if they have greater insight (cf. Deut. 7:6). Instead, they belong to God because

---

[82]. The same word, *enduō* ('clothe', 'put on') is used in 3:10 and 3:12. Similarly, the cognate *apekduomai* ('undress', 'strip off', i.e. 'put off', 'take off') is used in 3:9. For the clothing metaphor elsewhere in Paul see comments on 3:10.

of his infinitely wise purposes and gracious initiative to choose some even though all were 'alienated . . . enemies [in our] evil behaviour' (1:21) and deserving of wrath (3:6).[83] The next two descriptions, *holy and dearly loved*, are grouped together as further explanations of *chosen*. The adjective *holy* in this context refers not to 'holiness' of life, but to the status of being set apart by God to belong to him before any holiness of life is even possible (see comments on 'holy' in 1:2; the combination here echoes Deut. 7:6–7). *Dearly loved* highlights the affection of God towards his people and his desire and purpose for their good. This love in this context is not referring to God's general love for all humankind, but rather his special love for his people (as e.g. Eph. 5:25). In the context of 'chosen' and 'holy', 'dearly loved' highlights his initiative and again is not based on the performance of believers. Although 'chosen' and 'holy' are adjectives, *dearly loved* is a participle in the perfect tense, highlighting the status and state of being the object of God's great love. This is the basis then for what Paul will go on to say. It is *as* people such as these, chosen, holy, loved, that we put on the following items to reflect the new 'look' we have in Christ, not in order to become one of God's chosen, holy and loved people.

Just as the focus of the items in 3:8–9 was on interpersonal and relational breakdown, the focus in 3:12–14 is on interpersonal and relational wellbeing, culminating in love (3:14). The list picks up on the preceding reference to the renewal that is in accordance with Christ (3:10) and looks back in contrast to the list of 3:8. *Compassion* renders two words in the Greek text, *splagchna oiktirmou*, which can be translated as 'heartfelt compassion' (BDAG, p. 700; cf. NASB; ESV; 'tenderhearted mercy', NLT).[84] The idea is genuine, heartfelt concern towards others in trouble or hardship. It is often

---

83. The same term ('elect') is used in Luke 18:7; Rom. 8:33; 16:13; 2 Tim. 2:10; Titus 1:1; 1 Peter 1:1; 2:9. Cf. Eph. 1:4. Such initiative from God does not exclude the means by which we become his people – faith – since even that is something to thank God for (see 1:3–4).

84. The word *splagchna* is significant in Phlm. 7, 12, 20.

a description of God (cf. Rom. 12:1; 2 Cor. 1:3), and the verbal form is used of Jesus in Luke 7:13 (cf. Luke 10:33).

*Kindness* refers to actions of generosity or 'providing something beneficial for someone' (L&N 88.67). The term is found throughout the psalms to refer to God's kindness (e.g. Pss 25:7 [with ref. to God's forgiveness]; 119:65, 68; 145:7) and in Paul's writings to refer to God's kindness and patience with sinners (Rom. 2:4), and ultimately his kindness in sending Christ (Eph. 2:7; Titus 3:4).

*Humility* refers to that elusive quality that is best understood in contrast to its opposite, pride. It is the quality of not thinking too much of oneself, or too highly of oneself, or of being self-absorbed. It is likely to be present when someone has grasped the magnitude of God's grace, and is seen in how they reflect that grace to others. For this reason, the use of this word in a positive sense was rare in the ancient world.[85] In 2:18 and 23 the same term for *humility* was used and in that context referred to 'false humility'. *Gentleness* can also be understood in contrast to its opposite, harshness, in dealing with others (L&N 88.59). The term was used by Paul to describe Christ (2 Cor. 10:1). Other possible translations of the term, 'courtesy', 'considerateness', indicate a meaning in this context of a quality, like humility, 'of not being overly impressed by a sense of one's self-importance' (BDAG, p. 861).

The final term in this list, *patience*, may in this context have the antagonistic traits of 3:8 in view as it refers to bearing up under provocation as well as showing forbearance towards others (BDAG, p. 612). As noted above, it is linked with 'kindness' in describing God's forbearance towards sinners (Rom. 2:4); God's patience means salvation (2 Pet. 3:15). Paul himself is a display of Christ's great patience (1 Tim. 1:16). Paul prays that the Colossians may display patience, being strengthened by God's power (Col. 1:11). 'Forbearance', 'kindness' and 'gentleness' are also found together as fruit of the Spirit in Galatians 5:22–23. Thus the Colossians are to display their new 'look', by God's grace and power, by reflecting in their relationships with people Christ's character, the embodiment of God's grace to humanity.

---

85. *NIDNTTE*, 4.452.

**13.** The two actions encouraged, *bear with each other* and *forgive one another*, are participles in the Greek text ('bearing with' and 'forgiving', ESV) rather than finite verbs and thus indicate a shift in style from the descriptions in the previous verse. Grammatically they modify the command to 'clothe' (or 'put on') in 3:12. The relationship to 3:12 may be that these two actions are the result of putting on the items listed in 3:12,[86] or they may describe specific ways in which the preceding items are seen in action.[87] To *bear with each other* includes patience in the sense of 'putting up with' others, recognizing the reality of one another's weaknesses and differences. This of course requires kindness and humility and gentleness to be present as well.

The requirement to *forgive one another* is undoubtedly experientially complex and unsurprisingly is accompanied with two clauses further defining what this might look like. The term itself, *charizomai*, may be defined as 'being gracious by forgiving wrongdoing'.[88] As the first qualifying phrase shows, forgiveness is only needed *if any of you has a grievance against someone*. The 'grievance' here is a 'cause for complaint' and the implication is that this is likely to arise within a community of people. Thus the setting in view is one in which personal interaction has been fractured by some ungodly action against someone else, giving rise to a genuine cause for complaint in response. The reality of the wrongdoing is not denied, downplayed or ignored. The gracious act of forgiving, therefore, must include no longer continually holding the cause for complaint against that person. Forgiveness of sins has been elaborated upon earlier in Colossians as that which we have in the Son (1:14; 2:14). That such gracious forgiveness towards us is in view here is seen in the comparison that Paul makes for the second qualifying phrase. It is 'just as' *the Lord forgave* us that 'so also' should we forgive (cf. NRSV, NASB, CSB), perhaps providing both the reason for forgiving ('because') as well as the pattern ('in the same

---

86. Campbell, p. 57.
87. Harris, p. 140.
88. Adapting BDAG, p. 1078. The same term is used in 2:13 of God's forgiveness of us, and in Phlm. 22 in the sense of 'gracious gift'.

way as').[89] Although in the other references to forgiveness in Colossians, God the Father is the One who forgives through Christ (1:12–14; 2:13–14; cf. 1:20, 22), in this context 'Lord' refers to the Lord Jesus (cf. 3:15, 16, 17); a reminder once again of the close association between the two (1:19; 2:9). It is remembering and grasping God's grace towards us that helps us to be gracious and forgiving towards those who sin against us (cf. Matt. 6:12; 18:15–35). This is key to restoring fractured relationships in community, and is most likely a large part of what Paul's letter to Philemon is about (e.g. Phlm. 16, 18–20). It also needs to be remembered in this context that our relationship with God is not restored automatically or without response from us. The gospel is received by faith (1:4), we are reconciled through faith (1:22–23) and we are buried and raised, receiving forgiveness through faith (2:12–13). Elsewhere in the New Testament, Jesus taught that the process of reconciliation between two believers requires one who has sinned to hear and respond (see again Matt. 18:15–17). In other words, repentance is assumed (Luke 17:3–4). Even where there is repentance and forgiveness, depending on the nature of the offence, forgiveness does not mean there are no consequences. Trust might need to be earned, ministry opportunities might no longer be open, and in the case of illegal criminal actions, authorities should be notified and law enforcement should be involved. Such tragic circumstances do not mean that there cannot at the same time be genuine and demonstrated repentance and forgiveness and trust in God's righteous purposes to be worked out in due course.[90]

**14.** The opening phrase, *over all these*, continues the clothing metaphor (the verb 'clothe' or 'put on' is not in the Greek text but is implied from 3:12). The phrase suggests that what follows is not so much that this is the one item that must be prioritized, as the translation 'above all' (NRSV, CSB) might imply, nor that this is merely one more additional item to add, as the translation 'in addition to' implies (NASB; cf. NET). Rather, this will be the final, culminating item of clothing that is added to all the others but that

---

89. Moo, p. 280 (citing the similar structure in 1 Thess. 2:4).
90. See Brauns, *Forgiveness*.

also completes the outfit.[91] This culminating item is *love*, that concern for the good of others which may, depending on the context, arise from a warm affection for and high regard for someone with sincere appreciation.[92] It is a trait that can be distinguished from the others in that it is not identical with humility or patience. Yet at the same time love is the characteristic that gives all the other traits meaning. It is love for others that is seen in compassion, kindness, humility, gentleness, patience, bearing with and forgiving others (cf. 1 Cor. 13:1–7; 16:14). Like forbearance, kindness and gentleness, love too is a fruit of the Spirit (Gal. 5:22). Paul has already expressed his thanks to God that the Colossians have love for all of God's people (1:3–4), a love that is 'in the Spirit' (1:8). Paul's goal in proclaiming the gospel is that, as an outgrowth of their common understanding of the gospel, the Colossians will be united in love, and thus be greatly encouraged in their hearts (see comment on 2:2). Husbands are particularly singled out to display this love towards their wives (3:19). Most importantly, in this context, the Colossians have already been described as those who are 'dearly loved' (3:12). Thus love for others here is not understood in a vacuum, it has been seen and experienced by the believer who knows God's love in Christ. God's love, without downplaying wrongdoing, sought our good when it could not be earned. Thus our love for one another is to display and model God's love for us in Christ (cf. John 13:34).

It is not surprising then that Paul concludes that love is 'the perfect bond' (NET, NJB). It is not so much that love holds fellow believers together, although that is of course true, but that it holds all of the preceding items together because 'without love the virtues, as it were, melt away'.[93] As the final, culminating item that completes the outfit, enabling all the other traits to be displayed in a fitting way, love is 'perfect'. This might mean that love is itself

---

91. 'In addition to' in this context, with the verb 'clothe' implied, could still also mean something like 'add to' what is already in place and therefore 'over'. Cf. BDAG, p. 365 (meaning 7); MM, p. 234.

92. BDAG, p. 6; L&N 25.43.

93. Harris, p. 142.

'perfect/complete', or that it produces perfection/completion, or, more likely, love brings perfection/completion to the other virtues.[94] The idea is that the other items work in perfect harmony because of love. If biblically informed love is not present then the tendency of any of the above traits to veer off into naïve sentimentalism or unthinking misguided emotionalism is all too evident. Love, guided by the truth of the gospel of God's love for us in Christ, is the essential complementary and complete requirement.

**15.** Paul concludes this section with two third-person plural imperatives (*let the peace of Christ rule*, 3:15; *let the message of Christ dwell*, 3:16) and two second-person plural imperatives (*be thankful*, 3:15; *do it all in the name*, 3:17). Paul's focus continues to be the relational wellbeing of the Christian community in contrast to the activities and behaviour of 3:8–9 especially. Following the list of items that developed the clothing metaphor from 3:12, Paul now moves to direct the Colossians to concrete means by which these qualities can be encouraged among them.

The first means by which these traits will be experienced relates to what it is that should guide and direct them. It is *the peace of Christ*. The genitive phrase *of Christ* refers in this context to the peace that Jesus gives to believers.[95] As Paul has already emphasized, this is a peace that has been accomplished by Christ through his death on the cross for us, such that although we were enemies we are now reconciled and have peace with God (1:20–22). It is the harmony, *shalom*, between God and his people, anticipated in the prophets (e.g. Isa. 52:7; 53:5; 54:10, 13). Although Paul does not specifically contrast this peace to the *pax Romana*, it is a peace that transcends any worldly attempts to produce peace. The peace that brings us into harmony with God is one that therefore also brings us together as one people, indeed as *one body*. All believers therefore are united because they belong to Christ, who is the one and only head of this body. This reality is to *rule* or 'be in control' (NET) in our hearts.

---

94. H. Hübner, '*teleiotēs, ētos*' *TDNT*, vol. 3 p. 344. Cf. the use of the word for 'perfect' (*teleiotēs*) in the LXX Wisdom 6:15 ('perfect understanding'); 12:17 ('complete power').
95. Harris, p. 143.

A similar verb is used in 2:18. Perhaps a contrast is intended between the 'judgment' of the false teachers that separates the Colossian believers and the 'rule' of peace that Christ accomplishes. Whereas the next verse speaks of the message of Christ dwelling 'among you', this reference is to the 'hearts' of each believer. That this rule is to take place *in your hearts* means that the peace which has been accomplished by Christ is to be what guides our thinking as the basis for and directing determiner for decision making about disputes in the body of Christ. This cannot be construed to mean overlooking sin or avoiding repentance in order to preserve an outward veneer of 'peace'. If this were so, Paul may not have seen it necessary to warn of teachers who spread 'hollow and deceptive philosophy'. Rather, it means costly and open action guided by a goal to reflect God's hatred of sin and sacrificial pursuit of reconciliation.

As *members of one body* we were *called to peace*. 'Called' picks up the description of believers as 'chosen' in 3:12, and 'body' picks up the earlier references to the church as 'the body of Christ' (1:18, 24; 2:19). This was the goal to which we were called: a reconciled people of God who reflect his gracious saving purposes in Christ in one body. As we have noted throughout, it is possible that the schismatic effects of the false teachers are in the background throughout these verses. The guiding rule of the false teachers was their own human-oriented rules which set some above others, judging and condemning others (see again 2:18), and thus dividing the Colossian community into 'haves' and 'have nots'. The peace of Christ, rather than the false teachings, is to rule their hearts. If they let the peace of Christ be their rule, then they will be directed away from dividing against one another and towards Christlike love for one another.

The exhortation *and be thankful* almost seems like a throwaway line at the end of the verse. Careful readers of the letter to the Colossians, however, will remember that thankfulness has been mentioned by Paul before. In 1:3 thankfulness is key to Paul's own prayer for the Colossians and in 1:12 it is key to what Paul prays would be characteristic of the Colossians. In both places the basis for thanksgiving is God's gracious saving work in the lives of the Colossians. Likewise in 2:7 Paul sees life lived under Christ's lordship as a life overflowing with thankfulness. This link to Christ's lordship in 2:6–7 may offer a key to the apparently passing reference to thankfulness here too. It is the 'rule' of the peace accomplished by Christ that Paul exhorts the Colossians to submit to here, just as he highlighted Christ's lordship in 2:6–7. When glad recognition of Christ's saving and sovereign rule is present, so too is thankfulness.

It may be that Paul also has an eye on the false teachings in 2:7 since he focused on them in 2:8 and the following verses. One of the effects of the emphasis in the false teaching on human-oriented rules is to distract away from the sufficiency and sovereignty of the Lord Jesus. One of the antidotes to that possibility then is thankfulness to God for his accomplishments for us in Christ. Whereas the false teachings divide the body and distract from Christ, the peace that Christ has brought, as announced in the gospel, unifies the body and directs our attention away from ourselves and towards Christ. Thus thankfulness reminds us of God's gracious saving work in our lives, preserves humility, prevents pride in our estimation of our contribution to our standing before God and binds believers together as joint recipients of God's grace and Christ's peace. Paul's brief reference to being *thankful*, therefore, is a key part of how the relational wellbeing of the Colossian community is to be maintained as it accompanies a recognition of the *rule* of Christ's peace. Paul will return to this in 3:17 before he transitions to the next section.

**16.** The second means by which these traits will be experienced is to *let the message of Christ dwell among you richly*. These items of clothing, as 3:10–11 point out, are characteristic of the new self that is being renewed according to the image of Christ. Not surprisingly then, the *message of Christ* is key to reflecting Christ's character. The message of Christ is the gospel message about Christ that Paul has elsewhere called 'the word of truth' (1:5), the 'gospel' about 'God's grace' (1:6), 'the gospel' that holds out hope (1:23), 'the word of God in its fullness' (1:25), the 'mystery that ... is now disclosed' (1:26), the 'mystery which is Christ in you' (1:27), 'Him we proclaim' (1:28, ESV), 'the mystery of God, namely, Christ' (2:2), and 'the mystery of Christ' (4:3). Since Christ is both the mystery that was hidden for ages and generations (1:26) and also the reality to which Old

Testament festivals and celebrations were anticipating (2:16–17), it is likely that Paul has in view God's entire revelation that culminates and coheres in Christ and the teaching of Christ's authorized representatives, the apostles (1:1). Throughout this letter, but particularly in chapter 2, Paul also has in view another teaching, that which is not dependent on Christ (2:8) and that which is of human origin rather than God's revelation (cf. 1:26–27; 2:8, 18, 20–22). Thus it is *the message of Christ* that is to be at home among the Colossians, not the teaching that distracts from Christ.

For the word of Christ to *dwell* among the Colossians *richly* there must be an abundance of teaching, hearing and understanding of the content and significance of the good news of God's saving purposes in Christ. This is why Paul prays for the Colossians, asking God to fill them with 'the knowledge of his will through all the wisdom and understanding that the Spirit gives' so they may grow in the knowledge of God (1:9–10). It is also why he unpacks the significance of Christ's sovereignty and sufficiency in this letter, urging them to hear not only this letter to them, but also his letter that is coming from Laodicea (4:16). Paul's concern, therefore, is that the message of God's word that culminates and coheres in the gospel of the life, death and resurrection of Jesus the Messiah should be so at home among the Colossians that they live lives that reflect his grace and rule in their lives. Since the following participles most likely describe activities that they would do when they gather, the point Paul makes here is perhaps even more specific, that the word about Christ is to be at the centre of all they do and say in their gatherings.

The structure of the rest of the verse is somewhat complicated but it is clear that Paul follows this exhortation for the message about Christ to dwell among the Colossians with three participles in the Greek text that show how this rich dwelling of the message is to take place among the Colossians: by 'teaching', 'admonishing' and 'singing'. The first two, 'teaching and admonishing' are also found together in 1:28 (in reverse order) where Paul describes what his own ministry of proclaiming Christ involves. It is apparent, therefore, that Paul's ministry is a model for the Colossians. At 1:28 we suggested that the two terms, 'admonishing' and 'teaching', may cover the tasks of both warning about distractions from Christ's sufficiency, as well as positive instruction about Christ's sufficiency and Christlike behaviour. Just as Paul proclaims Christ to everyone (cf. 1:23) because Christ is the hope of every person in every place and culture (cf. 1:23, 28), so also the Colossians are to apply the message of Christ to *one another*. This is also part of the antidote to the false teachers. In the new covenant there are no longer different categories among God's people such as priests who mediate between God and his people, and 'ordinary' lay people. Rather, all of God's new covenant people 'know the Lord' and in this sense all, on the basis of the word of Christ, can teach and admonish one another. Nevertheless, the Colossians (and Paul) are to do this *with all wisdom*, so that God's people can live in a way that reflects God's gracious purposes for the world in Christ (cf. 1:28; 2:3). Although the fullness of Christ is applicable to everyone, the wide variety of settings and complexities of people's lives require wisdom in applying the grace and truth of the gospel with varied combinations of 'admonishing and teaching'. Just as mechanics are wise to use the variety of tools in their toolbox for the variety of tasks at hand, so too are believers wise to handle God's truth about the fullness of Christ's person and work with variety and thoughtfulness.

There is some debate about what the expression 'psalms, hymns and spiritual songs' modifies. Do the words 'psalms, hymns and spiritual songs' modify 'teaching and admonishing' as 'one way in which teaching and admonishing one another is to occur'?[96] Or do they modify the third participle 'singing', since 'three different words for "song" seem more suitable with "singing" than with "teaching"'.[97] It may help the following explanation to see the phrases in the order of the Greek text laid out visually:

let the word of Christ dwell richly
    teaching and admonishing one another (with all wisdom)
        psalms, hymns, spiritual songs
    singing to God (with gratitude in your hearts)

---

96. Campbell, p. 60. Cf. NASB, NIV, CSB, NKJV.
97. Harris, p. 145. Cf. NIV84, ESV, NET, NRSV, NJB, NLT. This is also reflected in the punctuation of NA$^{28}$ and UBS$^5$.

Although it does load up the word 'singing' with a lot of modifiers in contrast to the other two, I think it makes more sense to see these words describing various songs as better modifying the word 'singing'.[98] Even so, the word 'singing' indicates a means by which the message about Christ is to dwell among the Colossians richly. Thus all of the songs are still meant to convey edifying and understandable content that helps believers express their adoration and articulate their understanding of God's sovereign and saving purposes in Christ.

What then are 'psalms, hymns, and spiritual songs'? Although strict distinctions in meaning are not likely here, the following nuances might be possible.[99] *Psalms* most likely refers to Psalms from the Old Testament (this is the way the word is used elsewhere in the New Testament).[100] Psalm singing has had a rich tradition in the history of the church, and singing them helps the church to bring the wide variety of human experiences before God.[101] *Hymns* seems to be a more general reference to songs that are sung to God (cf. Isa. 42:10). *Songs* is also likely to be a general reference to songs that are sung to God (cf. Exod. 15:1; Deut. 31:19, 22, 30; 32:1–43; Hab. 3:1–19; Rev. 5:9; 14:3; 15:3). In connection with 'psalms,' the terms 'hymns' and 'songs' are likely new compositions in light of God's new revelation in Jesus the Messiah. In this context the word 'songs' is modified by the adjective 'spiritual' (most English translations) which is likely to be a reference to the Holy Spirit in some way. Some suggest that this refers to spontaneous songs inspired by the Spirit (cf. *songs from the Spirit*, NIV).[102] More likely, Paul uses the term 'spiritual' here, as he does elsewhere, to refer to that which

---

98. See e.g. with the dative case in the LXX 1 Maccabees 4:33 ('praise ... with hymns'); 3 Maccabees 7:16 ('exclamations of joy ... with hymns'); Nehemiah 12:36 ('praise with songs'); Sirach 39:14–15 ('praise ... with songs'); cf. also Ps. 136:3 (English 137:3; 'a hymn, sing to us one of the songs of Zion')
99. The terms are often used together in the Psalms.
100. Cf. Luke 20:42; 24:44; Acts 1:20; 13:33; 1 Cor. 14:26; Eph. 5:19.
101. Cf. Thompson, 'Consolation', pp. 37–51.
102. Dunn, p. 239.

is not 'natural' or 'fleshly' but that which is of the Spirit as it is in keeping with Christ and the gospel message about him (1 Cor. 2:13, 15; 9:11; 10:4; Eph. 1:3; 1 Pet. 2:5). There is nothing in the term that requires it to be spontaneous or a reference to 'tongues'. Since the word 'song' is the most general of the three words used here, Paul probably found it appropriate to modify this general word with a clarification: it isn't just any song that enables the word of Christ to dwell richly among the Colossians.

Finally, just as 'teaching and admonishing' one another were to be done *with all wisdom,* so 'singing' is to be done *to God with gratitude in your hearts.* That singing is 'to God' clarifies that when the Christian congregation gathers, although intelligible edification is to guide everything (1 Cor. 14:26), this does not reduce the gathering to a horizontal only focus. There is a recognition here that God hears and answers prayer and hears and receives songs of praise. These songs are directed to him rather than to us, even if they involve edifying content that enables the message about Christ to dwell among us richly. In a synonym for thanksgiving (cf. ESV), Paul concludes with a description of the manner or attitude that will be characteristic of such singing, *gratitude.* Gratitude will accompany such singing because the songs remind us of God's grace announced in the gospel about Christ (1:6).[103] Once enemies and alienated from God (1:21) and deserving of God's wrath (3:6), we know that we now have peace with God (1:20), forgiveness of sins through the death of Christ on the cross (2:13–14), having no fear before God of the accusations of anyone (1:22), let alone the powers and authorities (2:15), and are his chosen, holy and dearly loved people (3:12). That such gratitude is *in your hearts* refers to our internal and cognitive response (cf. 3:15) that accompanies the outward activity of singing. Singing (outwardly) with gratitude (inwardly) requires an intelligible grasp of the wonder of God's grace (1:6). Thus *gratitude* and wonder at God's grace in Christ characterizes the singing of God's people.

**17.** Paul concludes this section about putting on the practices of the 'new self' with a comprehensive summary statement about the

---

103. The same word, *charis,* is used in 1:6 and here.

way in which all of this is to be done. This comprehensiveness comes through in the translation, *and whatever you do, whether in word or deed, do it all* (there is even another 'all' at the beginning of the Greek phrase for emphasis).[104] The comprehensive 'word or deed' looks back to all the instructions of the preceding verses about compassion, kindness, forgiving, teaching and admonishing, and singing as well as all of the myriad of actions and words not specified above which make up the everyday interactions of life. It also looks back to Paul's opening prayer that the Colossian believers would 'bear fruit in every good work' (1:10). Paul gives a concluding guide that covers everything he has said and anything he has left unsaid here.

Doing everything *in the name of the Lord Jesus* looks back to the central exhortation of the letter in 2:6–7 in which recognizing the lordship of Jesus is key to continuing to live 'in him'. Elsewhere in Scripture 'the name of the Lord' is a common designation for Yahweh, the Lord God. In Micah 4:5 'walking' in the 'name of the Lord our God' is contrasted with 'walking' in the name of gods of the nations, idolatry.[105] The *name* of the Lord Jesus refers to his character and authority, something that has been in view throughout the letter, particularly in 1:15–20, but more immediately in this context as the 'image' that the 'new self' of believers is being renewed to reflect (3:10). This concluding exhortation to do everything in his name returns to the opening summary exhortation of this chapter to seek after and orient our thinking around the accomplishments and reign of Christ as proclaimed in the gospel. Since he is our life, we live with his honour in view. The final reference to *giving thanks to God the Father through him* modifies the imperative 'do', indicating that expressing thanks to God is meant to be 'the concomitant of all Christian behaviour'.[106] That this is done *through him* (i.e. Christ) reminds readers that Christ's crucifixion is the means by which we are reconciled to God and

---

104. Note the repetition of *pan/panta* ('all') in the Greek phrase: *pan ho ti eav poiēte en logō ē en ergō, panta.*

105. Pao, p. 251 notes this passage and others in which 'the name of the Lord' is used.

106. Harris, p. 149. See above on 3:15.

therefore the reason why we are able to enjoy access to him (1:21–22). What it means to 'do everything in the name of the Lord Jesus' in everyday responsibilities and relationships will be the subject of the following verses.

*Theology*
The focus of 3:12–17 is on the way God's people are to relate to one another and what they do together when they are gathered. Christology also permeates this section as it is Christology that shapes Paul's ecclesiology. Again, discontinuity and continuity from the Old Testament is assumed here. Like God's people in the Old Testament, God's new covenant people are chosen, holy and loved (see 3:12). Picking up on the final verses of the previous section, however, God's new covenant people consist of those who belong to Christ; indeed Christ is 'in' them so they all experience inward renewal according to his image. This means that they are 'one body' and they are to reflect Christ's love in their relationships with one another. Although not explicitly countering the false teachers here, divisions may have resulted from their teaching. So reminding the Colossians of the gospel of Christ includes showing them the common bond they have in Christ by grace. Thus, when they gather together, what is to characterize their gathering is the word of Christ as it permeates their speech in teaching and singing and all they do with thankfulness. There is continuity and discontinuity here too as believers sing psalms and new songs in light of Christ's appearing. Each believer, not priests and prophets, has the privilege and responsibility to teach and admonish each another with the word of Christ.

### iv. *The supremacy of Christ in earthly relationships (3:18 – 4:1)*
*Context*
Paul continues to apply Christology in this section, as he turns to the realities of the Colossians' everyday earthly responsibilities. The preceding exhortation to do everything in the name of the Lord Jesus shapes all that Paul says here, with the word 'Lord' (*kyrios*) occurring eight times in these verses. Since there are fourteen occurrences of this word in Colossians this is quite a concentration. The word occurs in 3:18, 20, 22, 23, 24; 4:1, showing

that the Lordship of Christ is to be determinative in every relationship. Three features of this passage need to be briefly addressed here: (1) this passage is one of a number of passages called 'household codes' that are found elsewhere in the New Testament with similar forms being found in ancient literature; (2) in particular this passage is similar to that which is found in Ephesians; and (3) this passage raises the question about how Paul's instructions to slaves and masters should be understood. There is not space to treat these matters comprehensively here; I will just provide a few orienting details and will touch on further exegetical issues in the verses where they arise.

First, these verses have been called 'household codes' because they concern the various members of the (first-century) household (for similar passages in the New Testament cf. Eph. 5:22 – 6:9; 1 Tim. 6:1–2; Titus 2:1–9; 1 Pet. 2:18 – 3:7) and there are similar treatments in ancient literature. Many point to Aristotle (*Politics* 1.2.1–23; esp. 1-4; 1.5.1–12), but there are also similar texts in Hellenistic Jewish writers such as Philo (*Hypothetica* 7:1–9) and Josephus (*Against Apion* 2:199–219). Two features in particular set these verses apart from their counterparts in Hellenistic Greek literature:

1. The determining factor for each person's behaviour is the Lord Jesus. Thus Paul is not simply following the ethical standards of his day. As with everything else he says in Colossians, his convictions about Jesus Christ determine his understanding of how we are to relate to one another. This can be seen in the way the phrase 'the Lord' modifies each of the following statements:

    as is fitting in the Lord (18)
    for this pleases the Lord (20)
    reverence for the Lord (22)
    as working for the Lord (23)
    you will receive an inheritance from the Lord (24)
    it is the Lord Christ you are serving (or 'serve the Lord Christ') (24)
    you also have a Master (Lord) in heaven (4:1)

This means that 3:18 – 4:1 should be understood in its immediate context. Not only does the emphasis on the honour of the Lord Jesus in 3:17 prepare for these verses, but all that Paul has said in the preceding verses should be kept in view here: all believers are to 'seek the things above' (3:1–2) and to 'put on' the new self (3:10); the countercultural reality of 3:11 ('no . . . slave or free') is true for all believers. This context, and the way 'the Lord' permeates these instructions, sets this passage apart from any apparent similarities in ancient literature.

2. Not only is there a significant difference in the way that the reference to the 'Lord' is pervasive, but unlike Hellenistic household codes in particular, each group is addressed. Unlike other ancient household codes, Paul does not focus on the 'rights' or the honour of the husband or the master, but on their responsibilities, and he addresses each member of the household so that there are reciprocal responsibilities. Also unlike the Hellenistic codes, Paul does not relate what he says about the household to the stability of the wider society, but to the Lordship of Christ. Thus the similarities to household instructions in ancient literature is largely superficial and due to the inclusion of similar members in ancient households in instructions to parents and children, slaves and masters. This brings us to the next two observations.

Second, the closest parallel passage is found in Ephesians. Even here there is one major difference that stands out if one were to set the two passages out side by side (see Table 2).

Table 2: Instructions for households in Ephesians and Colossians compared

| *Ephesians* | *Colossians* |
| --- | --- |
| Wives 5:22–24 (40 words) | Wives 3:18 (9 words) |
| Husbands 5:25–33 (147 words) | Husbands 3:19 (10 words) |
| Children 6:1–3 (35 words) | Children 3:20 (13 words) |
| Fathers 6:4 (16 words) | Fathers 3:21 (10 words) |
| Slaves 6:5–8 (59 words) | Slaves 3:22–25 (56 words) |
| Masters 6:9 (28 words) | Masters 4:1 (18 words) |

The number of words in the Greek text (give or take a couple of words depending on textual variants) show that for the most part the list in Colossians is a shorter version of the list in Ephesians. Proportionally, the instructions to slaves in Colossians is much longer than the succinct instructions given to the others in Colossians. Why might this be? A plausible explanation is found in the common names in both Colossians 4:7–17 and Philemon 1, 10, 23–24 and particularly the reference to Onesimus (Col. 4:9) who is accompanying this letter. There is even a verbal link between 3:25 and Philemon 18 (*adikeō*, 'do wrong'). The commonalities between Colossians and Philemon suggest that the letters are written to the same people at the same time, indicating that it is this that explains the lengthier material on slaves in Colossians.[107] Thus in Colossians there are instructions to slaves in a context that relativizes the authority of masters (3:11; 4:1) and in Philemon we have a request to a master on the basis of the new context of membership in the family of God.

Third, this brings up the place of this passage in the wider context of ancient slavery. We will add some more exegetical details in the treatment of 3:22 – 4:1 below, but for now we will summarize some important considerations:[108]

1. Slavery in the Greco-Roman world was not based on race or skin colour.
2. Slavery, often enough, was still a horrible fate, since slaves had no rights; there are plenty of descriptions of the horror that resulted from the degrading practice of human ownership.
3. The experience of slaves depended on the master who owned them and on the work they had to perform.
4. Slaves occupied a wide variety of positions – some slaves were teachers, doctors, business managers – with estimates that approximately a third of the population in the city of

---

107. McKnight, pp. 357–358.
108. The discussion here is indebted to the following summaries: Bartchy, 'Slavery', pp. 65–73; Harris, *Slave of Christ*; Moo, pp. 96–297, 371–377; Beale, pp. 370–373, 455–457; Pao, pp. 348–351.

Rome were slaves, making the institution of slavery an integral part of the economy and livelihood of everyone in the Roman empire.
5. This means that there are reports of slaves gladly gaining their freedom and never returning to slavery again.
6. Freedom, however, was not an automatic goal when there was also the lack of a wider social safety net and continuing obligations to one's master.
7. The small, insignificant, and marginal position of the early church in the wider setting of the whole Roman imperial economic and political context means that we should not think of them as though they had the opportunity or influence to change the entire system or that they could at least voice their critique of social conditions as though they lived in a modern democratic society.[109]
8. Nevertheless Paul never endorses the institution of slavery, and neither he nor any other writer in the New Testament encourages Christians to own or buy slaves.[110]
9. Instead, Paul says that slaves should gain their freedom if they can (1 Cor. 7:21) and slave traders are listed among those who are under judgment and who oppose the gospel (1 Tim. 1:8–11).
10. In Colossians the gospel is applied in ways that undermine the institution of slavery since slave and master are explicitly identified as equal recipients of the inner renewal according to the image of Christ (3:11): both are explicitly said to have the same master in heaven, making earthly masters 'slaves' too (3:23 – 4:1), and both are implicitly included in the many references to the unity of believers as part of one family, one body, and as recipients of God's gracious forgiveness and inheritance (cf. 1:12; 3:24).
11. This unity in Christ becomes the basis for Paul's appeal to Philemon to welcome Onesimus 'as a beloved brother . . .

---

109. Dunn, p. 253.
110. The wording here follows Moo, p. 376 (citing Harris, *Slave of Christ*, pp. 62–68).

in the Lord' (Phlm. 16), perhaps implying that he might grant Onesimus freedom (Phlm. 21).

12. All of this is vastly different to what Paul and other New Testament writers say elsewhere about husbands, wives and children (e.g. 1 Cor. 7:10–16): they are not inherently opposed to the gospel nor are husbands or wives encouraged to depart 'if they can'. Unlike with slavery, neither Paul nor Jesus nor anyone else in the New Testament gives any indication that the institution of marriage or the family unit should be abandoned if possible, or that those who participate in marriage or have a family are evil (even though Jesus takes priority, Luke 14:26). Rather, the consistent pattern of the New Testament, based on Genesis 1–3, is that marriage is between a man and a woman, that children can be produced in this setting and that Christian husbands and wives should remain together unless there is marital unfaithfulness or abandonment (see on 3:18).

13. Therefore, Paul here neither simply conforms to a contemporary first-century ethic that implies the need for further development or abandonment of his ethics of family life, nor does he address wider economic and political policies. We know from his other writings that Paul treats the topics of slavery and family differently. They are placed together here, not to endorse the institution of slavery, but to address the realities of everyday life that many believers as individuals and as families found themselves in, with an ancient household that included the groups of people addressed here.

*Comment*

**18.** As Paul continues to unpack what the lordship of Jesus looks like in the everyday lives of believers he turns now to the specifics of household relationships. Indeed, references to 'the Lord' will continue through this section qualifying everything Paul says. It is clear that he does not mean for the household to be a reflection of whatever the cultural and societal norms or injustices reflect. Thus we will observe that Paul's first instruction is qualified with *as is fitting in the Lord*. Paul first addresses wives and exhorts them to *submit yourselves to your husbands, as is fitting in the Lord*. Several observations can be made here about this exhortation that, if taken out of this setting, can be made to say something that it is not saying (see also the reference to both 'parents' in 3:20). First, note that wives themselves are being addressed (and they are addressed first). This command is not addressed to husbands to 'make wives submit'. Thus there is no room for coercion from the husband (indeed the husband is commanded in the next verse to love). Second, as the NIV correctly translates, the exhortation is for wives to submit 'themselves', again reinforcing the idea that this is an action initiated by the wife and not by the husband.[111] Third, this is an exhortation for wives with reference to their husbands only. This is not a general command for all women to submit to all men, nor does this command mean that unmarried women must submit to men in general. Fourth, the word 'submit' means to recognize the leadership and authority of another. This leadership and authority, however, is not absolute because, as is often pointed out, Paul does not use the word 'obey' here (as he does in 3:20, 22; note too that both husband and wife are to be 'obeyed' in 3:20). Fifth, this submission is done *as is fitting in the Lord*. The word 'as' refers to the manner, and so to do what *is fitting in the Lord* is to do what is appropriate, what is in keeping with one who belongs to the Lord.[112] The submission in view, therefore, must reflect what it means to be a follower of the Lord Jesus. Thus, whether speaking of husbands, or anyone else in the New Testament (whether governments, or leaders in a church), no one in the New Testament has authority over a new covenant believer in the sense that they rob individuals of their own responsibility before the Lord to obey him or in the sense that they exercise authority in every detail of life. The word of Christ is the directing guide (see 3:16).[113] In this

---

111. The translation reflects the middle voice of the verb here, but this would be the meaning even if this understanding of the middle voice is not in view here, or if it were in the passive or even active voice.
112. Harris, p. 154. The word for 'fitting' is used elsewhere in the New Testament only in Eph. 5:4 and Phlm. 8 (that which is 'right').
113. Cf. Acts 4:19; 5:29 (with ref. to Rom. 13:1; Titus 3:1; 1 Pet. 2:13; 5:5).

context, the husband who seeks to shape his life and marriage by that word and reflecting the character of the Lord seen in the traits of the preceding verses is to find support, not resistance, from his wife, as she herself also seeks to reflect the character of her Lord highlighted in the traits of the preceding verses.[114] Thus, the focus of this first exhortation continues the Christ-centred focus of the letter as a whole.

**19.** Husbands are given both a command and a corresponding prohibition. First, in contrast to other ancient household codes, husbands are to *love your wives*. As is often pointed out in discussions of ancient household codes, when attention is directed towards husbands it is usually to emphasize their 'rule' over their wife and children.[115] Paul, however, commands them to *love* their wives. As we noted above in 3:14, in this context, the Colossians have already been described as those who are dearly loved by God (3:12). Thus the husband's love for his wife, like the Colossians' love for one another, is not understood in a vacuum; it has been seen and experienced by the believer who knows God's love in Christ, a love that has sought our good when it could not be earned. Thus the husband's love for his wife is to display and model God's love for us in Christ (cf. John 13:34; Eph. 5:25–33). Love, as the perfect bond that holds the virtues of 3:12–13 together (3:14), will be seen in the wearing of the clothing of 3:12–13 in the home. Conversely, the husband is also exhorted not to *be harsh with them*. The word translated by the NIV as *harsh* is also translated as 'be bitter' (CSB), or, reflecting the passive voice of the verb, 'be embittered' (NASB), or 'become bitter' (BDAG, p. 812). The term refers to an internal bitter resentment or bitter hatred towards someone such that 'bitterly hateful' could also be a translation here (L&N 88.202). In

---

114. Passages that provide the occasion for divorce might also be noted here. No wife is required to 'stay and submit' where the husband is immoral or abusive, abandoning the Lord in his marital obligations (cf. 1 Cor. 7:15).

115. As reflected in the often cited statements of Aristotle, *Politics* 1.2.12. Instructions to love, though rare, have been identified in a couple of places. Cf. Talbert, p. 232.

this sense the additional words, *with them* could also be better translated as 'against them' (NASB). What does it look like to be 'bitterly hateful against your wife'? Such bitterness would reflect the traits listed in 3:8 that are the opposite of love, hence Paul's pairing of this command and prohibition together here.

**20.** Having addressed husband and wife individually, Paul now turns to address children and how they are to treat both parents together. The assumption is that although not every marriage will produce children, one key feature of marriage in the Bible is that a husband and wife can and generally do so.[116] Children are to *obey your parents in everything*. The contrast from 3:18 highlights the distinctions that Paul is making. Using *obey* rather than 'submit yourselves', adding 'in everything' here, and including the wife along with the husband together as 'parents', serves to show that wives and husbands are together the ones responsible for the godly order and atmosphere of the home. Paul does not specify the age of children here, but it is likely that he has in view those who have not yet reached 'maturity' or adulthood so as to exercise their own independent responsibility.[117] The additional motivation that *this pleases the Lord* also reminds parents and children alike that this obedience 'in everything' is also meant to be understood within the broader framework of living lives 'worthy of the Lord' such that we 'please him in every way' (1:10).[118] Thus this additional motivation assumes parents who know and submit to the Lord Jesus and who therefore seek to wear the 'clothing' of 3:12–14, obey the instructions of 3:15–17 and by both example and instruction point to the sufficiency and sovereignty of the Lord Jesus as Paul has been doing throughout this letter.

**21.** Although some suggest that the opening address to fathers refers to 'parents' together (since the plural *hoi pateres* may refer to

---

116. This is the assumption in Jesus' reply in Luke 20:34 to the issue raised in 20:28–33.
117. Cf. the use of the word 'children' (*tekna*) in 1 Thess. 2:7, 11; 1 Tim. 3:4; Titus 1:6.
118. The phrase can be rendered, 'for this is pleasing in the Lord' (NET; *en kyriō* as 3:18b).

both the male and female parent),[119] the different term for parents in the preceding verse (*gonous*) suggests that husbands are being addressed again here, now in their role as fathers. Once again, in contrast to ancient household codes that emphasize the rule of fathers, Paul addresses fathers in terms of their responsibilities. Even though this obviously applies to both parents, fathers are specifically addressed and are exhorted not to *embitter your children*. To 'embitter' children is to 'irritate' (NJB), 'aggravate' (NLT) or 'exasperate' (CSB) them. It is to act in such a way, perhaps by belittling, berating, bating or neglecting, or perhaps even in this context with an unrealistic or overbearing emphasis on 'obedience', so that they grow resentful.[120] Why would fathers be addressed specifically when this would also apply to mothers? Although different words are used, it may be due to the similar exhortation given to husbands in 3:19. Just as husbands are not to be bitter towards their wives, they are not to be the cause of bitterness in their children. As with the instruction to children in the preceding verse, the exhortation is followed by a motivation. The following motivation indicates what the outcome of such provocation of their children would be: 'discouragement'. The discouragement in view here is that of losing motivation, they 'lose heart' (NRSV). Although this can take place for any number of reasons, fathers are urged not to be the cause of their children shutting down and closing both them and the Lord out because they have been the subject of repeated needling or provoking, or worse. What might help fathers not to do this? Paul has given some guidance on this already and it has to do with what is worn around the home. Replace the clothing of 3:8–9 with the clothing of 3:12–14 and the instructions of 3:15–17. The instruction of 4:2 will help too.

**22–23.** Having briefly stated how husbands, wives, children and fathers are to relate to each other, Paul turns to an expanded set of instructions and motivations for Christian slaves in 3:22–25, followed by a brief instruction to Christian masters in 4:1. As we stated in the introduction to this 'household code', Onesimus will

---

119. BDAG, p. 786.
120. L&N 88.168.

accompany this letter with Tychicus (4:9), returning to Colossae, not only as a slave, but as a beloved brother. As a new believer, how should Onesimus and other Christian slaves relate to Philemon in the everyday realities of life as a slave in an ancient household? In keeping with the emphasis throughout this section, the motivations provided here reflect the impact that the Lord Jesus has in every area of life. Having just announced that there is no 'slave or free, but Christ is all, and is in all' (3:11), why does Paul continue to address Christian slaves as though they still have masters? Paul is not attempting to overthrow an institution that ran through the fabric of Greco-Roman society. He addresses all those who would generally be members of a household in the first century so that they would know what it looks like to reflect Christ's character in the realities and complexities of daily life. If he did not do this then a significant portion of the early church would not know how they were to behave as Christians, even though texts such as 3:11 (and 1 Cor. 7:21; 1 Tim. 1:10) undermine the validity of the institution (see the introduction to this 'household code' section).

What is a first-century Christian slave to do then? Slaves are to do what they can to serve the Lord in this setting. They are to *obey their earthly masters in everything*. As with 3:20 where a similar injunction is given, the assumption is that Christian masters are in view (see 4:1), although the application would be broader. Thus 'in everything' is not an excuse for exploitation, but directs the slave to steer away from selective obedience. This obedience is then explained with two further clarifications. First, slaves are to obey *not only when [the master's] eye is on you and to curry their favour*. Since slaves may be teachers or estate managers one can readily see why Paul instructs them in this way. An estate manager who is only looking after the operation of the estate when the master can see him is not going to end up with a well-run estate (Luke 16:1–2). Such a slave would only be concerned about working 'while being watched' (NRSV). The NIV's *curry their favour* translates the term *anthrōpareskoi* which refers to a 'people-pleaser' (BDAG, p. 80; ESV). This contrasts with Paul's concern here and throughout this letter for believers to live in such a way as to 'please the Lord' (1:10; 3:17, 20).

Second, therefore, slaves are to obey *with sincerity of heart and reverence for the Lord*. This contrasting clarification implies that the preceding description of working only 'while being watched' may also have referred to a service that was external only, without going beyond what the eye can see.[121] Instead, internal sincerity and a genuine desire to serve are to characterize those who belong to the Lord Jesus. This kind of obedience shows *reverence for the Lord*. In keeping with the high Christology of this letter, a common phrase in the Old Testament, 'fearing the Lord', to refer to Yahweh (e.g. Prov. 1:7) is used here to refer to the Lord Jesus. 'Fear' of the Lord in this context may also contrast with the more common cultural fear that many slaves might have for their master. In light of 3:25 and 4:1 this serves as an encouragement to the slave that the Lord Jesus is ultimately the sovereign ruler and judge of all.[122]

In this regard, Paul's designation of these masters as *earthly masters* ('masters according to the flesh' NKJV, LSB), while still encouraging obedience, at the same time qualifies the master's authority.[123] Ultimately what Paul encourages here is not obedience to the master for the master's sake, but obedience to the master as an outworking of one's ultimate concern to honour in their earthly responsibilities their 'Master/Lord' in heaven (cf. 3:1–3; 4:1). The same Greek word, *kyrios*, is used throughout here for 'master' (3:22; 4:1) and 'Lord' (3:22, 23, 24; 4:1b; i.e. referring to the Lord Jesus five times). In this framework, no master has ultimate authority, and slaves are concerned first and foremost to reflect the character of their heavenly Lord, being ruled by the peace of Christ in their hearts (3:15).

Before transitioning to the motivation in 3:24, Paul reiterates the preceding exhortation to serve with genuine heart. Paul clarifies that this applies across the board to *whatever you do* and that the motivation for such 'heartfelt' work is that this is done as (or 'with the thought that') *working for the Lord, not for human masters*. This uses the same wording as 3:17 as a way to bring the lordship of

---

121. Harris, p. 157.
122. Pao, p. 273.
123. See Phlm. 16 (lit. 'both in the flesh and in the Lord'). 'Flesh' here does not refer to humanity in sinfulness, but humanity in contrast to the Lord.

Jesus into everyday life, and points again to their ultimate Lord. Thus, although Paul addresses slaves here, he relativizes the authority of their masters. The primary focus for slaves as for all believers, is 'reverence for the Lord', and 'working for the Lord' so that 'whatever' we do is 'in the name of the Lord Jesus'.

**24–25.** The motivation for this service turns to the future in 3:24–25. Just as Paul highlights a future-oriented hope throughout Colossians (e.g. 1:5, 12, 22–23, 27–28; 3:4), so here he reminds slaves of this hope in terms that reinforce the earthly–heavenly distinction between their earthly masters and their ultimate master, the Lord Jesus. First, their heavenly Lord is not only the one they are ultimately serving, he also is the one who rewards with an eternal inheritance. They are promised *an inheritance from the Lord as a reward*. This is something that they *know* already, probably because this is part of the gospel hope that they have believed.[124] Thus, although they may be slaves of an earthly master with little hope of freedom, and no hope of an earthly inheritance, they are actually heirs who are 'qualified to share in the inheritance of the saints' (1:12), as brothers and sisters in God's family (cf. 1:2). The similarity in wording with 1:12 here likely means that the 'inheritance' is the same promise that is given by God's grace since he 'qualifies' us to receive it (see comment on 1:12).

The final part of this verse is usually translated as an indicative, *it is the Lord Christ you are serving* (NIV; cf. ESV, NASB). However, the following verse begins with an explanatory 'for' which suggests that this should instead be translated as another imperative, resuming the imperative 'work' from 3:23, and supported by the following explanation. Thus the final part of the verse reiterates the point here with the exhortation, 'Serve the Lord Christ' (NET, LSB).[125] In fact, the placement of 'from the Lord' towards the front of this sentence in the Greek text (see e.g. ESV, LSB), and this concluding imperative, together with the emphatic combination of

---

124. The participle 'knowing' is probably causal, giving a further reason for serving the Lord (hence, 'since you know', NIV, NRSV).
125. See the discussion in support of the imperative in Harris, pp. 160–161; Moo, p. 313; Pao, pp. 275–276. For the indicative see Beale, p. 332.

titles *Lord Christ*, all reinforce the emphasis throughout this section on who the ultimate Lord is.

Second, as well as one who graciously rewards with an eternal inheritance, the Lord Christ is a just Lord and he will ensure that ultimate justice will come. In the immediate context, the link with the end of 3:24 is evident in the word 'for' (ESV, NRSV; omitted in the NIV). Thus, in saying 'serve the Lord Christ, for . . .', Paul reinforces the superior blessing of knowing that one's ultimate master is the Lord Jesus; there is the promise of justice as well as an eternal inheritance. The reference to *anyone who does wrong* is general enough to include both slave and master. Thus this is both a warning for 'the one who does wrong' and a reassurance for the one who has been wronged. This is reinforced with the concluding statement that *there is no favouritism*. Whether it is the slaves who disobey and defraud their earthly masters, or the masters (to whom Paul will turn to more directly next) who mistreat their slaves, there is a future judgment coming. Slaves are not exempt because of their low social status, and masters are not exempt because of their position of power. The Lord does not judge on the basis of human status. Whoever 'does wrong' will be *repaid for their wrongs* (see 3:6). The assurance here is that although there are many times in this life where it appears that justice is not done, not least for the slave who because of an Empire-wide system has to work for a master without gaining freedom, still there is the promise that this life is not all there is and there will be a reckoning to come for those who perpetuated injustice. In the wider context of Colossians, this reality of judgment assumes the absence of repentance and faith that brings reconciliation with God and forgiveness of sins (cf. 1:14, 21–22; 2:13–14). However, what happens to an 'earthly' relationship where 'wrong' has been done? Philemon 18–19 elaborates upon this, even using the same word for 'doing wrong' as here. The assurance that there is no favouritism before God is developed in the following and final verse of this section.

**4:1.** The future orientation as a motivation, first for slaves (3:24), and then more generally for all (3:25), is now continued for masters. Masters must give slaves that which is *right and fair*. Again, rather than focus on the 'rule' of masters over the slaves in their household, Paul instead addresses the responsibilities of Christian masters.[126] To *provide* ... *what is right* (NIV) can be translated 'treat ... with justice' (NET) which is best understood in relation to what Paul has just said in 3:25. The deliberate link between this verse and 3:25 is seen in the contrast between that which is *right* (*dikaios*) and the one who does *wrong* (*adikeō*) who will be repaid for the 'wrong' (*adikeō*) that has been done. Thus, in contrast to the warning of the preceding verse, Paul now exhorts masters to do the opposite. To provide 'justice' or to do 'what is right' in this context is that which is in accordance with the word of Christ and his character that Paul outlines in the preceding section. This is also radically different to Aristotle, who didn't think slaves deserved justice.[127]

To do *what is right/just* is further defined as that which is *fair* (*isotēs*). This likewise picks up on the preceding reference to the Lord's impartiality (3:25) and refers to an 'even-handedness of treatment' among the master's slaves.[128] Just as the Lord shows no partiality or favouritism, neither should masters. Indeed, the motivation here is that masters (*kyrioi*) also have a *Master [kyrios] in heaven*. The deliberate repetition here is why all English versions translate the last word as 'Master' rather than 'Lord'. Knowing that they have a Master in heaven is the reason (*because you know*) that 'earthly masters' in the Colossian Christian community are to treat their slaves 'justly and fairly' (ESV). The implication of this is not spelled out, but following the preceding verse, the likelihood is that Paul implies that they are not a law to themselves, nor are they 'free' to treat slaves however they like. Rather, they are accountable to the Lord. In a sense then, even the (believing) 'masters' are 'slaves' too. Thus Paul alludes to the rationale behind phrases such as 'fellow slave/servant' in 1:7 (for Epaphras) and 4:7 (for Tychicus): all believers have a common Master/Lord. Thus the authority of the master is relativized since both master and slave are accountable to the same Lord (note the word 'also').

Although Paul's admonitions to masters are brief, they are about the same length as the instructions to wives, husbands, children

---

126. Pao, p. 277.
127. Cf. Witherington, pp. 195–196, referring to Aristotle, *Politics* 1.2.4–5.
128. Harris, p. 162.

and fathers, spanning one sentence each. There are not many specific instructions to anyone here (except for the slaves). Nevertheless, some may wonder why this is all Paul says to masters and why he does not tell the masters to set their slaves free. As noted above, elsewhere in the New Testament it is clear that Paul does not endorse slavery, while at the same time it would be anachronistic to think that Paul or the small Christian communities in the Lycus valley could alter the wider societal cohesion of this widespread Greco-Roman institution (see pp. 163–166 above). Paul's focus is on how the individual Christian can reflect Christ's character within the daily reality of a typical household setting and is not an endorsement of this wider political reality. Even in this context the relativization of masters and the lack of distinction between master and slave in their renewal in Christ (3:11) and their common accountability before the Lord (3:25) lay the seeds for a later overhaul of wider political systems. It is also possible that Paul hopes Philemon might free Onesimus (though this is debated; see Phlm. 21).

*Theology*
The Christological emphasis of Colossians continues in this section with, as we noted in the introduction, eight out of the fourteen references to 'Lord' (*kyrios*) in the whole of Colossians occurring in just these nine verses. The focus of this section is on the application of Christ's lordship to the daily activity of the Colossian believers, following the comprehensive 'whatever you do' reference in 3:17. What is striking here is that the reality of the lordship of Jesus is seen in the ordinary realities of family and work (with both viewed together in the ancient setting of the household). If the 'clothing' of 3:12–14 reflects the interpersonal and relational impact of one's inward renewal upon others in the body of Christ, the relationships of 3:18 – 4:1 are where 'the rubber meets the road', so to speak. This is where the reality of one's faith is seen. It is a sad fact that many are outwardly pious before people that do not know them very well, but those that live with them know all too well whether or not the character of Christ is evident in the renewing of the new self. The application of these master–slave relationships to modern employer–employee relationships needs to take into account the vast differences in freedom, opportunity and employment laws that

many modern contexts have. Modern employment laws generally offer employees and employers more immediate recourse for unfair treatment and opportunities for a change of circumstances than was the case for first-century slaves, but even this varies considerably across the world. Human trafficking and slavery affect many today, as do abusive employers. Paul's advice to 'gain your freedom' if you can (1 Cor. 7:21b) would apply in these instances and those who have the means and ability should help those in this predicament. Still, the overarching emphasis in this context on sincerely serving the Lord (first) in whatever setting one is in, together with seeking to do what is right and fair, with an eye on our final inheritance and reward from the Lord, can apply to any believer, whether they oversee a large corporation or stack shelves in a warehouse. It is motivating and encouraging to think that one's everyday work is able to reflect the character of our heavenly Lord and so bring honour to him in the ordinary.

### *v. Prayerful presentation of Christ to those outside the community (4:2–6)*

*Context*

These verses wrap up the section that began in 3:1 on what it means to live a Christ-centred life. They also conclude the main body of the letter; beginning in 4:7 Paul turns to refer to specific individuals known to the Colossian Christian community in his conclusion to the whole letter. These verses complement the preceding exhortations from 3:1. In this preceding section Paul focuses on how the Christian community in Colossae is to relate to one another (e.g. 3:9, 13, 16), including those within their household, as they live for the Lord (3:17 – 4:1). These verses, however, focus on how the Colossians (and Paul) are to relate to those outside the Christian community.

There are many links to the opening of the letter, signalling a 'frame' that surrounds the letter. Paul opened the letter with his own prayer of thanksgiving and his prayer requests for the Colossians. Now he concludes the letter with an exhortation for them to pray and a request that they pray for him. Central to his own prayer for them in 1:9–10 was that they might be filled with 'wisdom' so as to 'walk' worthy of the Lord. So here Paul urges them, in one of his final two imperatives of the body of the letter, to 'walk in wisdom' (4:5). In the opening verses of the letter Paul referred to their reception of the gospel and to the worldwide proclamation of the gospel, so here Paul requests prayer for the continued proclamation of the gospel (picking up on 1:22–23, 25–27) and urges the Colossians to be on the lookout for their own opportunities for gospel conversations.

*Comment*
**2.** Paul focuses particularly on a request for prayer in the following verses, but he introduces his request with the general exhortation *devote yourselves to prayer*. The word for *devote* is used with reference to prayer elsewhere in the New Testament (Acts 1:14; 2:42; 6:4; Rom. 12:12); the Greek form of the imperative emphasizes continuing activity (cf. NKJV, ESV; 'keep persevering in prayer', MLB:BV; 'persist in the practice of prayer', Harris, *Colossians*, p. 166). Paul then fills out the way in which this persistence in prayer is to be carried out, by *being watchful and thankful*.[129] What does Paul mean by *being watchful*? The idea is that of being vigilant, on the alert (NRSV, CSB, NASB; BDAG, p. 208). But alert for what? The assumption is that there is a danger to watch out for. Although some see this as a call to be vigilant in the period of eschatological 'watching' for Christ's return, in the context of this letter Paul has highlighted the danger of false teachers distracting believers from Christ and the sufficiency of his work for believers (cf. 2:4, 8, 16–17).[130] Prayer, therefore, is an important reminder of our own weakness and inadequacy and of Christ's sufficiency and sovereignty. The accompanying 'watchfulness' is due to our tendency to be taken in by substitutes for Christ, especially the tendency to rely on ourselves and our susceptibility to teaching that encourages us to do so. Like Paul's own prayer at the beginning of the letter,

---

129. Taking the participle 'being thankful' as a participle of manner (as in the NIV) rather than as an imperative (as e.g. CSB). Cf. Campbell, p. 67.
130. For watchfulness with reference to Christ's second coming see e.g. Dunn, p. 262; Moo, pp. 320–321; Pao, p. 291. For watchfulness against false teachers see e.g. Beale, p. 335, who cites Acts 20:29–31.

prayer is also carried out by *being . . . thankful*, or perhaps more specifically, this watchfulness in prayer is to be accompanied 'with thanksgiving' (CSB, ESV, NRSV). The two, prayer and thankfulness, are inseparable in this letter. As we noted above on 3:15, part of the reason for this is the corresponding emphasis on Christ's lordship since the opposite of thankfulness – ingratitude – expresses a dissatisfaction with Christ's rule. Prayer, as an acknowledgement of our own weakness, expresses dependence on Christ, with an eye on distractions from him and with thankfulness for his sufficiency and sovereignty.

**3–4.** The opening words of 4:3, *and pray for us too*, indicate that Paul wants the Colossians' continued prayer for themselves to also include ('at the same time', NRSV, ESV, CSB) prayer for Paul.[131] Our discussion here will be helped if we first lay out the phrases that will be explained below:

pray for us too
    that God may open a door . . . (*hina ho theos . . .*)
        so that we may proclaim the mystery . . .
        (*lalēsai to mystērion . . .*)
    that I may make it known . . . (*hina phanerōsō . . .*)

The first phrase of Paul's request for prayer unpacks the content of what he would like the Colossians to pray for him (*that . . .*).[132] Since Paul is in prison, it is interesting to see what he is most concerned about and it may come as no initial surprise to see that Paul asks for prayer that God would *open a door*. However, it is not the door of the prison that Paul is most interested in at this point but *a door for our message*. It is possible that he is alluding to his own release from

---

131. The opening word of this verse, 'praying' (NASB) is a participle that parallels the preceding participle 'watching' as a further way in which Paul wants the Colossians to 'devote themselves to prayer' (4:2).
132. The plurals 'us' and 'we' may refer to Paul and those currently with him, perhaps specifically his 'fellow prisoners' Aristarchus (4:10) and Epaphras (Phlm. 23). Verse 4, however, suggests that his own role in God's purposes is primarily in mind.

prison (Philemon 22 indicates that this too could be an item for prayer) so that he can continue to proclaim the word. However, the focus here is simply on the message and not on the location of Paul. We know from Philippians 1:12–13 that prison was no impediment to Paul's proclamation of the gospel, and Acts closes with Paul's two-year proclamation of the gospel while in Rome (Acts 28:30–31). The use of the term *door*, therefore, is metaphorical, meaning an opportunity or 'opening' for the message ('word', ESV, CSB).[133]

Paul then states that the reason or purpose for this opening is *so that we may proclaim the mystery of Christ*. Paul's prayer for an opening, therefore, must mean that he's praying for an opportunity so that there is effective proclamation that finds a receptive audience such that the gospel bears fruit among those who hear it (cf. 1:6; 2 Thess. 3:1). Since the gospel is a *message*, it is something that must inherently be communicated or 'spoken' (cf. CSB, LSB). Paul summarizes the message he proclaims as *the mystery of Christ*, meaning that the mystery is Christ himself (see comments on 1:27 and 2:2).[134] The use of the summary term 'mystery' is a reminder that the message too is from God. Contrary to the false teachers, Paul's message is not one of human origin and of this world (cf. 2:8, 20–22). The message that Paul proclaims, therefore, is *the mystery of Christ* in the sense that it is God's revelation of his saving purposes for sinners at enmity with him and under his wrath. God's saving purposes are embodied in Jesus and accomplished in his death and resurrection for sinners.

This message is the reason Paul is *in chains*. This is the first indication of Paul's actual situation that he is in as he writes. Earlier in the letter we have only had general references to his suffering (1:24) or to his struggles (1:29; 2:1). Now we know that he is bound up somewhere ('bound', LSB), most likely meaning that he is imprisoned (NRSV, ESV), due to his proclamation of the gospel (see also 4:18). As we noted in the introduction, the most likely location and setting for this imprisonment seems to be Rome during the two years noted at the end of Acts. The final chapters of Acts describe

---

133. Cf. 2 Cor. 2:12; Acts 14:27.

134. The genitive 'of Christ' is epexegetical in that it further defines the word 'mystery'; Harris, p. 168.

the 'binding' of Paul and his transfer from Jerusalem to Rome.[135] Paul repeatedly says in Acts that he is in such a predicament because of his hope in the resurrection of the dead, that is, his proclamation of the risen Lord Jesus.[136] Even the imprisonment of the apostle Paul, however, is no cause for despair about the progress of the gospel. For Paul it is a further reminder of our dependence on God and a consequent spur to pray.

In 4:4 Paul adds more to the content that he asks the Colossians to pray. He has already asked 'that God may open a door' (*hina ho theos* . . .). Paul then followed that up with a purpose statement, 'so that we may proclaim the mystery' (*lalēsai to mystērion* . . .). Now Paul requests that the Colossians include in their prayers a prayer *that I may proclaim it clearly as I should* (*hina phanerōsō* . . .).[137] The 'it' that Paul refers to here is 'the mystery'. There is a fascinating link back to Paul's first explanation of the 'mystery' in 1:26. The NIV's *proclaim clearly* translates the verb 'to reveal/make known' (*phaneroō*). This same verb was used in 1:26. In 1:26 Paul said that the mystery is 'now revealed', meaning that although it was hidden for ages and generations, God had now made his saving plan known in Christ. Paul's use of the same verb here with reference to the 'mystery' seems to be a deliberate allusion back to his discussion of the mystery in 1:26. Paul is saying more here than just that he would like to make the gospel clear or easy to understand. Rather, Paul says that the 'mystery' (God's saving plan in Christ) is being revealed in his proclamation of that mystery. Or, to put this another way, God reveals his long hidden mystery as Paul reveals it/makes it known. Thus 'that I may reveal it' or 'that I may make it known' might better show this link to 1:26 (cf. NET, CSB, NRSV). God is the one who has revealed his saving plan, and Paul's preaching is what God is continuing to use to reveal it. The final phrase, *as I should*, refers to Paul's commission, obligation and God-given role in salvation-history as the one through whom the plan to include

---

135. The same word for 'bound' (*deomai*) is used along the way in Acts 21:11, 13, 33; 22:29; 24:27.
136. E.g. Acts 26:5–8, 16–23.
137. The CSB takes this as a purpose clause ('so that'). Cf. Harris, pp. 168–169.

Gentiles together with Jews into the one body in Christ was made known.[138] Paul's request for prayer, therefore, highlights his understanding that all of this is dependent on God's gracious work

**5.** As Paul turns to give concluding instructions to the Colossians, the final two imperatives of the body of the letter, like the preceding exhortations to pray, also focus on those outside the faith. Paul has already used the metaphor of 'walking' in the letter to refer to how people 'go about', 'conduct' or 'live' their lives. Notably, this verb to 'walk' was the first imperative in the letter in 2:6, pointing to the significance of 2:6 for Paul's overall aims in writing to the Colossians. This is the verb that Paul uses again here in the first of two final imperatives of this section as he exhorts the Colossians to 'walk in wisdom towards outsiders' (ESV; *be wise in the way you act toward outsiders*, NIV). What does it mean to 'walk in wisdom'? Paul's meaning is clarified when we look back to his previous command to 'walk' in 2:6. There Paul exhorted the Colossians to live their lives 'in him', that is, in Christ. In the verses immediately preceding 2:6 Paul identified Christ as the 'mystery of God' (2:2). Then Christ is described as the one 'in whom are hidden all the treasures of wisdom and knowledge' (2:3). Thus, in 2:6, to 'live your lives' ('walk') 'in him' is to depend upon Christ as the one who has all the treasures of wisdom and knowledge. Now Paul uses the walking metaphor again but instead exhorts the Colossians to 'walk in wisdom'. Thus it seems likely that this means, in the context of Colossians and with deliberate links back to 2:3, 6, something like: 'continue to go about your lives with the knowledge of God's saving purposes in Christ for you and for the world as that which guides you on your way'. This of course runs counter to the false teachings in this letter since they only have 'an appearance of wisdom' (2:23). Since this is to be done specifically in this context *towards outsiders* (i.e. those outside the faith and therefore likely to be outside the Christian community; cf. NLT), it probably has the idea of living in such a way with others that is guided by the

---

138. E.g. 'so that I may make this known in the way I am obliged to tell it', MLB:BV. Cf. Acts 22:14–15; Rom. 1:14; Eph. 3:2–9; Col. 1:26–27.

sufficiency of Christ and the gospel, reflecting Christ's character and pointing to him.[139] Remembering that the Christian community in Colossae was a small minority in the wider culture is helpful at this point. Paul wants them to focus on Christ as the centre of their lives, and yet also to be wise in the way that is expressed.[140]

The reference to making *the most of every opportunity* further explains the manner which characterizes the everyday conduct of believers (their 'walk').[141] The word translated as 'make the most of' (*exagorazō*) is often used in commercial contexts for 'buying back' something.[142] Since the object is 'time' (ESV, CSB) the idea is to 'gain' time in the sense of 'taking advantage of all the possibilities at hand' (R. Dabelstein, *EDNT*, II, p. 1). To 'gain time' here is to look for more and more appropriate ways to reflect and show Christ in one's life among those who don't know him. The use of the verb in Daniel 2:8 (LXX) with reference to time in the context of God giving 'wisdom' to Daniel (2:20, 21, 23) and revealing the 'mystery' to him (2:19, 30) may also suggest a link between the 'time' and the 'mystery' referred to in the immediately preceding verses (4:3–4, which allude back to 1:26–27).[143] The 'time', therefore, that the Colossians are to make the most of may refer to this time in which the mystery is 'now made known' (1:26).

**6.** The final command of the body of the letter is only in this verse by implication since there is no imperative 'let . . . be' in the Greek text. Nevertheless, an implied verb here indicates that this is closely linked to the preceding focus on living the Christian life

---

139. The same construction (*tous exō*), referring to those 'outside' the Christian community, is used by Paul in 1 Cor. 5:12–13; and 1 Thess. 4:12. The Colossians too were once in this predicament (Col. 1:21).
140. Cf. McKnight, *Colossians*, p. 377.
141. Thus taking the participle 'making the most of' as a participle of manner; Campbell, p. 69.
142. BDAG, p. 343.
143. See Beale, p. 344. Though Moo, p. 328 correctly notes that, unlike Colossians, the idea in Daniel is more like 'stall for time'.

in such a way that opportunities for pointing to Christ's sufficiency are looked for. The reference to speech also looks back to Paul's prayer request in 4:3–4 and suggests that speech was also in view in 4:5. The term Paul uses here for *conversation* – 'word' (*logos*) – was just used in 4:3 for the gospel message. Thus *your conversation* is probably still referring to gospel speech with those outside the Christian community, although it obviously applies to all speech. In 3:17 Paul says that 'whatever' we do, whether in 'word or deed' is to be done in the name of the Lord Jesus. Here Paul specifies that such speech be characterized by two qualities: *always full of grace* and *seasoned with salt*. The reference to *grace* recalls references to grace earlier in the letter. Paul's opening prayer for the Colossians thanked God for their understanding of the gospel, the 'word of truth', summarized as 'God's grace' (1:6). The Colossians in turn are exhorted to let the message about Christ dwell among them richly, in part by singing with gratitude for God's grace to them (3:16). The meaning here probably relates to 'gracious' speech (cf. ESV, CSB) in the sense of winsome, attractive, agreeable speech in general (BDAG, p. 1079). However, in the context of what Paul says about grace in the letter, it is likely to also specifically include speech shaped and governed by an awareness of God's grace in the gospel. Such speech, therefore, would be characterized by the descriptions of the new self in 3:12–17. Speech that is *seasoned with salt* may be another way of referring to winsome, attractive speech (perhaps 'convincing', A. Sand, *EDNT*, I, p. 57). The additional feature of salt-seasoned speech, however, may be that such speech helps to provide a preserving influence in a world characterized by the vices of 3:5–9.

The goal of having such speech, says Paul, is *so that you may know how to answer everyone*. Once again Paul's concern to orient the Colossian believers to those outside the Christian community is evident here, in particular with regard to their witness in speech. The reference to the Colossians' ability to *answer* indicates that he expects the Christian community to be engaged with the polytheists in the city to such an extent that they provoke questions. Their lives have changed from what they once were (1:21; 3:7): why is that? How did that happen? They seem to have a hope beyond the trials of this life that seems to sustain them (1:5, 23): how did they get that? They seem to be gracious and forgiving of one another (3:13): why do they respond in that way? Yet they also seem convinced of the truthfulness of what they believe (1:5; 2:2): what is that message and why is it true for everyone all over the world and not just them (1:6)? They don't seem to fear unusual events in creation or spiritual forces (1:16; 2:15): why not? Such questions could arise if the Colossians are not distracted from the assurance of the gospel to the false teaching based on human initiative rather than on Christ. Paul's focus is not so much on the answers they could give, since such answers can be seen throughout the letter. Paul's focus here is on 'the way' in which they answer: *how to answer* in the sense of the 'fitting manner'.[144] The reference to *everyone* is not so much everyone in general but more specifically to 'each one' (NKJV) or 'each person' (ESV, CSB). Thus Paul's hope is that believers would have enough grace and thoughtfulness, shaped by the gospel, to provide 'perceptive answers ... suited to the varying needs of individuals'.[145] All need to hear about the message of Christ. One, however, may need a rationale for the awfulness of sin, another the magnitude of God's grace, still another some details about who Jesus is. There may be differing starting points and differing emphases as the universally applicable gospel is applied with wisdom and grace to each one.

*Theology*
When we compare Paul's opening references to prayer in 1:3–7 to these verses, we get a glimpse into the way Paul's theology of salvation integrates divine and human involvement. In 1:3–4 Paul thanks God for the Colossians' faith, indicating that God is the source of their faith (they are God's 'chosen people', 3:12). Yet the Colossians were involved since they heard and understood the message and they learned this message through another human instrument, Epaphras, who brought that message to them (1:6–7). In 4:2–6 Paul refers to his own role in proclaiming the gospel, yet even this cannot take place without prayer since God must provide

---

144. Harris, p. 171.
145. Ibid.

an effective opportunity, an open door for the message to go through. Similarly, in 1:6 Paul describes the worldwide spread of the gospel as the work of the gospel itself bearing fruit and growing. In 1:23, however, he attributes this worldwide spread of the gospel to the proclamation of the gospel, and in 4:2–6 Paul expects the Colossians to be thoughtful, wise, 'on the look out', thinking not only about what to say but how they say it, and thinking about answers to questions that others have. Paul clearly has a distinction in mind between the believing Christian community and 'outsiders' (4:5), yet he also clearly understands that it is possible to transfer from alienation to reconciliation and that this is due to God's gracious initiative. Thus in these verses Paul's request for prayer to proclaim Christ indicates that his view of God's sovereignty in salvation extends to the means by which he saves, through human instruments who pray and who talk and who think about how they walk, and are by God's grace used by him in the lives of others.

# 4. CONCLUDING GREETINGS AND INSTRUCTIONS (4:7–18)

*Context*

Paul concludes the letter with a series of final greetings and instructions. The details about names and instructions, with descriptions like 'fellow prisoner' and promises about further information coming from visitors, in addition to Paul's final signature (and the reappearance of 'I, Paul' from 1:23) have implications for matters of authorship and place (see the Introduction). The details indicate Pauline authorship: a genuine Pauline disciple is unlikely to create such a fabrication, and a forger of such details wouldn't have got away with it. We will note the similarities with Philemon in the exegesis below and in the introduction to Philemon.

The section has a clear structure. First, there is information about the visit of Tychicus and Onesimus (4:7–9) with a threefold repetition of the detail that they will bring news of Paul's circumstances. Then there is a series of greetings from co-workers (4:10–14) with an even balance of greetings from three Jewish believers and three Gentile believers. Then there are instructions about reciprocal greetings between the believers at Colossae and Laodicea (4:15–17) with three references to Laodicea. Paul then concludes with his own personal greeting, framing the letter with grace (4:18).

*Comment*

**7–8.** As Paul turns to his final greetings and instructions in the letter we learn why we have so few details about the actual circumstances of his own situation apart from general references to his suffering (1:24) and struggle (1:29–2:1) and that he is bound in chains (4:3). The reason is because he is sending Tychicus (and Onesimus, 4:9) to them and he *will tell you all the news about me*. Indeed, Paul states three times in 4:7–9 that additional verbal information will be given to the Colossians about his own circumstances. Since Paul has not met them personally there will be much about him and his travels that they would like to know (1:9). There doesn't appear to be an adversarial relationship between Paul and the Colossians and nor do they appear to need reassurance about his authority (1:1–3; Phlm. 1–3, 22). Paul has, however, just asked them to pray for him (4:3–4) and he does hope to visit Colossae at some stage (Phlm. 22). Thus further information about his circumstances, his safety, the opportunities he's having to proclaim the gospel in answer to their prayers and his hoped-for travel plans would all round out the picture for them.

Tychicus was originally from the province of Asia Minor and was one of those who accompanied Paul on his way to Jerusalem (Acts 20:4). He appears to be one of Paul's reliable messengers as he was later sent to Titus on Crete (Titus 3:12), and to what may have been his home town, Ephesus (from Rome; 2 Tim. 4:12). At the time Paul writes this letter he is planning to send Tychicus to Ephesus (Eph. 6:21, assuming that letter to be a circular letter to places, including Ephesus, around Asia Minor) as well as to Colossae.[1]

Paul's view of Tychicus comes through in the three descriptive phrases he uses for him: He is *a dear brother, a faithful minister and fellow*

---

[1] If Colossians and Ephesians are written at the same time and carried by Tychicus (cf. Eph. 6:21–22) it seems unlikely that Paul is imprisoned in Ephesus. See the discussion in the Introduction on 'Where is Paul when he writes to the Colossians (and Philemon)'.

*servant in the Lord*. The expression *dear brother* uses the word *agapētos* ('beloved') that is also used for Epaphras (1:7, with 'servant'), Onesimus in the next verse (4:9, with 'brother' as here) and Luke (4:14, used without modifier). This description will become especially significant in Philemon where Philemon is described as 'beloved' and Onesimus is likewise described as a 'beloved brother' (see comments on Philemon vv. 1, 16). We have already noted the significance of Paul's use of 'brother' in Colossians 1:1–2. The term reappears again in the letter here and in 4:15 as a description of the believers in Laodicea as 'brothers and sisters'. This too will become a significant term in the letter to Philemon (esp. vv. 7, 16, 20). Although all believers are loved by God (3:12) and are to love one another (3:14), Paul can also speak of a more particular, special love, such as that between husbands and wives (3:19). In these references to fellow workers as 'beloved' or 'dearly loved' (CSB) 'brothers' Paul evidences deep personal affection that comes from working with like-minded, gospel-focused believers such that the relationship is like that of a loving, supportive and reliable family sibling relationship.[2]

Tychicus is also a *faithful minister and fellow servant in the Lord*. Paul similarly describes Epaphras as a *faithful minister* (1:7), and Paul describes himself, using the same word translated here for 'minister', as a 'servant' (*diakonos*) of the gospel (1:23) and of the church (1:25). Thus the idea here, of course, is not that Tychicus is a 'minister' in the modern, narrow sense of the word that refers to someone responsible for a congregation, or that he is a 'deacon' in some official sense. Instead, Tychicus is a servant in the sense that he seeks to serve others, the Colossians in this case, rather than himself. As a 'faithful' servant he is someone who can be relied upon to remain true to the gospel in his concern for the Colossian believers (see 1:7). The final description, *fellow servant* (*syndoulos*) also connects Tychicus to Epaphras (1:7).[3] The use of this term for

---

2. Thus, as has been implied above, 'beloved' probably means loved by God as well as Paul and fellow 'brothers and sisters' in God's family.
3. This word is used by Paul only in 1:7 and 4:7. Elsewhere in the New Testament it is used only in Matt. 18:28, 29, 31, 33; 24:49; Rev. 6:11; 19:10; 22:9.

just Epaphras and Tychicus perhaps highlights their similar role between Paul and the Colossians: Epaphras has brought news of the Colossians to Paul (1:7), and Tychicus will bring news of Paul to the Colossians.[4] The term here is actually 'fellow slave' (NET, LSB), indicating that Tychicus, Epaphras and Paul belong to a common Master, Christ (cf. 4:12). More broadly though, although in this letter the renewal of the new self comes to all without distinction between slave or free (3:11), and although masters are told they have a Master in heaven (4:1), there is also the reality that all believers have Christ as their Master and therefore are united together as 'fellow slaves' of Christ. Such a definition then is not meant to remove the significance of other more intimate descriptions of a believer's relationship with God as loved and chosen in Christ (3:12). It points to the lordship of Christ and his exclusive rule for the believer. In this sense, the final modifier, *in the Lord*, most likely modifies all three descriptions as a way of saying that Tychicus is all of these because he is a believer, one who belongs to the Lord Jesus through faith (1:4).[5]

In 4:7 Paul says that Tychicus will tell them 'all the news about' Paul. In 4:8 Paul essentially repeats that Tychicus is specifically sent *for the express purpose that you may know about our circumstances*. There is not much difference here except for the emphatic note that he is sent 'for this very purpose' (NRSV, ESV, CSB), and that he will also bring news of those with Paul ('our'). However, there is an additional benefit for the Colossians. Tychicus has also been sent *that he may encourage your hearts*. Undoubtedly this will arise from news about Paul, but as an additional note here it is likely that this encouragement will be focused on the application of gospel truths to their lives, seeking to spur them on in the sufficiency of the Lord Jesus, the assurance of the gospel, and the unity they have in love (see 2:2 where the same verb is found). All of these descriptions of Tychicus show Paul's confidence in him; he comes as a representative of and with the backing of Paul.

---

4. Pao, p. 310.
5. Campbell, p. 70.

**9.** Tychicus will be sent along with Onesimus. This statement provides one of the most direct connections with the letter to Philemon (in addition to Epaphras) where Onesimus is named in Philemon 10 (the only two places he is mentioned in the New Testament). Here we learn that, like Epaphras and Tychicus (see 1:7; esp. 4:7), he is a 'beloved brother' (*dear brother*, NIV). Furthermore, again like Epaphras and Tychicus, he is *faithful* (see 1:7; esp. 4:7). Also like Epaphras (4:12), he is *one of you*, meaning not that he is a believer, though that is true as well, but that he is from Colossae originally. In the letter to Philemon we learn that he was a slave there, of Philemon's (something we only deduce from Philemon 11, 16), but that he had left Philemon and Colossae, had met Paul and became a believer (Phlm. 10–11, 15–16). Paul now sends him back to Philemon. And it is in this light that the significance of these terms in Colossians, 'beloved' and 'brother', will become very significant in Philemon, since the whole message of Philemon is about 'love' for Onesimus who is coming back as a 'beloved brother' (see comments on Philemon 7, 16, 20).

Interestingly 'faithful' modifies 'brother' and not 'servant' (as for Tychicus and Epaphras), nor is Onesimus called a 'fellow slave' (as Tychicus and Epaphras are, metaphorically). Perhaps Paul did not want this designation to be misunderstood in Onesimus' case, with Onesimus serving as a perfect example of God's renewal making no distinction between 'slave or free' (Col. 3:11; cf. 1 Cor. 7:22). *Faithful*, since it is paired with *brother*, may focus on the genuineness of Onesimus' conversion (see comments on 1:2). The main point is Onesimus' status as one of God's dearly loved family members. We are told that both of them will have news to pass on to the Colossians. The preceding two verses may give more prominence to Tychicus who is named first and whose task is described in more detail. Nevertheless it is interesting, in light of the letter to Philemon, that Onesimus too is sent by Paul and commissioned to inform the Colossian church of information from Paul that the Colossians need to know (*they will tell you*).[6] The specific information

---

6. The verb (*gnōrizō*) is actually 'make known' (BDAG, p. 203). The same verb is used in 4:7. A cognate verb (*ginōskō*), 'know', is used in 4:8.

will be about *everything that is happening here*. Perhaps some of the details will include how Onesimus became Paul's 'son' while Paul was in chains (Phlm. 9–10). We await further clues as to who was with Paul at this time if we would like to try and work out where 'here' is. Included in this information is probably some update on Paul's possible release (Phlm. 22), as well as God-given gospel opportunities that Paul is making the most of even while he is in chains (cf. 4:5).

**10.** As Paul turns from giving instructions about those being sent by him to the Colossians, to passing on greetings to the Colossians from those with Paul we encounter more direct links with the letter to Philemon with five of the six names here reappearing there. The first is Aristarchus. All we are told about him here is that he is a *fellow prisoner* with Paul (and with Epaphras, Phlm. 23), indicating that he too is 'in chains' (4:3).[7] From Acts we learn that: Aristarchus was originally from Thessalonica in the province of Macedonia (Acts 19:29; 20:4; 27:2); he was with Paul during the riot in Ephesus (19:29);[8] he accompanied Paul and others (including Tychicus) to Jerusalem (20:4); and was with Paul (and Luke) on the boat to Rome (27:2). Thus, since we know Paul was in prison in Rome at the end of the book of Acts, Aristarchus' presence with Paul on the voyage to Rome is one of the indicators that Paul was in Rome when he wrote this letter.

Mark is also mentioned along with Aristarchus in Philemon 24 as being with Paul at this time and sending greetings. There are a number of references to a John Mark in Acts and it is likely that this companion of Paul is the same Mark (cf. Acts 12:12, 25; 13:5–13). Since Mark left Paul and Barnabas in Perge and returned to Jerusalem, when Barnabas wanted Mark to accompany them again

---

7. Though some take 'fellow prisoner' metaphorically, the references to prison/chains in 4:3, 18; Phlm. 10, 13 suggest a more literal meaning here and Phlm. 23. Cf. Acts 27:1–2.

8. This was at the end of the two to three years Paul was in Ephesus and thus probably at a time during which Epaphras may have been commissioned to bring the gospel to Colossae (see comments on Col. 1:7).

from Syrian Antioch, Mark was the occasion for a sharp dispute that resulted in Paul and Barnabas parting ways with Mark who then accompanied (his cousin) Barnabas to Cyprus (Acts 15:36–39), Barnabas' home (4:36). In 1 Peter 5:13 Mark is with Peter in Rome and sends greetings to the churches in the area of Colossae (1 Pet. 1:1). In Paul's last letter he states that Mark (interestingly, like Onesimus, cf. Phlm. 11) is 'useful' in ministry (2 Tim. 4:11; *euchrēstos*).[9] What is interesting here (and Phlm. 24; 2 Tim. 4:11), however, is that Paul and Mark are together again. It is possible that this too is an indicator that Paul is in Rome (if 1 Pet. 5:13 is a clue then Mark is in Rome). The close association between Peter and Mark evident from Peter's description of him as 'my son' (1 Pet. 5:13) lends support to the tradition from the early church of Peter's influence (and preaching) behind Mark's Gospel.

There are a number of additional details concerning Mark: he is *the cousin of Barnabas*, they *have received instructions about him*, and, in the event that he visits them they are to *welcome him*. These additional details could be interpreted to mean that the Colossians may have heard negative reports about Mark, perhaps about the dispute mentioned in Acts 15:36–39. Or, perhaps more likely, these additional instructions merely indicate that Mark is less known to the Colossians than some of the others. Certainly the note that he is the cousin of Barnabas is more likely to be an identifier linking him with his better known cousin and companion of Paul rather than an indicator that they held some suspicion towards him. The *instructions about him* they received, therefore, could refer to information that Tychicus and Onesimus will pass on to them along with other details about Paul (4:7–9), or that others unknown have already given them instructions, perhaps to provide Mark with hospitality, should he visit.[10]

**11.** The third person to pass on greetings here is *Jesus, who is called Justus*. Although Jesus was a common name among Jews (the Greek

---

9. On Barnabas see Acts 4:36; 9:27; 11:22–24. On this dispute see Thompson, 'Unity', pp. 523–542.
10. The aorist tense of 'received' (4:10) may parallel the aorist tense of 'sent' (4:8).

name *Iēsous* renders the Hebrew name *Yehoshua*, Joshua), and although Justus as an additional Roman surname is given to two others in the New Testament (cf. Acts 1:23; Acts 18:7), this appears to be the only reference to this particular 'Jesus Justus' in the New Testament. What is more complicated is the interpretation of Paul's next statements. The first phrase in the Greek text, 'of the circumcision' (ESV; cf. CSB, NASB) is correctly translated in the NIV as referring to *Jews* ('Jewish converts', NET; cf. e.g. Acts 10:45; 11:2) rather than a party such as the Pharisees or those who more emphatically emphasized the law (cf. e.g. Gal. 2:12) since Paul would surely have qualified this if the latter were in view given what he has said about spiritual circumcision and the shadows of Old Testament regulations earlier in the letter (cf. 2:11–12, 16–17).

What does Paul say about Jewish believers here and who does he refer to? The complex Greek sentence is literally, '. . . Justus, the ones of the circumcision [i.e. Jewish believers], these only are my co-workers for the kingdom of God'. Harris succinctly summarizes the main options.[11] Does this mean that these three (Aristarchus, Mark and Jesus Justus) were Paul's only co-workers at this time, or Paul's only Jewish co-workers at this time?[12] The difficulty increases when the following verses are also taken into account. Does this mean that the following people who are named (including Luke) are not co-workers, or not Jewish co-workers? It is unlikely that he means the following are not co-workers at all, especially since Demas and Luke are called such in Philemon 24. It is equally unlikely that he means that he never had any other Jewish co-workers since he names others elsewhere (e.g. Rom. 16:3, 21). Thus Paul seems to be saying that these three men are his only Jewish co-workers currently with him (in Rome), perhaps with the range of other Jewish converts in view.

That they are *co-workers* means that they work together *for the kingdom of God* (cf. 1 Cor. 3:9). They are working with Paul to proclaim the gospel (1:13–14). Perhaps they joined Paul in doing this during his two years of proclaiming 'the kingdom of God' in Rome

---

11. Harris, p. 178.

12. A third option is less likely, that Paul only has Jewish co-workers.

(Acts 28:30–31). In the broader framework of the book of Acts, to be working together for the kingdom of God will include helping with evangelism and establishing a local church with elders who care for God's people (Acts 14:21–23). Paul's main point here, however, is to praise these co-workers as those who *have proved a comfort* to him. Aristarchus as a fellow prisoner, and all three as partners in gospel ministry, have shown themselves in the ups and downs of ministry with relationships coming and going to be a source of genuine trustworthy encouragement. It is possible that such a commendation may include a subtle warning about other Jewish converts or the influences of such in Colossae, but it is more likely in this context to be a simple expression of gratitude and praise on Paul's part for encouragement that is sometimes hard to find, even in Christian ministry.

**12.** As Paul turns from passing on the greetings from his Jewish co-workers to the next group who send the Colossians greetings, he refers again to Epaphras. As we noted at 1:7, Epaphras, also currently a 'fellow prisoner' with Paul (Phlm. 23), was likely commissioned by Paul to bring the gospel to Colossae ('on our behalf', 1:7). The following descriptions of Epaphras, together with 1:7, highlight his faithfulness to Christ and his genuine concern for the Colossians. As he was the one who brought the gospel to the Colossians, they should know how much he stands in contrast to the false teachers who, far from having their best interests in view, seek to deceive (2:4), take captive (2:8), judge (2:16) and condemn (2:18) the Colossians. In 1:7 and here, Paul describes Epaphras, like Tychicus in 4:7, as a 'slave of Christ' (NET, LSB) which, in light of 3:11 and 3:22–4:1 (all have a 'Master/Lord'), means that Epaphras belongs to the Lord Jesus, recognizing Christ's lordship in his ministry with Paul and for the Colossians.

Like Onesimus (4:9), Epaphras is also *one of you* in the sense that he was from Colossae. What is especially noted about Epaphras is his constant concern for the Colossians expressed in continued prayer for them and the content of that prayer in the context of this letter. First, he *is always wrestling in prayer for you*. Paul uses the same verb translated as 'wrestling' elsewhere in Colossians only at 1:29, where he says how he 'strenuously contends' or 'struggles' in his labour for the Colossians to reach the judgment complete in Christ.

The verb can be used for fighting or engaging in an athletic contest and points to the great love and intense concern Epaphras has for those who have come to faith through his gospel ministry in Colossae. That he is *always wrestling* further adds to the picture of his concern for them. They haven't been forgotten just because he is now with Paul, and nor is his recollection of them merely a passing occasional thought. They weigh heavily on his mind.

Second, what it is that concerns him can be seen from the summary description of the content of his prayers. He is always praying that they *may stand firm in all the will of God, mature and fully assured*. In this we again see how closely aligned Epaphras is with Paul's own goals for the Colossians. Paul's own constant prayer for the Colossians is that God would fill them with a knowledge of his will, that is, that they would know and therefore live out lives in accordance with God's revealed purposes as expressed in the gospel (see 1:9). Paul's concern for the Colossians is also that they would have an assurance or 'complete understanding' of the truthfulness of the gospel of Christ so as not to be distracted from it and so they would continue to depend on Christ, reaching the judgment complete in him (see 1:23, 29; 2:2, 6–7). This too is Epaphras' concern. It is likely that the descriptions *mature and fully assured* further define what the goal of 'standing firm' means. The combination of the adjective *teleios* (used only here and 1:28, in the context of the above-mentioned use of the verb for 'struggle'), 'mature' (NRSV, ESV, NIV), 'complete' (LSB), together with the perfect participle *plērophoreō*, 'fully assured' (most English translations), emphasizes the firm and unshakable conviction of the truthfulness of the gospel of Christ and the complete confidence in the purposes of God that Epaphras would love the Colossians to have. *The will of God*, similar to Paul's prayer in 1:9–10, refers to God's revealed will in Scripture and the gospel concerning his saving purposes, that in light of Christ and the teaching of his apostles, guides the believer to live a life pleasing to the Lord, with 'wisdom and understanding'.

**13.** The opening word 'for' (NRSV, ESV) indicates that this verse provides support to Paul's preceding statement about Epaphras' prayer for the Colossians. The NIV's *vouch for him* may sound weaker than it needs to be. Paul says that he 'testifies' (NRSV, CSB) or 'bears witness' (RSV, ESV), providing his own solid testimony to what he has just said in 4:12 as an additional supporting statement. The meaning of this should not, therefore, be abstracted from what Paul has just said. Paul's supporting assurance then is that Epaphras *is working hard for you*. The words, 'working hard' (*echei polun ponon*), could mean that 'he has much toil/pain for you'. The word *ponos* is used elsewhere in the New Testament only in Revelation 16:10, 11; 21:4 where it means 'pain/distress'. In the Greek Old Testament it can be used for toil or intense labour that produces pain.[13] In this context 'working hard' looks back to the preceding reference to his 'always wrestling' (NIV) or 'always labouring fervently' (NKJV) and partly reaffirms the effort Epaphras exerts in his constant prayers for them, but mainly emphasizes Epaphras' 'deep concern' (NASB, LSB) that he has for them.[14]

The reference to *Laodicea and Hierapolis* highlights Epaphras' special concern for the believers in this general area, likely because when he brought the gospel to Colossae, he probably also ministered in the nearby larger towns of Laodicea and Hierapolis located north-west of Colossae in the Lycus valley (see the Introduction). Since Hierapolis is only mentioned here in the New Testament we do not have any other information about how the gospel arrived there, but this verse suggests that Epaphras is the most likely candidate. Hierapolis was the home of Papias who was a disciple of John the apostle and knew Polycarp (who was also a disciple of John). There is a tomb in the ruins of Hierapolis that is reportedly that of Philip the apostle, which may confirm early church tradition that he was martyred there. Although Paul has already mentioned Laodicea in 2:1, this is the first of three references to Colossae's more famous neighbour in 4:13, 15, 16. The similarity to 2:1 and Paul's own 'contending' or 'struggling' for the Colossians and those at Laodicea highlights again the close alignment between Paul and Epaphras in gospel ministry goals and passion.[15]

---

13. L&N 24.77; BDAG, p. 852; MM, p. 528.
14. Cf. Beale, pp. 359, 364–365.
15. Cf. Rev. 3:14–22.

**14.** A final set of greetings to the Colossians comes from *our dear friend Luke, the doctor, and Demas*. Luke and Demas are also named, along with Mark, Aristarchus and Epaphras, in Philemon 23–24, reminding us again of the direct connections between the two letters. The only other explicit reference to Luke in the New Testament is in 2 Timothy 4:11 where we read, at the end of Paul's life, the touching and deeply moving words from Paul that 'only Luke is with me'. According to Colossians 4:11 (see above), Luke is one of Paul's Gentile co-workers, though this need not exclude Luke coming from a 'God-fearer' background with an extensive knowledge of the Greek Old Testament. Luke is of course more widely known for his enormous contribution to the New Testament in writing Luke's Gospel and Acts, making him the largest contributor per page (and by word count) to the New Testament.[16] From the explicit references to his name here, and in Philemon 24 and 2 Timothy 4:11, we know that Luke is a 'dearly loved' (CSB; like Epaphras, Tychicus and Onesimus, cf. 1:7; 4:7, 9) companion of Paul who was with him while Paul was in chains here (in Rome) and also with him at the end of his life in chains (again in Rome). As we noted in the Introduction, this reference to Luke is another indication that Paul could be in Rome at this time since Acts 27:1–2 places Luke, Aristarchus and Paul together in the journey to Rome where Paul is held for two years (Acts 28:30–31; and the 'we passages' in Acts indicate that Luke remains in Philippi during Paul's travel to Ephesus).

This is the only reference to a physician in the New Testament, apart from references to Jesus in the Gospels. On the one hand this passing reference provides insight into the validity of this profession even though Christians believed in prayer and in God's sovereignty. On the other hand this also provides us with a small glimpse into the identity of Paul's companion. There is no evidence of any unique 'medical vocabulary' in Luke's writings, but it is also true that Luke especially describes Jesus' compassion in his unique miracle accounts of the raising of a widow of Nain's son (Luke 7:11–17), the healing of a woman with a spirit of infirmity (13:10–17), the healing

---

16. Luke's name is found in the earliest manuscripts of the third Gospel.

of a man with dropsy (14:1–6) and the healing of ten lepers (17:11–19). Having a physician nearby in the ancient world may account for Paul's description of him as a *dear friend* or 'dearly loved', but in light of the other uses of this designation it is more likely to be attributed to Luke because of his faithful partnership in gospel ministry.

Although Demas is also one of those mentioned in Philemon 24, nothing more is said about him in these two references and the only other reference to him in the New Testament is in 2 Timothy 4:10, the verse before Paul's touching reference to Luke. Sadly, there Paul writes that Demas, 'because he loved this world, has deserted me and has gone to Thessalonica'. This description is evidence of the reality that, like Jesus' parable of the sower, not all who hear the word and respond initially prove to have genuine persevering faith (cf. Col. 1:23).

**15–16.** Paul now shifts from passing on individual greetings to the Colossians from those with him to asking the Colossians to pass on his own *greetings to the brothers and sisters at Laodicea, and to Nympha and the church in her house.* Noteworthy here is the description of believers at Laodicea in family terms as siblings in the family of God. Not just Timothy, Tychicus, Onesimus and Philemon are 'brothers', all believers at Colossae and Laodicea are 'brothers and sisters' in God's family (1:1; 4:7, 9; and see 1:2; Phlm. 1, 7, 16, 20).[17] Furthermore, the exchange of greetings and letters between the believers at Colossae and Laodicea accentuates the unity of God's people, something that Paul has highlighted throughout this letter (1:2, 6, 18, 22; 3:11, etc). Nympha, like Mark's mother, Mary in Jerusalem (Acts 12:12), Priscilla and Aquila in Ephesus and Rome (1 Cor. 16:19; Rom. 16:3–5), Titius Justus in Corinth (Acts 18:7), and Philemon in Colossae (Phlm. 2), had a room *in her house* that believers could use to meet together. Although the word *church* (*ekklēsia*, 'assembly', 'congregation') is used in 1:18, 24 with a broader reference to all of Christ's people, the word is used twice in these two verses to refer to a local gathering of believers in Laodicea, as it is in Philemon 2 to refer to a local gathering of

---

17. As we noted in 4:9, familial language is key in Paul's letter to Philemon.

believers in Colossae. In this sense, the local gathering is an expression of the wider people of God who belong to Christ. The additional reference to the church in Nympha's house following the greetings to the believers in Laodicea in general suggests that this is one gathering among others in Laodicea.[18] Paul's reference to her and his greeting to her specifically as well as to the church in her house emphasizes her hospitality and the important role hospitality had for the existence of the early church when there were, of course, no separate church buildings to meet in.

Continuing in his instructions concerning the believers at Laodicea, Paul wants not only his greetings passed on to them, he wants his letter to the Colossians passed on to them as well. We're given a glimpse into first-century church life. They meet in someone's home, and they listened to teaching that was read to them. Indeed, the word for 'read' is used three times in just this verse. Just as Moses was read aloud in the synagogue (Acts 15:21), so Paul expects his letters to be read aloud to the gathered people of God (cf. also 2 Cor. 1:13; Eph. 3:4; 1 Thess. 5:27).[19] Paul thinks that what he has written to the Colossians about the gospel and the sufficiency of Christ has significance for believers beyond Colossae even if the specifics of the false teaching are not found elsewhere. The close proximity of Laodicea, however, may mean that they too were susceptible to these same false teachers (cf. Rev. 3:14–22).[20]

Paul adds that he also wants the Colossians to *read the letter from Laodicea*. This is the only reference in the New Testament to this letter. The shift in the Greek text from 'in the church of the Laodiceans' (*en tē laodikeōn*; referring to them as 'Laodiceans'), to 'the letter from Laodicea' (*tēn ek laodikeias*; referring to the location

---

18. There is a possibility that the name could be accented to refer to a male name and therefore a variant in some mss. refers to the church in 'his house' (NKJV). The reading 'her house', however has better manuscript support.
19. Pao, p. 320.
20. The wider applicability of what Paul says in Colossians, evident in this verse, may even be one reason why more specific details of the false teachers are not given in Colossians.

of 'Laodicea'), indicates that the phrase 'from Laodicea' likely means that it is not written by the Laodiceans, but that it is 'coming from Laodicea' (NASB, LSB). Thus this letter was probably also written by Paul. Since the letter to the Ephesians was most likely a circular letter that included Ephesus as well as surrounding locations (there is debate about whether or not Eph. 1:1 includes the reference to Ephesus), it is possible that the letter to the Ephesians is the one that is 'coming from Laodicea'. Perhaps Tychicus was bringing it (cf. Eph. 6:21; Col. 4:7)?[21] In the early church lists of Paul's letters, Marcion's list refers to a letter to the Laodiceans which many take as a reference to Ephesians. These hints suggest then that the letter to the Ephesians may be in view here. We do not have much else to go on, however, so it is also possible that this is referring to a letter that we do not have in the New Testament (perhaps like Paul's earlier letter mentioned in 1 Cor. 5:9 or his 'tearful letter' noted in 2 Cor. 2:3–4). Either way, these instructions highlight the wider applicability of Paul's letters about Christ's supremacy, the significance and apostolic authority of Paul's letters, and the unity of God's people. And, God has preserved all we need to know in the letters we have in the New Testament.

**17.** The final name is Archippus, which also forms a link with the letter to Philemon since in Philemon 1–2 Paul addresses Philemon, Apphia and Archippus, where Archippus is also called 'our fellow soldier'. Although there is no way to be sure, the following instruction that Paul gives here, together with his reference to Archippus in Philemon 2, indicates that Archippus had some responsibility among the Colossian believers. Even so, Paul does not address Archippus directly but instead instructs the Colossian congregation to tell Archippus: *See to it that you complete the ministry you have received in the Lord*. The exhortation to 'see to it' could also be translated 'pay attention' (CSB) or 'take heed' (LSB) and implies that for some reason Archippus has been neglectful of his task. The use of the word 'ministry' elsewhere in the New Testament may indicate that the 'ministry' he received could be a reference to the

---

21. See the extensive discussion in Lightfoot, pp. 37, 242, 272–298, esp. pp. 272–279.

task of evangelism (e.g. Acts 20:24; 21:19; 2 Tim. 4:5), or to any spiritual gift that is used to serve others in the body (e.g. 1 Cor. 12:5; Eph. 4:12). It is impossible to know for sure without further information. Paul's instruction to the congregation here, however, could be an encouragement to them to get behind and support Archippus in his gospel ministry. The similar wording to Paul's own 'ministry/service' (*diakonos*) that he was to 'fulfil' (*plēroō*; 1:25) may also serve to place Archippus alongside Paul in gospel partnership.[22]

**18.** Finally, Paul takes up the pen (perhaps from Timothy, Col. 1:1) and adds a final greeting in his own handwriting. This is something Paul does elsewhere in the New Testament (1 Cor. 16:21; 2 Thess. 3:17; cf. Gal. 6:11; but Philemon 19 has a different emphasis) and served to authenticate his letters. Paul's name opens and concludes the letter as does his wish for the Colossians to know God's grace in the gospel as part of their daily lives (1:2, 6). Since the act of remembering is often included in Paul's description of his prayers, many see his request for them to *remember my chains* as a request to pray for him (e.g. Phlm. 4). However, the imperative 'remember' is used elsewhere in the New Testament in Ephesians 2:11 and Hebrews 13:7, without specific reference to prayer (cf. also 1 Thess. 2:9; 2 Thess. 2:5). Although prayer need not be excluded from this request, it is perhaps a final personal appeal for the Colossians not to depart from the gospel of Christ that Paul preaches, and for which he is 'in chains' (4:3; 1:24; cf. Phlm. 10, 13). It is this gospel of the supremacy and sufficiency of Christ in contrast to a human-oriented false teaching that drives Paul's concern for the Colossians in the midst of suffering and that has been the framework throughout the letter. So a final reference to God's grace, although common to Paul's letters, is a fitting conclusion to frame this letter (cf. 1:1–2).

*Theology*
Even in the customary greetings at the end of the letter, Paul includes pointers to the renewal of believers in their everyday lives which he has been highlighting since 3:12. The interpersonal and

---

22. Pao, p. 322.

relational evidence of the 'new self', expressed in love, was described in 3:12–17, elaborated upon with reference to the household in 3:18 – 4:1, demonstrated in prayer in 4:2–6 and now displayed in the concrete realities of specific individuals. This passage is rich not only in the names of individuals but in the descriptions Paul gives of many of them: 'beloved brother' (Tychicus, Onesimus), 'beloved' (Luke), 'faithful . . . brother' (Onesimus), 'faithful servant' (Tychicus), 'fellow slave' (Tychicus), 'slave of Christ' (Epaphras), 'fellow prisoner' (Aristarchus), 'co-worker' (Aristarchus, Mark, Jesus Justus) and 'brothers and sisters' (Laodicean believers). Tychicus will encourage them, Epaphras is wrestling in prayer for them and Aristarchus, Mark and Jesus Justus have been an encouragement to Paul. Christlike love for others is not an abstract ideal only to be talked about in general terms. It is seen in daily interactions with real people. It is evident in these verses that Paul experienced close bonds in gospel partnership, and was not a 'lone ranger' forging ahead by himself in his 'calling'. Such are the close bonds that gospel partnership can bring in God's family, those who together depend upon Christ's sufficiency. The evidence of love in the lives of specific individuals is also the subject of Paul's letter to Philemon, to which we turn next.

# PHILEMON

## INTRODUCTION

Philemon is the shortest and most personal of Paul's letters, written to Philemon (though with others in view, cf. v. 2), about the return of Onesimus (v. 10). In this well-crafted letter we are given an insight into Paul's personal interaction in what appears to be a delicate situation, as well as how the gospel is applied and how love is shown in the context of a first-century Christian master–slave relationship.

As we indicated in the introduction to Colossians, there are a number of links between these two letters (noted below) that point to them being written at the same time to the same location, with Onesimus accompanying the letters (with Tychicus, Col. 4:7–9).[1] Specific links between the letters primarily relate to the names that are included (with different instructions or descriptions):

---

1. Philemon and Apphia are addressed here rather than in the letter to Colossians due to the specifically personal nature of this letter.

Table 3: Names common to Colossians and Philemon

| Name | Colossians | Philemon |
| --- | --- | --- |
| Paul | 1:1, 23; 4:18 ('apostle') | 1, 9, 19 ('prisoner') |
| Timothy | 1:1 ('our brother') | 1 ('our brother') |
| Philemon |  | 1 ('beloved', 'fellow worker') |
| Apphia |  | 2 ('our sister') |
| Epaphras | 1:7 ('beloved fellow slave', 'faithful servant'); 4:12–13 ('slave of Christ') | 23 ('my fellow prisoner') |
| Onesimus | 4:9 ('faithful and beloved brother') | 10 ('my son') 16 ('beloved brother') |
| Aristarchus | 4:10 ('my fellow prisoner'); 4:11 ('fellow worker') | 24 ('fellow worker') |
| Mark | 4:10 ('cousin of Barnabas'); 4:11 ('fellow worker') | 24 ('fellow worker') |
| Jesus Justus | 4:11 ('fellow worker') |  |
| Luke | 4:14 ('beloved physician') | 24 ('fellow worker') |
| Demas | 4:14 | 24 ('fellow worker') |
| Archippus | 4:17 ('received a ministry') | 2 ('fellow soldier') |

Since the introductory matters of authorship, place of writing and destination have been treated in the Introduction to Colossians, they will not be repeated in depth here. Unlike with Colossians, there are generally no objections to the Pauline authorship of Philemon. As with Colossians, Paul's name occurs three times in this short letter. Even though (as in Colossians) Timothy's name is also mentioned in the opening verse, the first person singular 'I' from verse 4 and throughout the letter, as well as the nature of the request, indicate that Paul is the sole or primary author. It is also evident that Paul is 'in chains' (1, 9, 10, 23). As argued in the Introduction, I think the traditional location of a Roman imprisonment is still the best option. In addition to the probable placement of Luke and Aristarchus (and perhaps Mark) in Rome and the lack of any reference to an Ephesian imprisonment elsewhere, the inscription on the tomb of the merchant Flavius Zeuxis in Hierapolis

INTRODUCTION

referring to his seventy-two voyages shows that Rome was not viewed as too far to travel to and there were regular opportunities to make that journey. I will argue in the exegesis below that I don't think verse 13 means that Paul wanted Philemon to send Onesimus back to Paul again (this is sometimes presented as a reason against a Roman provenance). But what is Philemon about and why did Paul write this letter? The answer to this question is not as immediately obvious as one might expect.

## 1. Why was this letter written to Philemon?

As the letter unfolds, it is not until verse 10 that we learn Paul is writing about Onesimus. From Colossians 4:9 we know that, like Epaphras (4:12), Onesimus is from Colossae. In this letter to Philemon we learn that he was a slave of Philemon's, though this is something we only deduce from Philemon 11, 16. It appears as though he had left Philemon and Colossae (15) and was with Paul, having become a believer through Paul (10–11, 15–16). Paul, however, was sending him back to Philemon (12). The traditional explanation for these movements is that Onesimus was a runaway slave (a *fugitivus*), and that Paul was sending him back, now as a believer, asking Philemon to extend grace and receive him back as a fellow believer.[2] Paul also offers to pay any debt that Onesimus has incurred in order to ensure a full welcome for Onesimus. However, we are not told how Onesimus came to meet Paul as a runaway slave. The only hint we get is that it was an outworking of God's providence (15). The exegesis in the commentary will show that I think the details of the text are best explained by this traditional 'runaway' scenario. Two other main options, however, have arisen in recent discussions as to why Onesimus came into contact with Paul.[3]

First, some suggest that Philemon (and the church) sent Onesimus to Paul to assist him in some way. This seems unlikely in view of

---

2. E.g. Harris, pp. 207–209; Nordling, pp. 3–19.
3. See Brogdon, *Philemon*, pp. 1–32; Young, *Brother*, pp. 23–60;
   Pao, pp. 343–347, for recent summaries of the following options.

the following descriptions of Onesimus before he met Paul: he was 'separated' from Philemon in God's providence (15), he was formerly 'useless' in some sense and not a believer (10–11, 16) and he somehow 'wronged' Philemon previously (18; Paul is at pains to assure Philemon that he will cover the expense from this 'wrong', 18–19). Second, some suggest that Onesimus was seeking Paul's help as a mediator (as an *amicus domini*, 'friend of the master') in a prior dispute between Philemon and Onesimus. This also seems unlikely in view of the following: Paul speaks not of Onesimus' initiative in returning but of 'sending' Onesimus back, even deliberating over the appropriateness of keeping Onesimus with him (12–14); Paul only mentions Onesimus' 'wrong' (18–19) and makes no reference to any wrong on Philemon's part but speaks only of his faith and love (4–5); and the central point of Onesimus' new status as a believer is the determining factor in Paul's argumentation rather than anything else (10–11, 16). We are not told why Onesimus ran away, but Paul's description of Philemon's love (4–7) does not suggest that Philemon had mistreated Onesimus.

Thus, although we are not told how Onesimus came into contact with Paul, it is nevertheless this new development in Onesimus' life – his coming to be a 'brother in the Lord' (15–16) through Paul (10) – that has given rise to his return and is the basis of Paul's reasoning (and thus his repentance is assumed). The central appeal of this letter then is that Philemon 'welcome' him back as he would welcome Paul (17) and so have him back as a 'beloved brother' (15–16). In this regard, instructions to prepare for Paul's future visit (22) reinforce the central appeal to welcome Onesimus as he would welcome Paul. Thus I do not see the main aim of the letter as a request for Paul to have Onesimus sent back to help Paul in ministry (since Paul is planning to come there). Nor do I see the main aim of the letter as a request for Onesimus' manumission, although that could be a valid implication of the 'something more' of verse 21.[4]

---

4. Philemon is not praised because he is a master (he is not even called a master), nor is Onesimus described negatively because he is a slave, and this context of a small gathering in the setting of an entire first-century

## INTRODUCTION

The introductions to each section in the commentary will draw attention to specific words that link and strengthen Paul's appeal across the letter. These key terms include the following:

Table 4: Key repeated terms in Philemon

| Term | Verses |
| --- | --- |
| 'prisoner/chains' | 1, 9, 10, 13, 23 |
| 'grace' | 3, 22 (ESV), 25 |
| 'beloved' | 1, 16 |
| 'love' | 5, 7, 9, |
| 'brother/sister' | 1, 2, 7, 16, 20 |
| 'refresh' | 7, 20 |
| 'heart' | 7, 12, 20 |
| 'share/sharer' (*koinōnia/koinōnos*) | 6, 17 |

The links listed above can help us see the main message of Philemon. As we have noted above, the central appeal of the letter is found in verse 17 where Paul first makes his request known that he wants Philemon to welcome Onesimus back as a full and genuine believer and brother in the Lord. The basis for this appeal is the whole message of Philemon. That is, the letter to Philemon revolves around love. This comes through in the way that Paul first calls Philemon 'beloved' and then anticipates Onesimus' return as 'beloved'. It is seen in the way Paul praises Philemon for his love for all of God's people in anticipation of his description of Onesimus as now one of God's people too. It comes through in the way that Paul speaks of Philemon's love as having 'refreshed' the 'heart' of God's people before he describes Onesimus as his very 'heart' and then urges Philemon to 'refresh' his 'heart' in welcoming Onesimus. This is why Paul says in verse 9 that he is going to appeal on the basis of love. It is Philemon's love for Paul

---

imperial system is not an endorsement of slavery. Both are described with equal affection as believers. Indeed what is said here and in Colossians undermines the whole system (on Paul and first-century slavery see comments on Col. 3:18 – 4:1; and Pao, pp. 348–351).

and for God's people as an expression of the faith that he shares with God's people that he wants to see demonstrated towards Onesimus, his new 'beloved brother'.

Given the explicit links to the church in Colossae in the names noted above, it is also worth reflecting on how the letter to the Colossians might help interpret the letter to Philemon. More broadly, Colossians has highlighted the peace with God that believers have, that because of Christ enemies are reconciled with God, receive gracious forgiveness, and no longer face the wrath of God (1:14, 20, 21–22; 2:13; 3:6; cf. Philemon 3, 22, 25). More specifically, as noted in our discussion of Colossians 3:18 – 4:1, there are proportionately longer instructions for slaves than there are for any of the others referred to there. In light of this accompanying letter to Philemon it is possible that those instructions are a corresponding reminder that Paul is not advocating irresponsible behaviour by slaves to their 'masters according to the flesh' (3:22; cf. Philemon 16). However, the emphasis in the letter to Philemon on the new and equal status that master and slave have together in Christ is also emphasized in Colossians. There is no distinction in the renewal of the 'new self' that each has in Christ (3:11), anyone who does wrong will be repaid (3:25; cf. Philemon 18), and all have a Master in heaven (4:1). Colossians also highlights, therefore, the significant difference that conversion makes. There is a 'once ... but now' change that has taken place (1:21–22; 3:7–8; cf. Philemon 11), and this is characteristic of all who belong to Christ. Thus, all who belong to Christ are part of the one family of God and are 'brothers and sisters' together (1:1–2; 3:12–17; 4:15–16). The 'clothing' that believers wear is described as behaviour that reflects their new likeness to Christ in their relationships with one another, with all of the items in 3:12–13 orienting around how believers relate to one another. The item of clothing that gives meaning to them all is love (3:14). Thus love is also important in Paul's letter to the Colossians, in a section that focuses on how believers are to display the 'new self' in their relationships with one another. Paul's letter to Philemon, therefore, may be seen as a concrete instance of how love guides the virtues of Colossians 3:12–13, as an outworking of the unity in Christ in 3:11, and the difference that Christ makes in everyday and complex relationships in the family of God.

# ANALYSIS [1]

A. Greeting (1–3)
B. Thanksgiving and prayer: Philemon's faith and love (4–7)
C. Paul's general request for Onesimus (8–16)
D. Paul's specific request for Onesimus (17–22)
E. Final greetings (23–25)

---

[1]. The 'general' 'specific' terminology is from Harris, p. 209.

# COMMENTARY

## A. Greeting (1–3)

*Context*

As was customary in ancient letters the opening of Philemon identifies the author, recipients and greetings from the author. In Paul's letters these features are all transformed by the gospel and anticipate themes to come in the rest of the letter. In this brief letter, terms and themes that anticipate more to come include:

Paul as a prisoner (v. 1 and then 9, 10, 13): hinting at the sacrifices involved in belonging to Christ and signalling an appeal that will be made on the basis of sacrificial love;
believers as 'brothers' and 'sisters' in the one family of God (1, 2, 3 and then 7, 16, 20): Philemon is addressed as 'brother' and is encouraged to receive Onesimus as a 'beloved brother';
believers as 'beloved' (1 and then 5, 7, 16): the love Philemon has experienced and shown is to be extended to Onesimus as equally 'beloved';
the hospitality of Philemon (2 and then 17, 22): the use of his home for believers is to be continued with Onesimus and Paul.

The letter is also framed with references to 'grace' (3, 22, 25), highlighting the framework of the gospel of grace that is to shape believers' lives and Philemon's response to Paul's appeal. The letter is also framed with plural references to other believers. Others are named in verse 2 and the greetings of grace and peace are addressed to 'you' (plural) from 'our' Father in verse 3. Plurals return again at the conclusion of the letter in verse 22 ('your' prayers) and verse 25 ('your' spirit). This frame serves to remind readers of the impact that this personal interaction between Paul and Philemon and the treatment of Onesimus has on the rest of the congregation at Colossae. It is a letter after all about what it means to love fellow believers.

*Comment*

1. Paul's opening description of himself as *a prisoner of Christ Jesus*, although used elsewhere (Eph. 3:1; 4:1; 2 Tim. 1:8), is unlike any other opening of Paul's letters. It reflects the same situation mentioned in Colossians that he is 'in chains' (Col. 4:3, 18), but is significant for striking a different note from the opening to Colossians, and every other letter of Paul's. Rather than refer to his apostleship, or his relationship to the Lord Jesus as his slave, Paul refers to himself here as a *prisoner of Christ Jesus*.[1] In Colossians 4:3 Paul says that he is in chains for his proclamation of the gospel of Christ and that is likely the meaning here too. It is because of his ministry to proclaim Christ, the one to whom he belongs, that he is a prisoner 'of Christ Jesus'. Furthermore, even though he is confined with chains, Paul understands Christ to be the one who ultimately determines his life, since he is the one who rules over all thrones, powers, rulers and authorities (Col. 1:16; 2:15). This unique designation at the start of this letter may highlight more specifically the kinds of sacrifices one might make in the course of submitting to the rule of the Lord Jesus as a foreshadowing of Paul's expectation that Philemon would also prize the lordship of Jesus above his earthly obligations. The repetition of the phrase in verse 9 together with Paul's two equivalent references to being in 'chains' later in this short letter (10, 13) not only confirm that this is a reference to a real rather than a metaphorical prison, they also remind Philemon of the theme that this striking opening note sounds.[2]

---

1. 'Apostle' (Rom., 1 and 2 Cor., Gal., Eph., Col., 1 and 2 Tim., Titus 'slave' and 'apostle'); 'slave' (Phil.); no additional description (1 and 2 Thess.).
2. In verses 1 and 9 the word is *desmios* ('prisoner'), in 10, 13 the word is *desmos* ('chains' as in Col. 4:18). In Col. 4:3 Paul uses the verb *deomai* ('to bind').

Regarding *Timothy our brother*, see comments on Colossians 1:1. As with Colossians, Paul's name reoccurs later in this letter without reference to Timothy (cf. 9, 19), indicating that the reference to Timothy primarily highlights his presence with Paul at the time and that Paul is the author of the letter. The first person singular verbs from verse 4 ('I thank God', etc) confirm that Paul is the author of the letter.[3] In the context of this letter, however, the designation of Timothy as 'our brother' points to the familial equality that all believers have as members of one family because they belong to Christ and have come to know God as their Father. In the next verse Apphia is called 'our sister'. In Colossians Paul describes all the believers at Colossae as brothers and sisters in Christ (1:2), Tychicus is called a dear brother (4:7), as is Onesimus (4:9), as well as the believers across the valley at Laodicea (4:15). This designation is another significant indicator of where Paul is heading in this letter, since Philemon is called a 'brother' in verse 7 as well as in the climactic appeal in verse 20. As Paul says in Colossians 4:9, Onesimus too is a brother (in fact he became a 'son' in the faith to Paul, v. 10). It is the significance of this that will be the basis for Paul's hope in verse 16.

The letter is then addressed to three individuals as well as to the church more broadly in verses 1b–2. Since Philemon is addressed first, the singular pronouns that follow (incl. 'your [singular] house', v. 2) in Paul's thanksgiving and prayer (4–7) indicate that he is the main addressee.[4] This is the only place his name occurs in the New Testament so whatever we know about him is gleaned from this letter only. Two initial descriptions from Paul are that he is *our dear friend and fellow worker*. The NIV's *dear friend* translates the word 'beloved' (*agapētos*), the same description Paul gives in his correspondence with these Colossians to Epaphras (Col. 1:7), Tychicus (4:7), Onesimus (4:9) and Luke (4:14). Of these, 'beloved'

---

[3]. It is possible that Timothy is the scribe or amanuensis up until verse 19. Cf. Beale, p. 378.

[4]. It is for these reasons that the unlikely proposal of Knox, *Philemon*, that the primary recipient of the letter is Archippus has not been taken up by commentators. See e.g. Harris, pp. 207–208.

usually modifies a noun such as 'fellow servant' (1:7), 'brother' (4:7, 9) or 'doctor' (4:14), so that Philemon is the only one of whom 'beloved' is used absolutely. Since Onesimus is described as a 'beloved brother' in Colossians 4:9 and again in verse 16 of this letter, this description of Philemon in verse 1 is also a significant indicator of the direction Paul is heading in this letter. 'Beloved' here probably includes being the object of God's love as well as one who is loved by fellow believers, specifically Paul. As the letter progresses, Paul will want Philemon to receive back Onesimus as a 'beloved brother' (see comments on v. 16; using the same word *agapētos* found only in these two places in Philemon) as an expression of his love for God's people (see comments on 'love' in 5, 7, 9). Just as Philemon knows what it is to be loved by his 'brothers and sisters' in Christ, so too, Paul will say, should he extend such love to his new 'beloved brother in the Lord', Onesimus. Thus the importance of 'love' in this letter is sounded early.

The second designation, *fellow worker*, links Philemon with Aristarchus, Mark and Jesus Justus, who are also designated as Paul's (Jewish) 'fellow workers' in Colossians (see Col. 4:10–11), and Demas and Luke who are added to this list of fellow workers in Philemon 24 (with Mark and Aristarchus mentioned again there). The implication is that Philemon has been involved in some form of gospel ministry that sought to proclaim and teach God's saving rule in partnership with Paul's ministry aims and goals to see churches started and strengthened. It means too that he knows the joy of seeing someone respond to the gospel and come to faith in the Lord Jesus, something that he will soon learn about Onesimus. It probably also means that he is at least a well-known figure in the church, if not one of the leaders. His example, therefore, is something that others in the church will follow and this is also a reason why Paul will seek to encourage Philemon to live out the implications of the gospel in his personal interactions with Onesimus.

**2.** Since the additional addressees, Apphia and Archippus, are added before Paul refers also to *the church that meets in your home*, many commentators have concluded that Apphia is Philemon's wife and Archippus his son. This is possible given that they are addressed together, perhaps as members of this home. However, Paul's emphasis lies elsewhere. The designation that Apphia is *our sister* refers to her membership in God's family as a fellow believer.[5]

The family connections of Archippus are not referred to here either. In the only other place where his name is cited in the New Testament, Archippus was singled out for special mention in Colossians 4:17 where the church (not Archippus directly) was told to exhort him to pay attention to some area of service that the Lord had opened up for him. In Philemon the only description of Archippus is that he is our fellow soldier. This term is used only once elsewhere in the New Testament as one of Paul's descriptions of Epaphroditus in Philippians 2:25. However, soldier and military metaphors are used elsewhere by Paul in Ephesians 6:10–18; 2 Timothy 2:3–4; and 1 Corinthians 9:7. The imagery in Ephesians highlights the spiritual nature of these struggles for all believers as that which is against spiritual forces and is fought with the gospel, Scripture and prayer. The imagery in Philippians 2:25 and 2 Timothy 2:3–4 incorporates this spiritual understanding into gospel ministry more particularly where Paul highlights the hardship and sacrificial dedication to the gospel involved in serving the Lord's people. The inclusion of the term *our fellow soldier* thus highlights Archippus' sacrificial commitment to serving the Lord, but also his partnership along with Paul and the rest of the believers in Colossae in the hardship and opposition faced by believers.[6]

The reference to Apphia, Archippus and the final reference to *the church that meets in your home* shows that this is more than just a private letter about two individuals. Indeed, 'personal' rather than 'private' is a better description of the letter.[7] The 'your' (singular) likely refers back to Philemon as the first named addressee. Although the following singular pronouns keep the focus of the letter as a request from Paul to Philemon, the recurrence of plural

---

5. Later manuscripts have 'beloved' (NKJV) here instead of 'sister'. However, there is earlier and wider manuscript support for 'sister' here. It is possible that later scribes were influenced by the masculine form of 'beloved' in the preceding verse.
6. I am referring here not just to 'soldier' but to 'our' and 'fellow'.
7. Pao, p. 365.

pronouns in 3, 22 and 25 ensures that the entire Christian community in Colossae is kept in view. The interactions between Philemon and Onesimus are an outworking of the gospel that affects all those in this small Christian community. As we noted regarding Nympha and her house in Colossians 4:15, the implication here is that Philemon has a house with a room (or courtyard) large enough for believers in Colossae to meet in. In the context of this particular letter, this reference to Philemon's house indicates already that he seeks to serve the church in Colossae at least in the way in which he opens up his home, offering generous hospitality to others. It is this kind of hospitality that Paul will come back to again later in the letter, both for Onesimus (12, 17) and also for himself (22).

**3.** Regarding *grace and peace to you*, see the comments on Colossians 1:2. Paul's opening greetings transform typical letter openings into an expression shaped by the reality of the gospel. He wants believers to live out their lives within the framework of God's grace to them and the peace they have with God in Christ. By including both *God our Father and the Lord Jesus Christ* together as the one source from whom grace and peace come, Paul's greeting matches his other letter opening greetings (see Col. 1:2) in which the deity of Christ is assumed. In this context, Paul's reference to God's grace foreshadows the likelihood that Philemon will need to show grace in receiving Onesimus back just as Paul too in one sense hopes to be 'graciously given' back to Philemon (22, ESV). The word 'grace' occurs only one other time in Philemon, in the last verse (25). This frame, like Colossians and all of Paul's letters, places the content of the letter within the setting of the gospel. Likewise, the peace and reconciliation believers have with God anticipates the welcome reception Paul hopes Onesimus will receive that will reflect this peace that believers have with God as their Father and therefore also with each other as brothers and sisters in the one family of God.

*Theology*
As Paul typically does in his letters, this opening anticipates a number of themes that will develop throughout the letter. That God the Father is the source of grace and peace together with the Lord Jesus highlights the equal authority of Jesus with the Father

and is a reminder to Philemon that he too has a master and that all of God's people belong together by grace in the same family as brothers and sisters. Thus each individual believer, without distinction, can be described as a 'brother' or 'sister' in God's family. This is the product of the proclamation of the gospel of Christ and a commitment to the gospel is not without sacrifice and suffering in this world. Thus Paul is a prisoner, Philemon is a fellow worker and Archippus is a fellow soldier. It is a gospel worth proclaiming, for it enables believers to speak of God as 'our Father' and Jesus as 'Lord' and to experience the joy of belonging to his people with terms for one another such as 'beloved' and 'brother and sister'.

## B. Thanksgiving and prayer: Philemon's faith and love (4–7)

*Context*
Paul usually begins his letters with prayer for the recipients and expresses his thanks to God for what God has done in the lives of those he is writing to, and this letter to Philemon is no different. As with his other letters, the features of Paul's prayer and thanksgiving anticipate themes to follow in the rest of the letter, showing that ultimately what Paul hopes to see worked out in the lives of Philemon and Onesimus will be an outworking of God's grace in their lives. In these opening verses Paul particularly focuses on Philemon's faith in the Lord Jesus as something that is evidenced in his love for the Lord's people. In the comments on verse 7 we outline the probable structure of these verses that proceeds in the order of faith and love (5), faith (6), love (7). This anticipates a major focus of the letter on love as the outworking of belonging to Christ by faith: Philemon's love for Paul and for Onesimus. Specific links to the rest of the letter, therefore, include the following (and will be developed in the commentary below):

> Philemon's 'love' for 'all' the Lord's holy people anticipates
>   an appeal that will be made on the basis of 'love' to receive
>   Onesimus as 'beloved' (5, 7 and then 9, 16);
> the 'good thing' that flows from faith for fellow believers in
>   Christ is something that Philemon could do for Onesimus
>   (*agathos* occurs only in 6 and 14);

the faith that Philemon 'shares' in common with other believers means that he also is a 'sharer' with Paul in the gospel (*koinōnia*, 6; *koinōnos*, 17);

Philemon's love is seen in the way he 'refreshes' the 'hearts' of the Lord's holy people, and he will likewise 'refresh' Paul's 'heart' by welcoming Onesimus who is Paul's 'heart' (7 and then 12, 20);

Paul addresses Philemon as 'brother' when he speaks of his love, and again when he asks Philemon to refresh his heart, and he will appeal for Philemon to have Onesimus back as a 'beloved brother' (7 and 16, 20);

Paul 'prays' with thanksgiving because he recognizes God's work in Philemon's life, and will conclude the letter looking ahead to another answer to prayer when in God's grace Paul is able to visit Philemon and Onesimus in Colossae (4 and then 22).

Although not linked by the repetition of specific vocabulary, Paul's opening reference to Philemon's 'faith' as something which he thanks God for may also anticipate his references to conversion later in the letter. Onesimus has also come to faith through Paul's gospel ministry (10). This is something that Philemon should likewise thank God for and is something that Philemon has experienced too since it is apparent that like Onesimus, Philemon also came to faith through Paul's gospel ministry (19). In this carefully crafted letter Paul's opening prayer of thanksgiving looks ahead to the rest of the letter in anticipation of the continued outworking of God's grace in Philemon's life of love for the Lord's people.

*Comment*

**4.** As we noted in our comments on Colossians 1:3, it is Paul's view of God's sovereignty that leads him to *always thank my God* as he remembers believers in his prayers.[8] The pronouns in this verse add

---

8. In the structure of this verse, 'always' probably modifies 'give thanks' and this takes place each time (or 'when', ESV) he 'remembers' Philemon in prayer. See Harris, p. 214.

additional insight. First, although not unique to this letter (cf. Rom. 1:8; 1 Cor. 1:4; Phil. 1:3), and common throughout Scripture (e.g. Pss 91:2; 104:1), Paul's description of God as 'my God' reminds readers that even though the Lord's people are a community of believers and even though the gospel has implications for how that community is to relate to one another (e.g. Col. 3:12–17; and the reference to the church in Philemon 2), still it is individuals that come to Christ recognizing their own personal sin and responsibility for that sin and hence their own personal need for forgiveness. Thus it is a great privilege that by God's grace believers can speak of God, the sovereign Creator of all things and Saviour of his people, as 'my God' due to the relationship each one has with him through Christ. For Paul to thank God as he 'remembers' Philemon in prayer reflects the Old Testament combination of thanksgiving by remembering God's acts for his people.[9] The specific reasons for Paul's thankfulness will be developed in the following verse.

There is also a shift from the plural 'Paul and Timothy' to the singular 'I' and 'my' as well as from the plural addressees of verses 1–2 to *you* (singular). This shift to the singular signals the focus that the rest of the letter will have on Paul's relationship with Philemon.[10]

**5.** The reason Paul 'always thanks God' when he prays with Philemon in mind is *because* he has heard of Philemon's *love for all his holy people and your faith in the Lord Jesus*.[11] The NIV (and CSB, NRSV) reflects the chiastic structure (A-B-B-A) of this verse in the Greek text that can be seen in the following layout:

your love
   your faith
   toward/in the Lord Jesus
for all the saints

---

9. Pao, p. 367.
10. The plural reappears in verses 22 ('restored to you in answer to your prayers'), and 25 ('your spirit').
11. Thus, as with most EVV the participle 'hearing' is understood to be causal ('because I hear').

Since Paul never describes God's people as the object of faith, this translation decision to reflect a chiastic structure is more likely than simply following the word order and making love and faith directed to both the Lord Jesus and God's people (as e.g. ESV, NKJV).[12] This structure highlights both the distinction between love and faith and their respective objects, as well as the inseparability of them. Genuine faith in the Lord Jesus will be seen in a love for his people, and love for his people flows from trust in the Lord Jesus (see comments on Col. 1:4). As with the Colossians, Paul assumes that God is the initiator and cause of Philemon's love and faith and so gives thanks to God for these in Philemon's life even though Philemon is the one who expresses them and they are called *your love* and *your faith*. God's people are all 'holy' (see Col. 1:4) because they all belong to him, and so love for his people is to be love for 'all' of God's people. This strikes a similar note to Colossians: because the gospel highlights the universal sinfulness of humanity and therefore the universal need of grace, God's people are not defined by the 'haves' and 'have nots' of those who may or may not have adhered to other additional achievements. Thus there is a unity among the people of God on the basis of God's saving grace. Philemon's love for 'all' of God's people is emphasized and will be the backdrop to Paul's appeal. Paul returns to Philemon's love in verse 7; love is the basis for Paul's appeal in verse 9, and in verse 16 Paul hopes Onesimus will return as 'beloved'.

**6.** At this point, after giving the reason for his thanksgiving in verse 5, the content of Paul's prayer mentioned in verse 4 is now revealed. The meaning of the verse has been the subject of some dispute, which is reflected in the variety of translations. This may be illustrated in the shift in translation from the NIV84 to the NIV published in 2011 in the opening phrase. Thus 'I pray that you may be active in sharing your faith' has become *I pray that your partnership with us in the faith may be effective*. Two changes highlight the difficulties. First, should *tēs pisteōs sou* be translated 'your faith' (referring to Philemon's faith) or 'the faith' (referring to the Christian faith)? Second, should the Greek word *koinōnia* be translated

---

12. Moo, pp. 387–388; Pao, pp. 368–369.

'sharing' or 'partnership' or perhaps 'fellowship' (NASB), 'participation' (CSB) or even 'generosity' (NLT)?[13]

First, in light of the immediately following pronoun 'your', as well as the preceding reference to Philemon's faith, the best option for 'faith' here is to see it as a continuing reference to Philemon's faith. Second, the term *koinōnia* does not refer to personal evangelism as the word 'sharing' might imply (cf. also ESV). 'Partnership', although possible, may imply something more specific such as common involvement in gospel ministry than is in view here. In view of the preceding reference to Philemon's faith and also the close association between Philemon and all of God's people that Paul emphasizes in this context, this first phrase seems to refer initially to Philemon's faith, that is also a faith that is common to all believers. Thus, 'the faith you share with us' (NET) comes closest to what Paul begins with here. *Faith* in this view therefore is 'common', it is 'shared' (Beale, p. 394). The phrase 'your faith' and the continuing link between faith and love suggests that it is this 'faith' (that he and all believers 'share') that Paul prays would be *effective*.[14]

Paul's prayer is that Philemon's (shared) faith, a faith that he knows all believers have, would become 'effective in deepening your understanding of every good thing we share for the sake of Christ'. The reference to 'every good thing' could refer to the blessings believers have in Christ. That is, that this faith that he knows all believers have would result in a greater appreciation of the common blessings that all believers have. However, the use of the same word for 'good' (*agathos*), which is used elsewhere in Philemon only in verse 14, suggests that this is yet another anticipation of Paul's yet-to-be-made request. In verse 14 Paul refers to the 'good' (*favour*, NIV) that he is hoping Philemon will voluntarily do for Onesimus. If this is an anticipation of the direction Paul is heading, then what he prays for is that Philemon will see that the faith he shares with other believers should result in a deeper

---

13. A cognate of this word is also used in verse 17, the crucial turning point of the letter (*koinōnia*, 6; *koinōnos*, 17).
14. For 'fellowship' as that which is 'effective,' see Moo, pp. 389–394.

grasp of 'the good' that can be shared with others (see comments on v. 14).

The last phrase, *for the sake of Christ*, is also debated. The prepositional phrase *eis Christon* could also be translated 'for Christ', 'through/by Christ', '(leading) to Christ', 'in Christ', or 'with reference to Christ'. Although the last two options are not too dissimilar, the last option helps to show that the phrase *eis Christon* adds a clarification that 'every good thing' is specifically defined with reference to Christ and what it means to belong to him. In summary then, Paul is thankful to God for Philemon's faith and love, and, spelling out what is implied by combining faith with love in this way, he prays that Philemon's faith (a faith that Philemon has in common with all God's people) will be an active faith, a faith that will deepen his grasp of the Christlike good that can be shown to fellow believers in Christ. The implication is that his faith and love, mentioned in verse 5, will continue to be inseparable and demonstrable (and therefore he will welcome his new brother, Onesimus). That this is something Paul prays for reminds us that even the 'good' that we do is an outworking of God's grace at work in our lives (Eph. 2:10; Phil. 1:6).

**7.** Some have suggested that the opening word of verse 7, 'for' (omitted in the NIV), indicates that verse 7 provides another reason for thanksgiving in addition to verse 5, or that it provides a supporting explanation of verse 6. However, in light of the sequence of 'love' and 'faith' in verse 5, followed by a reference to 'faith' in verse 6, it seems more likely that verse 7 completes the sequence with reference to Philemon's 'love'. Thus, 'for' indicates that this verse is going to provide a confirmation of the earlier reference to Philemon's 'love for all the saints' (5) as part of the basis for Paul's thanksgiving ('I have indeed', NRSV). So a complementary way of saying 'I always thank my God as I remember you in my prayers, because I hear about your love for all his holy people . . .' (4–5) is, *your love has given me great joy and encouragement, because you, brother, have refreshed the hearts of the Lord's [holy] people*. The repetition of 'your love' and 'saints' (ESV) confirms the deliberate link to verse 5 (the link is slightly obscured in the omission of the word 'holy' in v. 7 of the NIV). Thus, the progression of thought in verses 5–7 may be structured as follows:

your *love* for all the 'saints', and
your *faith* in the Lord Jesus, is something Paul thanks
   God for
may your *faith* (which you have in common with others)
   be expressed in 'every good thing'
your *love*, in the way you refresh the 'saints', brings Paul joy
   and encouragement

Once again, this description that fills out Paul's thanksgiving anticipates Paul's request that will unfold in the rest of the letter. It is on the basis of the 'encouragement' that Paul has received from Philemon that he will in turn 'encourage' Philemon to continue with more of the same.[15] The words translated 'refresh' (the verb *anapauō*) and 'heart' (plural *splagchna*) appear together again in verse 20 where Paul, having made his appeal for Philemon to welcome Onesimus, concludes by exhorting Philemon to 'refresh' his 'heart' (i.e. just as he refreshes the hearts of the saints). Between these two statements that more or less frame this short letter, Paul also describes Onesimus as his 'very heart' (v. 12; using the same word).

Thus the letter proceeds along the following lines: Paul wants Philemon to continue in his love for the saints; this love is something Paul thanks God for and brings him great joy and encouragement; this love refreshes the hearts of the saints; Paul would like Philemon to welcome Onesimus as a concrete instance of this love; Onesimus is Paul's very 'heart'; thus receiving Onesimus would refresh Paul's 'heart' too. The word used for 'heart' (*splagchna*) is only used eight other times in the New Testament, but it occurs three times in this short letter.[16] It can refer literally to the internal organs of the body (Acts 1:18), but more often in the New Testament it refers metaphorically to the internal 'affections' or 'feelings' of people, hence the translation 'heart' in English versions. Thus, in this context, to 'refresh' the 'heart' is to give fresh strength and

---

15. A cognate verb of the noun 'encouragement' in verse 7 (*paraklēsis*) is used in verses 9, 10 but translated as 'appeal' in most EVV (*parakaleō*).
16. Cf. Luke 1:78; Acts 1:18; 2 Cor. 6:12; 7:15; Phil. 1:8; 2:1; Col. 3:12; 1 John 3:17.

new life or to 'revive' and revitalize the internal and emotional wellbeing of believers. This may also imply that Philemon is someone who is sensitive to and actively looks out for those who are in need of such mercy and care.[17]

One final indicator of the significance of this verse is that Paul also specifically calls Philemon 'brother', placed at the end of the sentence in the Greek text for emphasis. In a further link between this verse and verse 20, Paul calls Philemon 'brother' again there as he urges him to 'refresh Paul's heart'. Significantly the word also occurs only one other time between these references, in verse 16 where Paul exhorts Philemon to receive Onesimus 'no longer as a slave, but better than a slave, as a dear brother . . . in the Lord'. If we move beyond these specific references to Philemon and Onesimus, we see that Timothy is called 'our brother' and Apphia 'our sister' in verses 1–2, and in his letter to these Colossians Paul also calls Timothy (1:1), Tychicus (4:7), and significantly, Onesimus (4:9) 'brothers'. In fact the whole Colossian congregation (1:2) as well as the Laodicean congregation (4:15) are called 'brothers and sisters'. Thus the familial language of believers belonging to the same family of God through Christ also permeates this letter as a framework for Paul's appeal to Philemon as a 'brother' to welcome Onesimus as a 'brother' too. The significance of this will become more apparent in the following verses (esp. v. 10).

*Theology*
Paul's expression of thanks to God here, as in Colossians and in his other letters, is evidence of a theology of God's sovereignty as the one who has brought about a change in people such that they trust in the Lord Jesus and love God's people. Furthermore, because this is God's work of grace, faith and love are inseparable. Although faith in the Lord Jesus is distinct from love for God's people, genuine faith is expressed in love. Because this is God's work, Paul also prays that this would continue to be worked out in continuing 'good' for one another that is consistent with what it means to belong together to Christ. Lastly, since such love is evidence of

---

17. McKnight, *Philemon*, p. 75.

God's work, it brings great encouragement to see this demonstrated in an awareness of the need for mercy and care as well as a concern to give life to, or 'refresh', the hearts of others.

## C. Paul's general request for Onesimus (8–16)

*Context*
There are close links between the preceding verses and this section. Paul transitions from speaking of Philemon's love for all the Lord's people and the way this love is an encouragement to him in the preceding verses, to gradually developing his appeal for Philemon to extend this love specifically to Onesimus, and in turn further encourage Paul. There is some debate about where to end the main body of the letter which we will address in the introduction to verses 17–22. Broadly speaking, this section is characterized by a more general introduction to Paul's appeal to Philemon before he gets to specific requests in verses 17–22.

The details of the situation unfold only gradually in a compact but developing argument: Onesimus is first mentioned in verse 10, we only learn that Onesimus was a slave in verse 16, and Paul makes no specific appeal at all in this section except to say that it will be on the basis of love and concerning Onesimus (9–10). Building on his earlier references to Philemon's love, Paul makes love the overarching framework for the rest of his letter. After stating that he will appeal on the basis of love, Paul names Onesimus for the first time in verse 10 along with the significant detail that Onesimus has become a 'son' of Paul's (in the sense that he came to faith through Paul's gospel ministry). This is significant for Onesimus since he now knows the Lord Jesus, but it is also significant for Paul since their lives have been brought together in Christ. Therefore, this should be significant for Philemon as well.

The verses that follow the first mention of Onesimus in verse 10 are tightly connected with further details related to him (linked in the Greek text with words like 'whom' in 11, 12, 13; see e.g. KJV). In verse 12 Paul reveals that he is sending Onesimus back to Philemon and verses 13–14 further unpack the reasons for doing so, centring on Paul's concern for Philemon's involvement. The final two verses, 15–16, on the one hand complete the thought of verses

10–11 with reference to Onesimus' new status as a believer, and on the other hand form the climax of this part of the letter before Paul transitions to his specific requests in the next section. The central development in verses 8–16 that prepares for verses 17–22 is that Onesimus has become a believer. This now impacts the way that Paul, and more importantly Philemon, will respond to him. Although the details are yet to come, the reality is that they all now belong to the same family with the same status as 'beloved' and as 'brothers'. Paul indicates that Onesimus is coming 'back' (12, 15) to Philemon. What this love will look like when Onesimus arrives, and what happens to past wrongs is what Paul will get to in the next section.

*Comment*

**8.** Paul's opening word *therefore* confirms that what he is going to say will build on what he has just said about the outworking of Philemon's faith in love. Paul first contrasts one way in which he could go about the following interaction with Philemon before he proceeds with his appeal. In the context of the word 'command' (*order*, NIV), Paul's reference to having 'great boldness' (CSB; *be bold*, NIV) means confidence to speak plainly or frankly. Paul says he has much of this 'boldness', enough to 'command' (*order*, NIV) Philemon 'to do what is right' (CSB).[18] Why does Paul think he has this confidence to command Philemon? The reason he gives is that this 'great boldness' is *in Christ*. This prepositional phrase, however, has a notoriously wide range of possible meanings. Paul often uses this phrase to refer to union with Christ in the sense of belonging to Christ. Campbell suggests the idea of 'ground' or 'cause', meaning that it is '*because* of Christ he has boldness to command Philemon to do the right thing'.[19] Still, why does Paul think he can 'command' Philemon because of Christ? The word Paul uses for 'command' is mainly used with reference to one who has authority to give orders. Most interpret this as a reference to the unique authority Paul has

---

18. The same word translated here as 'right' (CSB) is the one used in Col. 3:18 for that which is 'fitting'.
19. Campbell, p. 84.

as an apostle (cf. 1 Cor. 14:37). If this is the case, then 'because of Christ' might mean something like 'because of Christ's commission' or 'because of my service for Christ'. However, as we will see, what Paul is about to ask of Philemon could simply be something that any Christian should do. Although Paul develops his request gradually, as he proceeds it becomes clearer that Onesimus has become a believer and Philemon is to welcome him as such. Thus, although Paul says that he could simply exercise his unique apostolic and Christ-given authority and command Philemon, nevertheless even this command should not be understood independently of what it means to belong to Christ since it will be the outworking of Christian love.[20] Thus, the contrast is not between Paul acting as an apostle with independent authority and Paul acting in some other way. Rather, the contrast is between an instruction that could be given to any Christian as a command but is better carried out from another motivation. To return to our original question: why does Paul think he has this confidence to command Philemon? It is because he is *in Christ*, that is, as a believer in Jesus and as an apostle of Christ is free to tell Philemon to do what is 'right' or 'fitting' for those who belong to Christ.

**9.** Instead of commanding Philemon, Paul sees a more appropriate way of motivating him; in keeping with his opening prayer, Paul would rather 'encourage' Philemon *on the basis of love*.[21] What he means by this will be developed in the following verses, but because this reference to 'love' picks up on what Paul has already said in verses 5–7, it means in the first instance Philemon's love for others.[22] This would seem to include a love for Paul, as an encouragement to him, and also love for Onesimus, as one of God's people and a 'brother' in Christ. At this point, however, Paul

---

20. Note too that Paul does not introduce this letter with reference to his role as an apostle (see on v. 1).
21. As noted above on verse 7, the cognate noun 'encouragement' is used there and the verb 'encourage' is used here and verse 10 (translated as 'appeal' in most EVV).
22. There is a definite article before the word 'love' in the Greek text that is likely anaphoric (pointing back to the previously mentioned love).

focuses on Philemon's view of Paul himself. Paul includes his own name again for emphasis and adds that he is *an old man*.[23] The implication of this is that Paul appeals to Philemon's compassion and respect for Paul as elderly, and perhaps therefore also pointing to Paul's wisdom as one who has lived long enough to see the benefits of particular ways of approaching matters of faith and love (cf. Titus 2:2).[24]

In addition to this, Paul adds that he is *now also a prisoner of Christ Jesus*. This is likely to be a reference again to Paul's actual, rather than metaphorical, location in prison because of his proclamation of the gospel (see comments on v. 1 and Col. 4:3, 18). In adding this reference to his imprisonment, Paul may be reminding Philemon of his commitment to the gospel and the (sacrificial) lengths to which believers may need to go in serving the Lord. Thus, rather than continue to appeal to his apostolic authority, or seek to manipulate Philemon's emotions, with these descriptions of himself Paul appeals to Philemon as someone that Philemon can learn from in matters of sacrifice and love. In the immediate context the initial reason for this reference to his imprisonment will become clear in the next verse.

**10.** Now for the first time Paul mentions Onesimus (the only time he names him in this letter) as the one who he is encouraging Philemon to consider. Paul's appeal is regarding or 'concerning' Onesimus (NET). Even here Paul does not quite state what he is encouraging Philemon to do. The actual appeal does not come until verse 17. First we are given a window into Paul's connection with Onesimus and how this request from Paul has come about, and more importantly we learn about a significant change that has taken place in Onesimus. Indeed, in the Greek text Paul leaves it until after he describes Onesimus before he actually uses Onesimus'

---

23. Some propose the word 'ambassador' instead of 'old'. However, there is no textual variant, and there is no good reason for reading the conjecture *presbeutēs* instead of *presbytēs*, which means 'old'. See McKnight, *Philemon*, pp. 80–81; Pao, p. 386; Moo, p. 405.
24. Cf. Dunn, p. 327; the age range in view here is late fifties to early sixties.

name (at the end of the verse) in order to emphasize first the momentous change that has come about (cf. NET).

Onesimus, says Paul, is *my son* and he *became my son while I was in chains*. If the language of 'brother' and 'sister' evoked the bond of close familial ties by being in the family of God, the language of 'son' and 'father' emphasizes this close bond even more.[25] Thus the reason for Paul's reference in verse 9 to his imprisonment for Christ becomes clearer. Yes, he is in prison, but while there he has continued to serve Christ and proclaim the gospel to 'all who came to see him' (Acts 28:30). Somehow, and Paul does not say how, Onesimus came into contact with Paul during Paul's time in prison. During this time Onesimus heard Paul explain the gospel to him, and he responded with repentance and faith in Christ. In this sense Onesimus became a child of God through Paul. Although not stated explicitly, the implication may be that in order to respond in this way with repentance and faith, Onesimus has acknowledged his own sin and recognized his need of forgiveness. By God's grace Onesimus is not who he once was, he has experienced a 'new birth' (John 3:3) and is a 'new creation' (2 Cor. 5:17).[26] In his letter to the Colossian believers Paul says that this would entail a 'new self' that is 'renewed' with a renewal that does not distinguish between slave or free, because Christ is all and is in all (Col. 3:10–11).

Paul's focus is on the closeness of this new relationship in Christ. Elsewhere, Paul speaks lovingly of Timothy as his 'son' in the faith (1 Cor. 4:17; 1 Tim. 1:18; 2 Tim. 2:1; cf. also 1 Cor. 4:15; Gal. 4:19). The closeness of this bond between Paul and Onesimus will become clearer in the following verses as will the implication of this new development in Onesimus' life for Philemon's relationship with Onesimus. It is for this reason, that although the specific appeal does not become clear until verse 17, this verse is a significant development in Paul's build-up to that request. It is likely that Philemon did not know that Onesimus had become a believer

---

25. The NRSV, ESV's 'whose father I became' translates *egennēsa*. 'Spiritual father' (NET) helps to clarify that Paul does not refer to becoming a literal father while in prison.

26. Moo, p. 408.

while Onesimus was 'separated' (15) from him.[27] Thus this first mention of Onesimus' name is accompanied with a crucial piece of information that makes all the difference for the subsequent development of Paul's appeal since it makes all the difference in the relationships between these three men.

**11.** As most translations indicate with a note in verse 10, Paul appears to continue his appeal with a play on the meaning of Onesimus' name as 'useful'. Paul describes Onesimus with a familiar 'once ... but now' framework that he often uses to contrast the 'before' and 'after' lives of those who become Christians. This is the framework in which Paul describes the reality of the Colossians' lives. Now that they have been raised with Christ and have died with Christ, having 'put off' the old self, they must 'put on' the 'new self' in keeping with their new life in Christ.[28] In this context, Paul employs this framework to encourage Philemon to now relate to Onesimus accordingly, and differently. In what sense, then, was Onesimus *formerly ... useless* to Philemon? The answer comes in the corresponding contrast. How has Onesimus *become useful both to* Philemon and to Paul? The answer to this must relate to what Paul has previously said. Onesimus has become a believer through Paul and has therefore joined Paul's side in gospel service. This was not something that Onesimus would have participated in before, in this specific sense he was not 'useful' (thus, this is not a criticism of Philemon). However, now he has participated with Paul in this and will, likewise, be of assistance to Philemon in gospel ministry in Colossae, and in this sense, be 'useful' (cf. 2 Tim. 4:11). Might there be some other reason for Onesimus being 'useless' before to Philemon? Paul gets to some specifics in verses 18–19 that indicate that a further barrier lies in the background.

**12.** At this point Paul again reveals the close bond he has with Onesimus as part of his appeal to Philemon. He is counting on Philemon's love for Paul. If Onesimus is so close to Paul and if Paul is wanting him to be welcomed, he should indeed be

---

27. McKnight, *Philemon*, p. 82.
28. See esp. Col. 1:21–22; 3:7–8, 9–10 for the 'once ... but now' contrast (cf. Rom. 6:21–22).

welcomed. Paul specifies that he *is sending* Onesimus *back to Philemon*. The implication is that Onesimus, as 'one of' the Colossians (Col. 4:9), must have come, in some sense, from Philemon if it is to Philemon that he is being sent back. Another implication is that this presents Philemon with an unavoidable opportunity that he needs to respond to one way or another. It means too, that, as Paul says in Colossians 4:7–9, Onesimus will accompany Tychicus in bringing the letter to the Colossians and the letter to Philemon, along with news about Paul's ministry and imprisonment. Therefore (as with Tychicus), this should not be interpreted to mean that Onesimus is coming unwillingly, just that he is coming with Paul's wholehearted support. Indeed, Onesimus is Paul's *very heart*. Paul uses the word used in verse 7 as referring to internal affections. Thus the appeal on the basis of love is back in view here. Just as Philemon's love for the saints (5) has meant that he has refreshed the 'hearts' of the saints (7), then his love for Paul will refresh Paul's 'heart' (cf. 20) in welcoming one who is Paul's *very heart*.

**13.** The suggestion of verse 11 that Onesimus' 'usefulness' referred to his new participation with Paul in gospel ministry is confirmed here. Indeed Paul wanted *to keep him with me*. The verb Paul uses can have the idea of 'restrain' or 'hold back' and highlights Paul's strong desire to have Onesimus continue alongside him in ministry in spite of having decided to send him back to Philemon. The purpose for holding on to Onesimus is *so that* Onesimus would 'help Paul' or 'serve' (*diakoneō*) while Paul was *in chains for the gospel*. The word 'chains' was used in verse 10 and indicates again that Onesimus' conversion during Paul's imprisonment has resulted in not only another believer but another believer who wants to help Paul in the cause of the gospel. In this broad sense Onesimus has become another gospel worker, serving alongside Paul. The reference to Onesimus 'taking the place' of Philemon in helping or serving Paul indicates again the love that Philemon had for Paul. Onesimus, therefore, has filled a beloved place, one that Philemon would have been only too pleased to have participated in himself if he were able to. In light of the change that Paul has recounted in verses 10–11 it is unlikely that Paul implies that Philemon actually sent Onesimus to Paul to serve in place of Philemon. Rather, each statement highlights the value Paul places on Onesimus and assumes Philemon would likewise see this same value. Some suggest that Paul hints at the possibility that Philemon should send Onesimus back to him to continue in this service. However, since Paul does not expect to be there for too much longer (22), it seems better to see this as simply emphasizing the esteem Paul has for Onesimus (cf. 15). Nevertheless, Paul may also model what it means to live sacrificially, and this may in turn serve as an example for Philemon as Paul gets nearer to his request in verse 17.

**14.** Paul adds that despite his desire to hold on to Onesimus, he *did not want to do anything without [Philemon's] consent*. The shift from the imperfect *would have liked* (13) to the aorist *did not want* (14) does not contrast a past and a present desire of Paul's but rather accentuates the high regard Paul has for both Onesimus and Philemon as he sends Onesimus back to Philemon. The word for 'consent' may not mean 'formal agreement' but 'opinion', 'way of thinking' or even 'input'.[29] In this context, therefore, Paul is assuming that even though he is sending Onesimus back to Philemon (12), Onesimus should not have stayed anyway without Philemon's knowledge and involvement. What Paul 'wills' is ultimately not determinative in Paul's mind for Onesimus, but rather it is what Philemon 'wills'. There is no explicit reference here to any particular obligations for slaves that Paul is having to adhere to.[30] Rather, while these obligations are assumed, Paul's focus throughout is on Philemon's love and the relationship between them all in light of Christ.

Nevertheless, the assumption seems to be that Onesimus needs to return to Philemon. The reason for sending him back is *so that any favour* Philemon would *do would not seem forced but be voluntary*. What then is this 'favour' or better, 'good deed' (NRSV, CSB)? Paul still has not specified exactly what he is hoping for except that it is an encouragement, on the basis of love, regarding Onesimus, who is on his way back to Philemon. The next step in this sequence, yet to be specified, is that Philemon would welcome Onesimus back (17). This, says Paul, is the Christian and loving thing to do (8–9).

---

29. BDAG, pp. 202–203, meaning 2, 3.
30. Old Testament laws such as Deuteronomy 15, 23 are not in view here.

Indeed, it is a 'good thing'. The word *agathos* is the same one Paul used in verse 6 where 'every good thing' was with reference to the outworking of a faith that is in common with other believers. It is likely that Paul's use of the word again deliberately recalls his earlier use in verse 6. This 'good thing', later clarified as welcoming Onesimus back, is precisely the kind of 'good thing' we can share with one another as those who belong to Christ: a restored relationship and a glad welcome into God's family. If Onesimus had stayed with Paul, without any input from Philemon, the implication is that what Philemon would do would have been *forced* and not *voluntary*. The term 'forced' is also translated as 'compulsion' (NASB, RSV, ESV) and 'necessity' (KJV). The implication of this is that even though Paul had welcomed Onesimus into ministry, since Onesimus was a slave (16) there was some need for Philemon himself to 'receive/welcome' Onesimus too. If Paul had decided that Onesimus would stay with him and help him, the assumption is that Philemon had to have approved of this. Without being involved, however, this 'approval' would have been forced upon Philemon. The backdrop to all of this seems to be the potential sticking point raised in verses 18–19.

**15.** Before concluding this general appeal to Philemon and moving to the specifics in verses 17–22, Paul provides one more rationale ('for' omitted in NIV) for sending Onesimus back and his (developing) appeal to Philemon. *Perhaps*, says Paul, there was a reason why Philemon *was separated from you for a little while*, the reason being *that you might have him back forever*. Paul once again refers to Onesimus' conversion (10–11) and alludes to what his request will be: to welcome Onesimus back. There is perhaps a play on words here between Paul's statement that he wanted to 'hold back' (*katechō*, 13) Onesimus, but now Philemon will 'have back' (*apechō*, 15) Onesimus. The additional emphasis is that Philemon will have Onesimus back *forever*, that is, 'eternally' (NET).

Paul encourages Philemon to consider ('perhaps') the events in light of God's providence, suggesting that in spite of whatever the circumstances were for Onesimus' departure from Philemon, this may have been part of God's greater purpose in the lives of both Onesimus and Philemon. The passive voice of the word *echōristhē* ('was separated') is a 'divine passive' in the sense that it was God who was ultimately behind this action. The meaning of the word does not specify how this departure came about. Given that Paul is aiming to convince Philemon of God's good purposes in this event, however, it is unlikely that this was something Philemon initiated or even wanted. Paul's appeal to God's ultimate purposes, therefore, is consistent with the scenario that Onesimus ran away. Paul's main focus though is that in God's providence Onesimus has come under the hearing of the gospel and his life and status has changed for ever. This has eternal consequences for believers since there is a new bond between them, as they are now joined together to the hope the gospel provides for eternity (Col. 1:5, 22–23, 28). This new eternal relationship is what Paul unpacks a little further in the rest of the sentence that continues in the following verse (and confirms that Paul does not mean that Onesimus is now a permanent slave).

**16.** As Paul completes this rationale based on God's purposes in Onesimus' life and the significance of this for Philemon, he once again highlights the new spiritual familial dynamic involved as well as the way in which Paul's own relationship with Philemon contributes to his appeal. For the first time we are given a window into the possible complications involved in this relationship between Onesimus and Philemon. Paul says that Philemon would have Onesimus back (picking up on the verb from v. 15) *no longer as a slave, but better than a slave.* This phrase indicates that the relationship between Philemon and Onesimus is one of master and slave. Therefore, the broader issues surrounding this whole economic system in the Greco-Roman world are the backdrop to this letter. Since we do not have access to all of the details in this case, we are left putting the pieces together from what hints are provided in this brief letter. Although the reasons for the separation are debated, the issue in the letter surrounds how these two men will now relate as Christians. To say *no longer as a slave* might initially appear as though this will mean that Philemon and Onesimus' connection as master and slave has ended with the change that has come to Onesimus in his conversion. However, Paul adds, *but better than a slave*, and all through the letter Paul assumes some kind of continuing relationship between them: Paul is 'sending him back' to Philemon (12); Philemon will 'have him back' (15) and should 'welcome him' (17).[31] If release, perhaps for gospel ministry (13), is in view, it is only in the background as a possibility, perhaps hinted at in verse 21. Thus the change in view relates primarily to how they will now relate as believers. If the earlier relationship was one of believing master and unbelieving slave, the new relationship is one of believing master and believing slave as in Colossians 3:22 – 4:1.

Therefore, 'more than a slave' means that Onesimus is now also a 'beloved brother'. Paul once again picks up on the emphasis throughout this letter on both 'love' and the familial bond of the family of God. Paul introduces this letter with his description of Philemon as 'beloved' (1), and these are the only two places in this letter where the term is used. 'Love' is the main theme of this letter: Philemon's experience of love from believers, his love for believers, his love for Paul, the benefit this love brings to the saints and to Paul, and therefore the basis for Paul's appeal. What Paul says about love in Colossians will also be in view here (Col. 3:14), and Onesimus was described as 'beloved' there too, indeed a 'beloved brother' (Col. 4:9). Thus, as a 'beloved brother', he is a member of God's family along with all believers equally. He is therefore as much a 'brother' in the family as Philemon is a 'brother' in the same family of God (see 7 and 20).

The closeness of their bond is such that Paul says Onesimus is *very dear* to him ('especially so', CSB). But Paul adds that Onesimus is *even dearer* to Philemon ('even more', CSB). Given what Paul has said above about Onesimus becoming his child, it is understandable why Paul would say that Onesimus becoming a 'beloved brother' or fellow believer is especially meaningful to him. But why is this even more so for Philemon? The assumption is that because of their prior relationship, this new development will mean much to Philemon. Close as Paul and Onesimus are, theirs is only a comparatively recent connection. Philemon and Onesimus, as we might say, 'go way back'. 'No longer' means that the 'formerly . . . but

---

31. Harris, p. 231, notes that the use of 'as' points to Philemon's view of Onesimus, whereas a simple 'no longer a slave' would have implied manumission.

now' (10–11) transformation in Onesimus' life by God's grace also transforms Onesimus' relationship with Philemon.

Paul's final phrase seems intended to explain the 'much more' aspect of this new development in their relationship. The NIV's translation, *both as a fellow man and as a brother in the Lord* seeks to explain a more word-for-word rendering of the Greek exemplified in translations such as 'both in the flesh and in the Lord' (NRSV, ESV). It is most likely that 'in the Lord' means something similar to what Paul has already been saying from verse 15. Thus Philemon will have Onesimus back 'for ever', 'better than a slave', 'as a beloved brother', that is, 'in the Lord'.

However, what does 'in the flesh' mean? The Greek phrase *en sarki*, has a notoriously wide-ranging meaning. In Paul's writings it often has a negative connotation with reference to humanity in weakness and prone to reject God (e.g. Rom. 8:8). Sometimes it can refer more obviously to the body or physical flesh (e.g. Phil. 1:22). Neither of those two options are likely here since it is about a relationship between Onesimus and Philemon. The phrase can mean something like 'by birth' (e.g. Eph. 2:11a). So one possibility might be that Onesimus and Philemon were physical brothers and the additional feature of their relationship is that they are now 'spiritual' brothers too. It is possible that this explains the emphasis on familial ties and the family of God throughout this short letter. However, this familial language is always employed in Philemon with reference to the spiritual reality (see on 1–2). Sometimes this phrase can refer to humanity, just being human or living as human beings (e.g. 2 Cor. 10:3). Thus a common interpretation is that Philemon relates to Onesimus as a fellow human being, but even more as one who belongs to the Lord Jesus, hence the NIV's translation *as a fellow man* for the Greek phrase *en sarki*. Another possibility, closely related to this, is that 'in the flesh' refers to life in this world (e.g. 1 Pet. 4:2, 'earthly lives'; perhaps also 2 Cor. 10:3). Before unpacking the significance of this it may help to visually lay out the flow of thought from verse 15.

> so that you might have him back for ever/eternally
>    no longer as a slave
>       but more than a slave

> a beloved brother (especially to me but more so to you)
> both in the flesh and in the Lord

The entire phrase 'beloved brother ... both in the flesh and in the Lord' further explains the new development expressed in the preceding phrase 'more than a slave'. Therefore, in view of the immediate context, it is possible that Paul uses the phrase 'in the flesh' to further explain what 'more than a slave' looks like for life in this world (i.e. not a separate category of 'fellow human' or 'physical brother'). This would fit with the development from verse 15 that began the further explanation in this verse. The new 'eternal' transformation that has taken place in the relationship between Philemon and Onesimus affects their relationship both in this life, or in this world, as well as eternally. Therefore, as noted above, their relationship is now no longer one of merely master and slave but believing master and slave. Paul uses similar language in Colossians. Philemon therefore would be, as Colossians 3:22 puts it, a believing 'master according to the flesh' (*kata sarka*), which is translated in the NIV as a believing 'earthly master'. Yet he also has a 'beloved brother' 'in the Lord' (*kyrios*) because they also both now have 'the Lord' as their master in heaven (Col. 3:23, 24; 4:1). Thus Philemon will have Onesimus back as more than merely a slave, but as a beloved brother, transforming their earthly master–slave relationship (*en sarki*) and bringing them into a common eternal relationship with one Lord (cf. NJB, 'both on the natural plane and in the Lord'; cf. also NET).

### Theology

Having begun by thanking God for Philemon's faith and love, Paul's emphasis on God's work of grace in changing lives is continued in this section. The basis of Paul's developing argument is the difference that the conversion of an individual makes. That person has a new status and a new loving family of brothers and sisters. Paul highlights the close relationship in the gospel that has developed with Onesimus' conversion. He has become so close to Paul that Paul can call him his 'son', his 'very heart' and 'beloved' as a 'brother'. The reality of Philemon's love for the Lord's people is already seen in his love for Paul, and Paul hopes that this love will in turn be expressed towards Onesimus. Furthermore, although Paul does not state the matter definitively, he appears to continue this emphasis on God's work of grace in people's lives by suggesting that God is ultimately behind the details of Onesimus' departure from Philemon (15). This appears to be something of a 'they meant it for evil but God meant it for good' argument much like Genesis 50:20. Just as Paul thanks God for the evidence of faith in believers' lives, so he recognizes God's hand in the varied and mysterious circumstances that brings them to faith.

### D. Paul's specific request for Onesimus (17–22)

*Context*
Having reached the culmination of his general appeal in verses 15–16 with the grand vision of Onesimus' return to Philemon as a 'beloved brother', Paul will now identify his specific request for Philemon. Whereas the previous section had no imperatives, there is a noticeable shift in verse 17 with Paul's first imperative of the letter, and with imperatives to follow in 18, 20 and 22. Having said that Paul is 'sending back' Onesimus (12) and that Philemon, in God's providence, will 'have back' Onesimus as a 'beloved brother', Paul now specifies the main aim of his letter with an imperative for Philemon to 'welcome back' Onesimus (17).

There is debate regarding where this section ends and where Paul's concluding comments begin. Some observe that Paul often concludes his letters with a reference to his own 'hand' (cf. Col. 4:18) and argue that verse 19 should therefore be the point at which Paul's conclusion begins, marking off verses 17–18 as Paul's final appeal.[32] As I will argue below, however, verse 19 is deliberately linked to verse 18 as a supporting assurance and therefore does not begin a new section introducing Paul's concluding plans and greetings.

Many argue that verse 20 is the conclusion to this section, given the clear links between verse 20 and earlier sections in the letter, especially with Paul's request for Philemon to 'refresh' his 'heart' (cf. 7), and the sequence of three imperatives in 17, 18 and 20.

---

32. Weima, *Paul*, pp. 226–227.

In this view, verse 21 is a summary of Paul's hope for Philemon, verse 22 provides Paul's concluding 'travel plans' as he does in other letters, and verses 23–25 wrap up the letter with Paul's greetings. However, I will argue below that verse 22 is also linked to the preceding section. Therefore, verses 17–22 form a complete unit in which Paul outlines his specific requests. Four (not just three) imperatives characterize this section ('welcome', 17; 'charge', 18; 'refresh', 20; 'prepare', 22).[33] More specifically, verse 22 is integral to how Philemon should welcome Onesimus. If Philemon is to welcome Onesimus back 'as he would welcome' Paul (17), then verse 22 provides Philemon with a concrete and specific reference to how he would welcome Paul. The imperative of verse 22, therefore, should not be separated from the imperatives that begin in verse 17.

The repetition of the verb 'write' in verse 21 also seems to specifically recall the only other use of that verb in verse 19. Since verse 21 looks back to Paul's request with an expression of his confidence, and since verse 22 is closely linked with verse 21 (as we will notice below), this is further evidence that verse 22 should not be separated from the preceding appeal.

Verses 17–22 are also characterized by a high density of personal pronouns – 'I', 'me' and 'you' – which focus on the specifics of Paul's request for Philemon. Although verse 22b includes the plural pronouns '(restored) to you' and '(in answer) to your prayers', the specific request to 'prepare' a room for 'me' is singular, for Philemon, and continues the personal pronoun use of 'me' in relation to Philemon from the preceding verses.

The broad outline of this section unfolds from Paul's specific request in verse 17. In 18–19a Paul follows this up with a request to charge him for any wrong that Onesimus might have done and an assurance that he will cover any such wrong, and also a reminder that in a sense Philemon is in debt to Paul anyway (19b). In many ways verse 20 summarizes the main body of the letter in which Paul again addresses Philemon as 'brother' and puts his request in terms

---

33. There is also an optative, expression of wish (for 'benefit/joy'), in verse 20.

that he has used earlier in the letter for Philemon to bring joy and 'refresh his heart'. In verse 21 Paul looks back to his specific imperatives of 17–20, and expresses his confidence that Philemon will indeed lovingly welcome Onesimus back as a believer just as Paul has asked. Paul's confidence in verse 21 arises out of what he has said about Onesimus' new status (8–16), and Philemon's character (4–7). Indeed, such is Paul's confidence that he is sure Philemon will go 'above and beyond' this specific request (21b). In verse 22 Paul returns to his original request for Philemon to welcome Onesimus as he would welcome Paul (17) by making his final request of the letter and asking Philemon to prepare for such a welcome for Paul.

*Comment*

**17.** Although Paul's relationship with Philemon has always been in the picture, Paul shifts from a more general reference to Onesimus' change, and therefore changed relationship with Philemon, to his more specific request to Philemon and subsequent supporting promises to Philemon in the event of any possible obstruction to carrying out this request. All along the hints have been there that Paul is explaining a return of Onesimus to Philemon. Paul has said that he would not command Philemon but encourages him on the basis of love, a love that Philemon has for Paul and for the saints in general that will be applied to a love for Onesimus. In verse 12 Paul says he is sending Onesimus back, and in verses 15–16 he explains how Philemon would have him back in a much richer way than before. Only now, however, does Paul explicitly make a request of Philemon. The opening word, *so*, indicates that what follows is a summary and concluding appeal on the basis of what he has been saying throughout the letter. In making his request, Paul grounds it specifically in the relationship Philemon has with Paul such that the connecting word 'so' looks back to all that Paul has said so far about this.

First, however, we will consider Paul's request. Paul asks Philemon to *welcome him*. The 'welcome' is that of 'accepting' (cf. NASB, LSB) or 'receiving' (cf. RSV, ESV), showing full acceptance without hindrance or barrier. Paul wrote to the believers in Rome to 'accept' one another (e.g. the 'weak'), not condemning or standing in judgment of one another, because God had 'accepted' them in Christ (Rom. 14:1, 3; 15:7). In verses 12 and 15 Paul stated that Onesimus is on his way back to Philemon. So to 'welcome him' will at least include in the first instance a willing and glad reception back to the home (BDAG, p. 883). In light of what Paul has been saying about Onesimus becoming a beloved brother, this seems to further refer to Philemon's acceptance of Onesimus as a genuine believer and fully accepted member of God's family. The following verse will indicate why there might be an obstacle to this welcome. Before this, however, Paul provides a further compelling rationale.

Paul introduces his request with a conditional clause that assumes the truth of the statement for the argument: *If you consider me a partner, welcome him*. The word that Paul uses for 'partner' is a cognate noun of the word he used in verse 6 (*koinōnia*, 6; *koinōnos*, 17). This word might include a reference to 'partnership' in gospel ministry (e.g. 2 Cor. 8:23). However, in verse 6 Paul spoke of the faith that Philemon 'shared' with God's people, a 'common' faith that is demonstrated in his love for God's people. The link with this word in verse 6, therefore, implies that Paul assumes that Philemon views Paul as a 'sharer' in the people of God; they are together joint 'participants' in the people of God. Thus, with this term Paul builds on what he has said about their relationship especially in verses 1, 4–7. To Paul, Philemon is 'beloved', a 'fellow worker', the one who Paul thanks God for, and whose love for Paul and God's people brings Paul such joy and encouragement and refreshes Paul's heart. They are 'sharers' together in a faith in the Lord Jesus that expresses itself in love for his people. Thus for Philemon to *welcome him [Onesimus] as you would welcome me* will involve the full and heartfelt recognition of Onesimus as one of God's people, no less than Philemon would view Paul as one of God's people, and a willing and glad welcome to the home (see v. 22). However, perhaps there is still more to Onesimus' return as the next verse implies.

**18.** The way in which Paul states this, beginning with *if*, may imply that there's a chance Onesimus has not done anything wrong. Perhaps Paul is just 'covering his bases' so to speak, just in case there's any unknown hindrance to Onesimus' welcome return. The form of this conditional statement, however, is the same as that of the previous verse. This parallel suggests that Paul assumes this statement is true. The strength of Paul's follow-up assurances in the next verse further indicates that something untoward has happened. Here we perhaps come to an underlying issue that has been in the background all along. Clearly there has been some delicate matter that Paul is working around in his request for Philemon to welcome Onesimus back. Philemon loves believers, Onesimus is now a believer, a brother like Philemon; why would he not welcome him as a believer?

Paul's statement that *if he has done you any wrong or owes you anything, charge it to me* helps to clarify why there might be such hesitancy, even if we still are not sure exactly what Onesimus has done. The parallel statement *done you any wrong or owes you anything* could refer to two distinct wrongs or one wrong restated. Paul's following instruction to *charge it to me*, together with his promise in the following verse points to a financial wrong of some sort.[34] Since Onesimus was a slave (16), it is possible that his very departure incurred a cost to Philemon. Philemon, therefore, might have needed to fill whatever gap Onesimus had left. His return comes with the awkward reality that his departure was costly to those who know him best. It is also possible that Onesimus has added to his problems by taking something from Philemon, perhaps to help him on his way in his departure. Or perhaps Onesimus defrauded Philemon which prompted his flight, seeking help from Paul, perhaps in order to avoid being punished by Philemon (the 'mediator' view mentioned in the Introduction). The specifics are unclear, but a 'wrong' does seem to have been done and a debt incurred.[35]

Interestingly, Paul uses the same word for 'doing wrong' twice in the one verse in Colossians 3:25 where he declares, in the context of masters and slaves, that 'anyone who does wrong will be repaid for their wrongs, and there is no favouritism'. In the context of

---

34. The same accounting verb is used by Paul in Romans 5:13 (the only other occurrence in the New Testament) for the role of the law in the 'reckoning' of sin to our account. In this commercial context the word refers to a 'financial obligation' (BDAG, p. 319).

35. Cf. Matt. 18:23–34; Luke 16:1–9.

Colossians, this refers to judgment before God, apart from repentance. Forgiveness of sins means the debt we are in due to our sin is 'forgiven' (Luke 11:4; Col. 1:14, 21–22; cf. 2:13–14), but what about wrongs done to one another and what about our 'earthly' obligations? Paul obviously does not assume that there are no earthly consequences to wrongdoing. Even though Onesimus became a believer, Paul does not assume that Philemon does not need to be repaid. At the same time, it seems as though Onesimus does not have the means to repay it. So what can be done? Paul, out of love for both Onesimus and Philemon, offers to cover the costs and askes Philemon to *charge it to me*. Is this an empty promise given that Paul is in prison? Far from it. Paul hopes to be there soon (22).[36] In fact, his commitment to pay Philemon is reinforced in the following verse.

**19.** Although a closing comment by Paul in his own hand is found in other letters of Paul's as a final greeting (see comments on Col. 4:18), this assurance of his own writing does not function as a closing greeting here.[37] It is possible that this reference to his writing with his *own hand* means that Paul has written the entire letter without a secretary or amanuensis, and not just a final greeting as he indicates elsewhere. However, that is not his point here, and therefore this reference to his own writing more likely refers to this specific emphasis on his promise of verses 18–19a.[38] This is Paul's further emphatic reassurance to Philemon of his commitment to see restoration take place between Onesimus and Philemon, by stating, as if in bold or capital letters, *I will pay it back*. The repetition of Paul's own name together with the emphatic pronoun in this context adds emphasis to his promise. The word Paul uses for *pay it back* is found only here in the New Testament

---

36. If Paul is in Rome, according to Acts 28:30 his 'imprisonment' was at his own expense (Acts 28:30), indicating that he had access to some funds.
37. The word 'greeting' does not appear here (as e.g. in 1 Cor. 16:21; Col. 4:18; 2 Thess. 3:17). The addition of 'letter' in the NET translation interprets this as a reference to Paul writing the entire letter and not just this emphatic promise.
38. Beale, p. 427.

but is used regularly in the Septuagint in contexts of restitution, compensation and repaying wrongs to those who have incurred a loss for various reasons. The word is found eleven times in Exodus 22:4–16 alone. The effect of verses 18–19a is to reinforce the obligation Onesimus has to Philemon as well as the close association between Paul and Onesimus in Paul's request for Philemon to welcome Onesimus 'as you would welcome me' (17).

Continuing the language of debt, Paul adds a reminder to Philemon of the very personal obligation he has to Paul himself. Once again, the background to Paul's statement is something we have to infer from elsewhere. Paul's statement *not to mention that you owe me your very self*, has the rhetorical effect of highlighting the possibility of a supporting argument from some larger more significant event in their lives that Philemon knows about and that hardly needs stating. Why does Philemon 'owe' Paul his 'very self'? One possibility is that Philemon too, has come to faith (and probably Christian ministry) through Paul. This may have come about indirectly through Epaphras who was sent by Paul to Colossae (see Col. 1:7; thus perhaps explaining the reference to Epaphras in the greetings of v. 23), or directly if Philemon visited nearby Ephesus during Paul's two to three year stay there (Acts 19:10). In that sense he 'owes' his spiritual life and ministry, humanly speaking, to Paul. Thus, in the larger perspective of Paul and Philemon's relationship in general, it is not as if Paul has been the recipient of one too many favours from Philemon and is having to apologetically come to him asking for another one. Far from it. Paul has been the one who, by God's grace, has had an enormous impact for good in Philemon's own life. As many have pointed out, this subtly and ironically places Philemon in a similar position to Paul as Onesimus is with Philemon, that is, indebted. There is a deliberate play on words with the word 'owe' in verse 19b echoing a similar word for 'owe' in verse 18.[39] However, Philemon has not personally wronged Paul and Paul is not commanding or even manipulating Philemon here. Rather, once again Paul draws on the familial love that Philemon has for Paul (Philemon became a 'brother in the Lord' through

---

39. Harris, p. 235; *prosopheileis*, v. 19b; *opheilei*, v. 18.

Paul himself) and highlighting the wonderful difference that coming to Christ has in one's life (Philemon can identify with Onesimus' experience of God's grace too; cf. 9–10).

**20.** As Paul draws his appeal to a close he returns to the theme of love that he opened the letter with. Although the word 'love' is not used here, Paul's formulation links directly to verse 7 where he spoke of the effects of Philemon's love for the saints. Specific links to verse 7 include the description of Philemon as 'brother', the verb 'refresh' (now the third imperative from v. 17) and the internal descriptive 'heart' (see comments on 7). Thus verses 7 and 20 broadly frame the letter with 21–22 wrapping up Paul's appeal. Philemon's love 'refreshed the hearts' of the saints and thus this 'brother' gave Paul 'great joy and encouragement' (7). As Paul concludes his letter, having made his appeal, he comes back to Philemon's love for the saints. Paul's appeal has been on the basis of love for Onesimus, who himself is Paul's 'very heart' (12). To 'welcome' Onesimus as he would welcome Paul (17) means that Philemon would be welcoming Paul's 'very heart'.[40] Thus Paul concludes with a reaffirmation ('yes', NRSV, ESV) and a vivid description that for Philemon to welcome Onesimus as he would welcome Paul (17) would be to *refresh* Paul's *heart in Christ*. Paul asks, therefore, for Philemon's characteristic love for the Lord's people to be extended and applied to the particular case of this new member of the Lord's people, Onesimus, who is now one of the 'faithful brothers and sisters in Christ' in Colossae (Col. 1:2).

The *benefit* to Paul is one that is *in the Lord*. That is, if Philemon shows Christian love and forgiveness to Onesimus and welcomes him back as a brother 'in the Lord' (16), allowing Paul to cover any outstanding debt (or not wanting Paul to pay), this would refresh Paul's heart, bring him further delight and reaffirm the common faith they have in the Lord (5, 17). Is there another pun here (similar to vv. 10–11) between the name Onesimus/useful (*Onēsimos*) and the verb in which Paul wishes for a 'benefit' (*onaimēn*), as if Paul is asking for some 'use' from Philemon?[41] In this context, given the

---

40. Pao, p. 411.
41. Cf. Beale, p. 428.

identification throughout between Paul and Onesimus (especially 10–13, 16), it is more likely that Paul's rare use of this verb here (the only occurrence in the New Testament) may be a deliberate reminder to Philemon that what he does to Onesimus would also be a means of joy, refreshment and here 'benefit' (or 'joy', NKJV) to Paul. The Greek word 'evokes a sense of joy more than the blander English term "benefit"'.[42] The repeated references to 'in Christ' and 'in the Lord' emphasize the framework that drives the whole letter. It is because of Christ that Paul, Philemon and Onesimus belong to God's family as 'brothers' and therefore can both express and receive such internal and emotional revitalization.[43] Given these clear links to verse 7 many see this as a frame or 'inclusio' and therefore the conclusion to the letter. However, the following two verses continue to express Paul's hopes for his appeal and conclude with one final related appeal.

**21.** Paul's final statement about the appeal he has been making throughout the letter is one of confidence. With a second reference to what he has 'written' (cf. v. 19), Paul looks back both to his emphatic assurance in verse 19 as well as to the entire letter. Paul's appeal throughout has been on the basis of love and the new relationship that has come about through Onesimus' conversion. In the immediately preceding context, Paul's appeal has also been made through the framework of his own relationship with Philemon. So far then, Paul has highlighted the following throughout the letter: the outworking of God's grace in Philemon's genuine faith in the Lord Jesus in common with God's people, and the evidence of this in his love for all of God's people; Onesimus' transformation (in God's providence) to become one of God's people too; the close ties between Paul and Onesimus; the historic relationship and close tie between Paul and Philemon; and

---

42. McKnight, *Philemon*, p. 106; MM, p. 451 translate the optative verb as 'may I have satisfaction'.
43. The following expression of confidence means that when Paul seeks to have his heart 'refreshed' it is not because he has anxiety about how Philemon would respond to Onesimus (*pace* Beale, p. 429).

Paul's own promise to cover any outstanding debts. Thus at this point Paul looks back over his letter and does not appear to be in any doubt that Philemon would indeed respond positively to his encouragements.

Due to the emphasis throughout the letter on Paul's appeal to love rather than issuing a command, the translation 'compliance' (NJB) to Paul's requests rather than 'obedience' (most translations) to commands might express Paul's point.[44] However, while it is still best not to see this as heavy-handed pressure to bend to Paul's authority, Paul's appeals on the basis of love in this letter are the imperatives to 'welcome' Onesimus as a beloved brother in the Lord and thus 'refresh' Paul's heart. 'Obedience' in this sense is something Paul is confident of. It is obedience after all to the command of the Lord Jesus to 'love each other' that gives evidence that one belongs to Christ by faith (John 15:9–17).

Paul adds that he writes this, *knowing that you will do even more than I ask*. What is the 'even more' that Paul hopes for here? It might help to start with what it is that Paul has been asking up to this point. So far he has been asking that Philemon 'receive' or 'welcome' Onesimus back (17). Since Onesimus is a slave (16), and now a believer (10, 16), and is being sent back by Paul, the request so far relates to Philemon's welcome of Onesimus as a fellow believer back into the household, with any outstanding debts being covered by Paul. Thus full and complete acceptance as a believer in the Lord has been in view throughout the letter. What then is *even more than I ask* referring to? Some have suggested that in light of verse 13 Paul hopes that Philemon would also send Onesimus back to Paul, perhaps to continue helping him in ministry. The following verse, however, seems to make that suggestion unlikely (and this was not Paul's point in v. 13).[45] Another possible conclusion is that *even more* alludes to Onesimus' manumission or release from

---

44. Harris, pp. 240–241.
45. *Pace* Beale, p. 430 who thinks a request for Onesimus' return is unlikely here because this is what Paul has already been requesting throughout the letter. Pao, p. 420 and McKnight, *Philemon*, p. 108–109 see a return to Paul in view here.

slavery.⁴⁶ So far, everything that Paul has been saying has been something that Paul could encourage Philemon to do as a Christian with all of the motivations that come from being a member of God's people by God's grace. The next step, however, of releasing Onesimus from the obligations he has to Philemon and to Philemon's household is a decision that belongs to Philemon alone (cf. 14) and comes with complications related to continuing tasks and provisions for Onesimus beyond Paul's awareness. Everything Paul has said would be in keeping with this next step, is pointing Philemon to this next step and indeed, is the basis for the undoing of this entire system of slavery, but it is beyond what Paul has explicitly asked for so far. It may belong in the realm of the 'something more' that Paul hopes for but it is difficult to be sure. Since Paul does not explicitly suggest this, perhaps it is better to focus on what Paul does say in this letter.

Throughout this letter Paul has alluded to the outworking of faith in serving others, whether in love for fellow believers (4, 7, 9, 20) or in sharing the gospel so others may respond in faith and join God's people (10–11, perhaps 19, and the descriptions of 'fellow worker' and 'fellow soldier' in 1, 2, 23, 24). Paul appeals to Philemon to 'welcome' Onesimus back as a believer and beloved brother, indeed as he would welcome Paul. What could be *even more* than this in this letter? It seems likely that this would also involve seeing Onesimus as a 'fellow worker' in gospel ministry, even though this may not involve a return to Paul (in light of the next verse). Philemon could still encourage a now 'useful' Onesimus in such ministry. In the following verse Paul will ask for such help in his own ministry. To welcome Onesimus as he would welcome Paul could therefore involve helping and encouraging Onesimus in ministry as he will do for Paul. Would such service be *even more* than receiving him as a beloved brother? Yes. Would such service have to be back with Paul? No. Would such service include manumission? Perhaps, but not necessarily, and it would be up to Philemon to release Onesimus.

**22.** The NIV's translation, *one thing more* implies that this verse appears like an incidental passing comment at the conclusion of the

---

46. Cf. e.g. Moo, p. 436; Witherington, pp. 86–90.

letter. However, this final request for Philemon to *prepare a guest room for me* is not as detached from the preceding requests as might first appear. First, the opening term, *hama*, better translated as 'at the same time' (e.g. NASB, ESV) is meant to indicate an action simultaneous to the preceding statements.[47] At the 'same time' as Philemon responds to Paul's appeal and considers what the 'even more' might be, he is to think about and prepare for a visit from Paul. Thus verses 21 and 22 are tightly connected. On the one hand this makes it unlikely that there is a break between verses 21 and 22 with verse 22 belonging to mere concluding travel plans and greetings. More importantly, since verse 21 looks back in confidence to the request of the entire letter, so verse 22 should also be seen in light of the entire letter. At the central point of the letter in verse 17 where Paul makes his specific appeal to Philemon to 'welcome' Onesimus, we suggested that in light of verses 12 and 15, this would be a welcome both to the household and as a fellow believing brother in the Lord. Paul's appeal there for Philemon to 'welcome' Onesimus is explicitly clarified with 'as you would welcome me'. Now Paul concludes this section from verses 17–22 with just such a scenario for Philemon to consider as he looks at Onesimus standing before him. He will indeed need to start thinking about how he would welcome Paul and Paul helps him to see what would be involved in this welcome.

First, Philemon would need to *prepare a guest room for* Paul. This is the final imperative of the letter, concluding the series of imperatives from verse 17 ('welcome', 'charge', 'refresh'). Since the imperatives 'charge' and 'refresh' relate to Paul's central appeal for Philemon to 'welcome' Onesimus, it is likely that this imperative 'prepare' also relates to the central request of the letter. The word that Paul uses for 'guest room' was commonly used outside the New Testament for showing a guest 'hospitality' (BDAG, p. 683). In this context, Philemon's welcome of Paul will likely involve provisions for his stay as well as a room.[48] In other words it involves

---

47. BDAG, p. 49; L&N 67.34.
48. The only other use of the word in the New Testament is Acts 28:23 (for Paul's room).

being considerate about what the guest needs and is an expression of love. The present tense of the imperative is best understood as a general, rather than specific, command. 'Philemon is to have a room ready for Paul – in case, and whenever, Paul might visit . . . since Paul's visit is undetermined'.[49] Many have seen a visit from prison in Rome to Colossae unlikely and so have seen in this request evidence for a closer location such as Ephesus (see the Introduction to Colossians). However, since this return is undetermined, and the request is general, part of Paul's overall concern in this context is for Philemon to consider how he would welcome Paul as he proceeds to welcome Onesimus.[50]

More importantly, this welcome will also be an occasion for joy and thanksgiving as it will be a 'restoration' or a 'gracious gift' (cf. ESV) *in answer to your prayers*. The pronoun 'your' is plural here, returning to the plurals last used in verses 1–3. The plural pronoun in this context highlights the communal nature of this prayerful concern for Paul as well as the communal nature of the 'restoration' in answer to that prayer. The reference to 'prayer' recalls Paul's own opening prayer (4) and underscores Paul's trust in God's providence (alluded to also in 15). That such a visit would be viewed as a 'gracious gift' to Philemon once again highlights the close relationship between Paul and Philemon. The word translated as *restored* (NIV) could misleadingly imply that there is a breach in the relationship between Paul and Philemon or the church. A better expression might be 'graciously given' (ESV; BDAG, p. 1078), which in this context with reference to answered prayer, highlights God's role. Although the word can refer to granting forgiveness in other contexts (e.g. Col. 2:13; 3:13), it can also be used in contexts where someone is released or granted a rescue or freedom from danger (cf. Acts 3:14; 27:24). This latter use is in view here as Paul is in prison at the time of writing. Thus, rather than a disconnected afterthought, or loosely connected concluding reference to

---

49. Campbell, p. 93.

50. Since Paul apparently did minister in Asia again after his imprisonment at the end of Acts, a location in Rome is not ruled out by this verse (cf. Titus 1:5; 3:12); Pao, p. 421.

his travel plans, or worse, a concluding threat, this final statement is a vital part of Paul's appeal specified in verse 17. Paul brings Philemon's mind back once again to the way in which Paul hopes that Philemon will 'welcome' Onesimus just as he would welcome Paul, with love for Onesimus and Paul and gratitude for God's grace.

*Theology*

The specifics of why Paul writes to Philemon are finally detailed in verses 17–22; he wants Philemon to welcome Onesimus back as a fellow believer in the same way that he would show his love for Paul in welcoming him. We see what it means in this particular case for believers to express love for someone who has become a fellow believer. Underlining all of this section, even if not apparent on the surface, is the significance of the gospel. Allusions to 'debt' and 'forgiveness' are present throughout, including verse 22. If the penalty for the 'wrongdoer' has been removed through Christ (Col. 2:13–14; 3:25), what might this look like in the context of the wrong done against us by one who has since become a 'brother or sister in the Lord'? The implication is that Onesimus has 'wronged' Philemon. It is in this context that the significance of Philemon's own conversion is alluded to in verse 19b. On the one hand the application of the gospel means that, knowing what it means to be forgiven and to receive grace, believers too are people who forgive, extend grace and 'accept one another' just as the Lord accepted us. Yet consequences for our actions still exist, financial wrongs cannot just be waived. In these verses Paul demonstrates what Christ has done for us, and he takes on board the debt himself and pays for it in the place of Onesimus who is unable to pay.

Aware of God's providence in all of life, Paul looks ahead to being with the Colossians again as an answer to prayer and as a gift from God (22). Thus, just as God's work of grace is seen in Philemon's faith and love (4–5), just as Paul prays for the continuing work of God in Philemon's love for others (6–7) and just as God's providence lay behind Onesimus' conversion (15), so too Paul sees God's gracious answer to prayer involved in his arrival in Colossae to see Onesimus already welcomed into the family of God just as they will welcome him (22).

## E. Final greetings (23–25)

*Context*

Having completed his appeal to Philemon concerning Onesimus, Paul wraps up the letter with final greetings. The broad emphases of the appeal have not been left behind. With references to a 'prisoner' in 'Christ Jesus' (1, 23) and a 'fellow worker' (1, 24), and 'grace' from the 'Lord Jesus Christ' (3, 25), to the congregation as a whole (the plural 'you' and 'your' in 3, 25), Paul uses terms that recall the introduction to the letter and frame the letter with themes Paul highlights throughout. Thus, although the names are known to us from the concluding greetings of Colossians, the setting here highlights the framework of the gospel of grace and a commitment to that gospel that entails sacrifice and belonging that Paul has been highlighting throughout the letter. Paul's double reference to the Lord Jesus in these closing verses re-emphasizes that all of this is an outworking of what it means to belong to him by grace.

*Comment*

**23–24.** As Paul writes his final greetings, he lists names that have already been mentioned in the greetings of Colossians, confirming the likelihood that the two letters are both going to the congregation in Colossae. See the comments on Colossians 4:7–14 (and the introductions to the letter to Colossians and to Philemon) for more detail about the individuals named here. Epaphras is named first as the one who, as a citizen from Colossae, brought the gospel to Colossae (see comments on Col. 1:7; 4:12–13). As a *fellow prisoner* with Paul and with Aristarchus (Col. 4:10), he is nevertheless still concerned about the church at Colossae and wants his greetings passed on to Philemon (*you*, singular). As suggested in the comments on Colossians 4:10, the term 'fellow prisoner' is likely intended as a literal description, picking up on Paul's opening description of himself as a 'prisoner of Christ Jesus' (see comments on v. 1) and his references to his imprisonment and chains throughout the letter (9–10, 13). By concluding his letter with another reference to imprisonment, this time with reference to the founder of their church, Paul again reminds Philemon of the kind of sacrifices that accompany gospel ministry.

Mark and Aristarchus are both mentioned together in Colossians 4:10 and Luke and Demas in Colossians 4:14 (see comments there). At this point Mark's relationship with Paul looks as though it has been restored after he left Paul and Barnabas, and Demas is yet to abandon Paul and the gospel (2 Tim. 4:10). Such are the stresses and strains of relationships which take on greater significance in a letter seeking a loving restoration than their brief mention may initially suggest. In this context, all four are called *fellow workers* of Paul (see comments on Col. 4:11). In this they join Philemon himself (v. 1) as those who serve together for the spread of the gospel and the strengthening of churches, along with Paul. This designation, 'fellow worker', frames the letter with reference to gospel service and serves to remind Philemon of the bigger picture of commitment to the gospel that his welcome of Onesimus is a part of.

**25.** In the final and closing statement to Philemon Paul returns to where he began, with reference to grace. The opening greeting expressed Paul's desire that the grace experienced in the gospel be the framework by which Philemon lives his life, daily aware of and dependent upon grace (3). The whole letter has demonstrated what that looks like. In this concluding statement, Paul's desire is for Philemon, as well as Apphia, Archippus and the church in Philemon's house, to know internally (*your spirit*) the knowledge of *the grace of the Lord Jesus Christ*. The full title (also recalling v. 3), 'Lord Jesus Christ', is emphatic, the word 'of' shows the source of this grace, and the pronoun 'your' is plural. Thus Paul concludes by reaffirming the public nature of this letter, highlighting again the need of everyone to know and experience grace, and by focusing on the most concrete demonstration of that grace as it has been embodied in the Lord Jesus Christ and his sacrifice for our sins so that we may be reconciled with God.

*Theology*
The concluding verses highlight both the significance of the Lord Jesus as well as the partnership in ministry and commitment to the gospel that belonging to Jesus involves. The emphatic full title, Lord Jesus Christ, highlights Jesus as the sovereign Lord and in this context the source of grace. Thus it is only because of him that

Paul, Philemon, Onesimus and all those at Colossae know God. Furthermore, it is his sacrifice for sin that gives shape to the way Paul appeals to Philemon to extend grace and love to Onesimus. The list of names, therefore, conclude the letter as those who belong to the Lord Jesus, are committed to his gospel and who serve together: a fitting conclusion that highlights for Philemon how the gospel of the Lord Jesus is the framework for life.